CHLOE'S
Cry

LYNN POTTER

Published by Potter's Heart Ministry
PO Box 11
York, SC 29745

ISBN: 978-1981243037

Cover design by Brenda Haun, www.brendahdesigns.com

Book Cover Image
A Little Child Shall Lead Them
Artist: Ken Helser
Used with permission
www.americanartshow.com

Disclaimer: The author is not a licensed clinical counselor. Therefore, the material in *Chloe's Cry* is not to be considered counseling, or a substitute for professional assistance in trauma recovery.

Dedication

I dedicate *Chloe's Cry* first and foremost to my Lord and Savior, Jesus Christ, without whom there would be no abortion recovery for me. His gentle leading and tender care throughout the entire process gave me the courage I needed to follow Him to the deepest, darkest place in my soul where I buried my abortion experience along with myself and my daughter Chloe Renee. Eternity will not be enough time to thank Him for His mercy and grace.

To the countless wounded men and women who are maimed physically, emotionally, and spiritually due to an abortion, I give you *Chloe's Cry* as my testimony to the unfathomable love of God that makes the unimaginable possible…healing and wholeness from an abortion through the love, mercy, and grace of our Creator.

To the millions of unborn children who
were not given the right to life,
I dedicate *Chloe's Cry* to you,
for her cry is yours as well…

O death where is your sting?
O Hades, where is your victory?
(1 Corinthians 15:55)

Let not your heart be troubled;
you believe in God, believe also in Me.
In My Father's house are many mansions;
if it were not so, I would have told you.
I go to prepare a place for you.
And if I go and prepare a place for you,
I will come again and receive you to Myself;
that where I am, there you may be also.
(John 14:1-3)

And God will wipe away every tear from their eyes;
there shall be no more death, nor sorrow, nor crying.
There shall be no more pain, for the former things have
passed away. Then He who sat on the throne said,
"Behold, I make all things new ...
(Revelation 21:4-5a)

Contents

Foreword

It is hard to believe that one can find words of consolation when a child is lost to abortion. Lynn Potter, or Ms. Lynn as I am blessed to know her, does just that. Not only are words of consolation to be found and digested in the deepest depths of your soul on the pages to come, but a powerful testimony of God's healing grace and freedom is on display as well. It is a testimony that will lead you toward your own healing and wholeness as you share *Chloe's Cry* with her.

When Ms. Lynn shared her story with me, I was in disbelief. I was in disbelief because she is a fearless prison chaplain who raids the gates of hell on a daily basis. How could someone as righteous and amazingly defined by Jesus have gone through such a thing? As I saw Ms. Lynn heal and become gloriously free in Jesus, I saw a warrior with a bow and arrow arise. From the ashes of the guilt and shame of what she had done, God has created a beautiful battle cry through *Chloe's Cry* that He would free everyone and anyone who would come to Him.

I was blessed to be able to read the pages as Ms. Lynn courageously wrote and battled through the penning of this book. There were times when what I read brought me to tears. Tears knowing that Jesus loves me and would forgive me of anything. Tears of joy and peace, as paradoxical as that may seem, to know that Jesus is with me, even in my darkest hour.

Perhaps the most glorious moment of this journey of *Chloe's Cry* being written was the day I received a text message from Ms. Lynn. In it was a chain of pictures of the memorial service that she had held for her aborted daughter, Chloe Renee. She had taken communion, run after the love of Jesus, and found freedom and forgiveness for what she had done. The pictures moved me to grieving over the pain and shame she had been living with for years.

Tears of repentance stormed my eyes for thinking of abortion so piously and religiously in my past years of ministry. Those tears were then filled with joy, when the image of her smiling face with a rabbinical robe covering her surfaced on my phone (which can be seen on the back cover of this book). I saw my sister in the faith, with the abundant life of Jesus radiating about her. I saw the teachings of Jesus come alive in 2017. I saw that guilt and shame no longer had authority over my righteous sister.

As a pastor, I'm so thankful for this book as a bridge to freedom for those who have had an abortion. As a brother, I'm so thankful for a sister who had the courage to pen what has been published. *Chloe's Cry* is a message everyone needs to hear, and oxygen for dry bones to come to life.

As I write this, I pray for you, dear reader. I pray you see the heart of Jesus revealed in the pages, and the love of Jesus seen in the courage of your sister in the faith, who has written *Chloe's Cry* for all who have been impacted by the dark hand of abortion. May the peace and promises of Jesus free you, and propel you into greater things.

— Dr. Nate Staton
Lead Pastor, Another Church
Author of *Faithful Father*

Introduction

And a Little Child
Shall Lead Them

Chloe Renee was eight weeks old in utero when she passed from this life into the arms of Jesus at the hands of an abortionist. I was twenty-two years old at the time and engaged to be married when she was conceived. We took our marriage vows in front of family and friends with Chloe Renee's tiny little body forming inside my womb. We thought we couldn't possibly afford a child, so the unthinkable was decided…after we returned from our honeymoon, the abortion would take place.

It has been thirty-eight years since I walked out of that abortion clinic. I am now sixty years old, and childless. Most of the details surrounding Chloe Renee's life and death are lost in the sea of time, but she is forever alive in the presence of the Lord Jesus. Through His mercy and grace, I have been given the courage to follow Him back to that place and time in order to begin my abortion recovery.

He carried me in His arms as a shepherd carries a wounded lamb that has been snatched away from a ravenous wolf. We trudged through dim-lit tunnels where bloodthirsty wolves appeared out of nowhere, snarling and salivating. He held me tight while fighting off the wild beasts, and at the sound of His voice, they retreated as if being struck by lightning. In the distance, I saw a tiny figure move. I began to shake as He carried me closer. "Who is that?" I buried my head in His chest, shielding my eyes and heart. "Fear not, I am with you," He said.

A young woman of twenty-two years cowered down in the corner of a dark, damp prison cell, half-buried under a pile of rubble. One lone dim light swayed above her, projecting an eerie sense of evil all around. Her once spotless wedding dress was soiled with blood and soot…a filthy rag covering a skeleton of a woman. She trembled as we approached the bars that held her captive. She would not look up. Her boney arms covered her head as though she expected to be stoned to death.

He touched one of the bars, leaned forward, and spoke tenderly, "Bath," which in Hebrew means, "Daughter." She looked up, stretching her empty arms toward Him, with tears caked on her face from years and years of endless wailing in the dark, filthy place. I reached through the bars to comfort her. She recoiled, pressing her back against the wall as though she could not get far enough away from me.

As she cried and shook, every fiber of my being became one with her. She was me and I was her. We were one in this deep, dark dungeon together. This powerful but gentle Shepherd who carried me through the dark tunnels and past the ravenous wolves, stood beside me as I came to the realization that this terrified, shame-and guilt-ridden young woman I was looking at was me.

As this gentle Shepherd took me step-by-step, tenderly walking me through stages of my recovery, He set me free from the deep, dark place I had banished this part of myself. He removed my soiled gown, brought me up out of the pit, and clothed me in His righteousness with a spotless, white wedding gown (2 Corinthians 5:21, Revelation 19:8). He has fed my starving soul, restored my emotional and spiritual health, and given me strength to help others seek their own healing journey.

One day as I was thinking about my daughter, Chloe Renee, I came across a beautiful painting of a young girl walking barefoot in the sand, carrying a bucket with three pink hearts painted on it. The hearts were intertwined, and I pondered their significance as I was drawn into the scene.

My imagination soared as I followed this young girl, wondering where she was headed. It was as if I had entered another realm of existence. I heard the distinct calling of sea gulls in the distance as they soared over the ocean searching for a catch and the thunder of waves as they pounded the beach. A warm breeze caressed my face as it passed by. Instinctively, I lifted my face to breathe it in and sigh. I felt sand squishing between my toes and stooped to pick up a broken shell as I followed her lead. As we crested the dune, I spotted a Man sitting in the sand. The young girl ran to Him. He scooped her up and held her high above His head. She giggled and squirmed with delight, pointing in my direction…

**Jesus! Can we build a great big sandcastle where
all three of our pink hearts can live together forever?
Yours, Mine, and Mommy's…
Please! Jesus, Please!**

This is *Chloe's Cry*…and our story…my gift to you…

The gentle, strong Shepherd who caused the ravenous wolves to retreat has turned my prison of dark tunnels into a mansion where one day all three of our hearts will live in harmony. May the pages of this book through the Word of God and my testimony bring you peace and comfort as you walk through your own journey toward healing and wholeness from abortion.

*Let not your heart be troubled;
you believe in God, believe also in Me.
In My Father's house are many mansions;
if it were not so, I would have told you.
I go to prepare a place for you.
And if I go and prepare a place for you,
I will come again and receive you to Myself;
that where I am, there you may be also.
(John 14:1-3)*

Chapter 1

Time Capsule: Unexpected Uncovering

I take a deep breath, steady myself, and prepare to disassociate from the presentation until it is over. Although outwardly poised with a false, nonchalant aura about me, somewhere deep inside I am screaming in agony. Thirty-eight years of learning to skillfully hide my secret horror makes this charade possible. I feel as though I am suspended between two very opposite spheres of existence. After several minutes of relying on my ability to disassociate, I am confident that I have succeeded in my quest to be present and absent at the same time…but I am about to be proven wrong.

Sharing a delicious Christmas dinner with friends quickly turns sour. My anticipation of Christmas carols and joy to the world disintegrate as we are introduced to our guest speaker and representatives from a local crisis pregnancy center. I'm caught off guard in a crossfire of monumental proportions. Words that I've learned to disconnect myself from are being shot at me from every direction. Frantically, I make an attempt to erect thicker walls around my heart in order to avoid being hit by this invisible machine gun.

Pro-life, choose-life, pregnancy, adoption, fetus, pre-natal, and worst of all...the **big A**...Abortion! They are talking endlessly, or so it seems, about abortion! I gasp as the condemning, guilt-ridden words I learned to avoid come crashing down around me, threatening to shatter my skillful disassociation. There is nothing in my thirty-eight years of secret silence that has prepared me for this.

My feeble attempt at erecting a stronger fortress around my heart provides short-lived relief until I am faced with our guest speaker's beauty and talent. She commands the keyboard and guitar with her extraordinary musical gift while telling her miraculous life's story through music and prose. My mind races and my heart pounds with every word, every song, with everything this beautiful women does. Look at her! She is amazing! She is beautiful! She is alive and ministering this evening because her mother chose life. I chose abortion. I ache and groan deep, deep in the recesses of my darkened past.

Thoughts of who Chloe Renee would have become threaten what little sanity I have left while the machine gun filled with guilt and shame relentlessly shoots at me. My weak fortress disintegrates, leaving me unprotected. I've been hit...and hit hard. Invisible wounds from an invisible weapon bleed bright red, slowly sucking the life out of me. I'm not sure how much more I can take.

I want to run, yet my body won't budge. I want to plug my ears, but my spirit cries out, "Listen!" I want to hide my eyes from the images on the screen, but my soul says, "Look!" My silent secret screams and wails as I force myself to look at the images of a baby in its mother's womb. Pictures of what I might have seen had I been offered an ultrasound while Chloe Renee was being formed inside of me condemn and accuse my tortured soul.

I hold my breath while the evil, guilt-ridden, shame-based thoughts shout without mercy. They're talking about you! You're the one that didn't choose life! Look at that screen! Look at what you did! You murderer! That's your child up there! I feel so alone, so hopeless, but for some reason tonight, I am unable to disassociate. I am unable to numb my way through. I am unable to be absent while present.

In fact, I am very present. I stare at the screen in utter horror. They are explaining the benefits of ultrasound in helping women understand all the facts when they find themselves in a crisis pregnancy and are considering abortion. Where was my right to an ultrasound in 1978? Where was the evidence that I was carrying a human life, not a blob of tissue? What kind of choice did I have when I wasn't presented all the facts?

The images on the screen shatter what is left of my crumbling fortress...a child's body forming with arms, legs, fingers, and toes. A heartbeat! There she is, my daughter, my child, moving around on a very big, big, big screen for everyone to see. I cannot stop staring at her. She is captivating and alive! Although there are about three hundred women in the room, and the year is 2016, at this moment in time, it is only Chloe Renee and me. It is 1978...and I am about to do the unthinkable...

Oh God! No! You are alive! I want to change my mind! I want to touch you! I want to hold you, rock you, and sing love songs over you! Look at you! I wonder what color your hair would have been. Would you have become a gifted musician like our speaker? Oh, my beautiful daughter, I want to build sandcastles in the sand and run along the beach with you! I want to teach you how to catch fireflies and hear you scream with delight when you do! Oh Chloe! Oh Chloe Renee! Thousands and thousands of unobtainable dreams attack my already shattered heart. Light and truth penetrate the darkness of my self-created delusional denial and disassociation, and I am bombarded with heart-wrenching facts.

I am a mother! I had a daughter! She was alive and growing within my womb. She was created by the same God in whom I worship. I chose not to let her live. I chose to end her life. I chose to bury my guilt and shame under a mountain of denial and disassociation. I chose to move on with life, pretending the whole thing never happened. It was my choice. Oh, my precious daughter, it was all my choice! Chloe Renee, how could you ever forgive me? Oh God! Help me!

For the first time since Chloe Renee's death, I see what she might have looked like had I been given the opportunity to view an ultrasound before my abortion. I cannot stop looking at the little limbs with hands; the form of a child of eight weeks safely tucked inside the womb, moving and full of life. Surely this is my child...

I am suspended between my past and the present. Even though there are about three hundred women in here, it feels as though Chloe Renee and I are the only two in the room. I don't know what is going on, but something incredible is happening. I am cradled in a Healing Presence. Something that feels like warm oil is pouring through my shattered heart. The dark, evil voices and despair of just a few minutes ago lose their power over me as I embrace the reality of what I am experiencing. I am at peace, a peace that passes all understanding...

I will forever be grateful to the women who hosted the Christmas party, and the ladies of Palmetto Pregnancy Center for being part of God's plan as His light penetrated the darkness of my soul, setting me free to seek healing and wholeness from my abortion. It was during the moments of utter contempt and self-loathing that heaven met earth in a way that can only be penned as miraculous to me.

And, it is an honor beyond my wildest dreams for me to share this journey with you. You see, it was not too long ago that the subject of abortion was, at its best, something I had learned to ignore. There was no reason for me to dwell on that decision I made so many years ago. It was swept under the rug, and no one was the wiser. In God's perfect timing, however, my silent secret, buried beneath piles of guilt and shame, suddenly came to the surface, and He tenderly called me to follow Him toward healing.

The very fact that you have chosen to read this book tells me I am not alone. It affirms my decision to offer my journey toward healing and wholeness as a testimony that when this silent, dark secret is exposed to the light of truth, it no longer has any power over us.

I am confident that you are seeking healing for yourself, or understanding and wisdom to help someone you care deeply about. The subject matter contained in these pages is not something people want to read about unless they are personally and dramatically affected by it.

It is the big "A" Abortion. The word itself creates violent debates for some, while creating traumatizing, debilitating, raw emotion for others. It is not easily swept under the rug, pushed to the side, or ignored when brought up. It is explosive. It is divisive.

There Is Nothing Neutral About Abortion

Men and women alike are affected by an abortion decision they have been part of making. Because I am a woman, what I am about to share with you will be from a woman's perspective. However, I am confident that men will be able to receive healing and wholeness as well, as the truths set before us within these pages are universal and offered to all.

My gift to you is my own story of healing and wholeness. My desire is that it will ignite a spark of hope deep within you, that you too, can find healing and wholeness from your abortion experience. Your story will be yours. It will always be yours. It cannot be altered, for the facts and truths about what happened are real. What can change, however, is how you view yourself in light of these facts and truths. My journey started with hope...hope that I would be able to face my silent secret and be free of the guilt and shame that was attached to it. This is true healing...free to be me...free to be whole again.

I come to you humbly, with tender affection, knowing this is one of the most important decisions you will ever make in your life...to be *intentional* about seeking healing from your abortion. As we journey together toward this end, I stretch out my hand toward you in sisterly love, willing that you be free from all the guilt and shame that is attached to your abortion experience. I will walk with you every step of the way. Come with me! I've found the way! Do not be afraid! Take my hand!

You will not walk alone...

17

Chapter 2

A Single Step

But now, thus says the Lord, who created you, O Jacob,
And He who formed you, O Israel.
"Fear not, for I have redeemed you;
I have called you by your name; you are Mine.
When you pass through the waters, I will be with you;
And through the rivers, they shall not overflow you.
When you walk through the fire, you shall not be burned,
Nor shall the flame scorch you.
For I am the Lord your God,
The Holy One of Israel, your Savior..."
(Isaiah 43-1-3a)

Who am I that I should be set free? Who am I that I should walk in newness of life, healed, whole, and forgiven? Who am I that I should hope? These degrading accusations surfaced the moment I *chose to* be *intentional* about seeking healing and wholeness from my abortion.

It is too much! I cannot go there! I cannot face what I have done! Intense fear and disgust rose together at the thought of facing the deserted, wounded part of me that I had left behind and imprisoned in deep darkness. I walked away from her thirty-eight years ago hoping she would cease to exist, for I felt she had no right to live. Although sentenced to death with the silent secret she held, her cries could be heard from the depths of her prison when events reminding me of my heinous crime occurred.

To my utter dismay, this deserted, wounded part of me lived on, tormented and in anguish, in a deep, dark dungeon, buried under piles of fear, guilt, shame, and regret. Relentlessly, my brokenness cried out for redemption and relief. My eyes pleading for recognition, forgiveness, and healing, dripped with repentant tears. Condemned to solitary confinement, I longed to be free of the silent secret I held.

One day I picked up a card that seemed to speak directly to this violent storm raging inside of me. Its thought-provoking words came to life, calling me back to the distant land from where I had secretly vowed never to return. This dark place where denial, suffering, guilt, and shame held me captive to my own self-loathing, this place where I had abandoned myself to eternal incarceration, seemed unwilling to hold me hostage any longer.

I was pulled, tugged, almost to my own anguish with an inner desire to answer its call, to follow her cries, and to bring her out of her torment. Somehow, I knew deep down it was part of me crying out to me. It was time to face my fears and set myself free. So far away, so long ago...how would I ever get to her? This beautiful card, placed in front of me by Divine Providence tenderly answered my plea. I read the front of the card out loud...

A JOURNEY OF THREE THOUSAND MILES IS
BEGUN BY A SINGLE STEP...IMAGINE...

IMAGINE...imagine what? With hopeful anticipation, I opened the card and wept as this intimate, personal invitation brought peace to my troubled soul...

Your journey has just begun. Embrace the opportunities that life has before you, and let the Lord be your guide. With God all things are possible. (Matthew 19:26)

Yes! I could face my fear and go back! Yes! I will embrace the journey! Yes! If God is with me, I can do anything! Even this! My lifelong vow of never going back was replaced with a new vow. Nothing was going to stop me from receiving my healing and wholeness. So, with everything I had in me, I earnestly began my journey toward abortion recovery.

However, as I jumped in full speed ahead, I realized very quickly that this journey was going to take a lot more out of me than I had anticipated. In my zeal to leap toward the finish line, I found myself running on empty and in desperate need of emotional and spiritual rest...

Now, Jacob's well was there. Jesus, being wearied from His journey, sat by the well. (John 4:6)

There is no shame in needing rest. The greatest Man to walk on earth needed rest. He knew it was a vital part of being able to continue to do what He was called to do. Periodic rest during this journey we are taking is vital to us staying mentally and physically healthy as we pursue abortion recovery.

We will take periods of time to rest, reflect, and refresh our souls before moving on. We will meditate on Scripture, share our experiences, and move forward only when you feel you are ready. I encourage you to take as much time as you need every time we stop to rest.

Make sure you are getting plenty of sleep, eating healthy, and avoiding stressful interactions during the process of your journey. Keeping a journal specific to your abortion recovery is something I highly recommend. My journal has become a way to honor and memorialize my daughter, Chloe Renee, and has become the centerpiece of my healing.

Secondly, I encourage you to set aside a time and place where you will have no distractions and feel safe. I have *intentionally* reserved a space in my home that invites me to be at peace while on my journey. A cozy, warm fire, lit candles, and a hot cup of tea work for me during the cold winter months, and our deck with its water fountain and ceiling fan provides a safe haven for me in the summer. Pick a place where you will feel comfortable and safe. Being *intentional* by preparing the atmosphere serves us well as we take this journey to places we have previously vowed we would never return to.

For my sisters and brothers who are incarcerated…do not despair! I pray that the Lord would give you the desire of your heart and provide you the time and place to begin your recovery journey. He is the God of all comfort and hope. He will provide for you as you reach out to Him with hope in your heart!

If at any time during our sharing, you experience increased anxiety, depression, or any other mental health conditions that concern you, it may be necessary to seek additional help from clergy or a counselor. Abortion recovery uncovers things that may or may not require professional help, but I encourage you to seek it if your symptoms become unmanageable and severe.

Let's pray as we prepare our hearts and minds for the journey ahead…

Father in heaven, our Abba, Daddy, I'm coming to You in the Name of Your Son Jesus, with all the trust of an infant without any knowledge or strength to take care of itself. I ask You to scoop us up, myself and my friend who is reading this book, in Your tender, loving arms. Help us to know we are safe in Your embrace. Help us to believe You are for us and not against us. Give us Your peace as we take this journey, knowing we will steer off course if we do not let You be our guide. Thank You, Abba Daddy, for loving us enough to send Jesus to die for us and cleanse us from all our sin, including our abortions.

We know that all things are possible with You, and believe this to be so as we take this first step. You are our Healer. You are the One who has invited us to take this journey toward healing and wholeness with You. We believe that when we see ourselves as You see us, we will be made whole. We offer ourselves to You today, and trust You as we step out together. May we take this journey toward healing and wholeness not only for ourselves, but in order to be able to help others, and ultimately for Your glory. Thank You, Abba, Daddy, for hearing us and loving us in spite of what we've done. Amen.

I would like to invite you to write your own prayer out to this gentle Shepherd who desires more than anything that you experience His love and care for you as you pursue healing and wholeness from your abortion. I have provided some space for you here, but you may find it inadequate to totally express your feelings. I encourage you again to acquire a special journal for this journey. If you do not have the means to purchase a journal, any paper will serve you just as well! I have found that returning to my personal abortion recovery journal on days where the sting of my loss resurfaces, I am comforted by what I read as I remember being tenderly held and loved by Jesus during my recovery. The foundation of *Chloe's Cry* is built upon my personal journal entries and meditations throughout my healing journey.

_____

_____

_____

_____

_____

_____

_____

REST-REFLECT-REFRESH

Much of what I have shared so far may have been difficult for you to read. My story may have triggered feelings in you that you were not prepared for. I want to applaud your decision to continue pursuing your abortion recovery! No one who has had an abortion wants to relive the horror of the traumatic experience, even through the stories of others, but until we begin the grieving process by returning to the source of our pain, part of us will be stuck in that time and place without any hope of escaping the debilitating results of that decision.

The title of this portion of our journey is *A Single Step*. Picking up and choosing to read *Chloe's Cry* may be your first attempt at taking a single step toward abortion recovery, or it may be that you have tried numerous times. In any case, you have not only *chosen* to pick up *Chloe's Cry*, but have *bravely shared* some of my most painful expressions of abortion grief and have *chosen* to continue reading! This is amazing! You are amazing! God is amazing!

> *But now, thus says the Lord, who created you, O Jacob,*
> *And He who formed you, O Israel.*
> *"Fear not, for I have redeemed you;*
> *I have called you by your name. You are Mine.*
> *When you pass through the waters, I will be with you;*
> *And through the rivers, they shall not overthrow you.*
> *When you walk through the fire, you shall not be burned,*
> *Nor shall the flame scorch you.*
> *For I am the Lord your God,*
> *the Holy One of Israel, your Savior..."*
> *(Isaiah 43:1-3a)*

You have weathered an abortion storm! It was my storm, but you held your head up high and *chose* to walk through even as your own experience may have cried out, *"STOP! PUT THIS BOOK DOWN! ENOUGH IS ENOUGH! I CAN'T TAKE ANY MORE!"* That's happened to me several times! You walked through wind that threatened to strip you naked and expose your pain. You trudged through deep puddles produced by your endless tears. You came face-to-face with your loss, but walked on with hope in your heart!

You have taken a *HUGE* step toward weathering your own abortion storm and recovering! You silenced fear that told you to

STOP! You held your pain up to the wind and said, *"I BELIEVE I CAN BE HEALED!"* You dried your eyes in response to a voice inside telling you, *"I WILL PUT YOUR TEARS IN MY BOTTLE" (Psalm 56:8).* You have trusted that voice and something in you cries out, *"YES! I WANT TO START THIS JOURNEY OF THREE THOUSAND MILES TOWARD RECOVERY...WITH A SINGLE STEP. I AM READY!"*

This is *AMAZING!* You have just responded to the same awesome, unconditional, healing Presence that I did during the Christmas party that invited me to follow it on a journey that was sure to set me free!

As God's partners, we beg you not to accept this marvelous gift of God's kindness and then ignore it. For God says, "At just the right time, I heard you. On the day of salvation, I helped you." Indeed, the "right time" is now. Today is the day of salvation. (2 Corinthians 6:1-2, Life Recovery Bible)

For me, the Right-To-Life presentation at the Christmas party was *my day to choose* not to ignore God's kindness. The minute His light invaded the darkness of my abortion experience *I had a choice to make.* Would I step toward the *truth* of His Healing Presence that enabled me to engage in what was going on around me, or would I return to the *false safety* of the prison I had built around myself?

How about you? Where are you *right now* in your thinking, your emotions, your spiritual connection to God? Are you willing to *trust* the *truth* of His Healing Presence or are you tempted to return to the *false safety* of the prison you have built around yourself? As God's partner, I beg you not to accept His kindness toward you and then ignore it! He says...

I have heard your cries! I want to help you! Right now, today is the day! Come to Me! I want to release you from your self-inflicted prison and set you free!

Take some time right now to meditate and pray. Let His Healing Presence speak to you. Jot your thoughts down in your journal including today's date. Tell God exactly what you are feeling. He knows anyway! It's facing the *truth* of what happened and allowing His Healing Presence to guide us into recovery that will set us free!

SCRIPTURES TO MEDITATE ON
FOR OUR JOURNEY:

Be strong and of good courage,
do not be afraid, nor be dismayed,
For the Lord your God is with you wherever you go.
(Joshua 1:9)

The Lord is my light and my salvation; Whom shall I fear?
The Lord is the strength of my life;
Of Whom shall I be afraid?
(Psalm 27:1)

Chapter 3

Fearless Against Fear: War in the Heavens

Do not be afraid. Stand still and see the salvation of the Lord, which He will accomplish for you today...
(Exodus 14:13)

E ven though I had intentionally taken the first step toward my abortion recovery, I was very timid about including God in my journey. I still held the belief deep in my subconscious that this particular sin was the sin of all sins, and had a very hard time believing I could ever be free from the guilt and shame that surfaced every time I tried to face what I had done. Although I knew I was forgiven by God, when it came to including Him in my abortion recovery, I simply could not lift my guilt and shame-stricken face to look Him in the eye.

I had been involved in prison ministry for over twenty years at the time of the Christmas party where my thirty-eight-year silent secret surfaced and I faced my abortion head-on for the first time. I had been able to minister the love and forgiveness of God to thousands of men and women who were incarcerated for a variety of heinous crimes without judgment or rancor. Why then, could I not minister to myself with the same nonjudgmental spirit that spoke the truth of God's love to them? Why then, could I not receive this same love and forgiveness from God for ending Chloe Renee's life?

There is something about abortion that strikes the core of a woman's makeup that is so detestable and unforgiveable in her own psyche that delusional denial and disassociation with that portion of her being is the only way to cope with the guilt, shame, and regret. As the pregnancy center's representatives continued their presentation at the Christmas party, my safe fortress of denial and disassociation began to crumble, providing the Healing Presence entrance into the deepest, darkest places of my soul...

As I responded to the gentle prodding of this Healing Presence, years of involuntary slavery forced upon me by fear, guilt, shame, and regret were threatened, and the battle between life and death, slavery and freedom had begun. The Healing Presence continued to sustain me until the program was over, but was challenged by the voice I had learned to follow so long ago, *"You need to get out of here. You don't need to dwell on this anymore. Enough is enough. Once you're out of here, you can forget the whole thing and get on with life as though it never happened. You can't get all emotional and let your secret out!"*

The longer I entertained the negative dark thoughts, the less protection I felt from the Healing Presence until I was completely consumed once again with fear, guilt, shame, and regret. My heart raced in agreement as irrational fear of exposure escalated and my breathing became labored. Anxiety rose as I waited to be dismissed, and my thoughts geared toward planning a quick exit. Completely oblivious to what was going on, I was once again falling victim to the cunning and debilitating spirit of disassociation whose only desire was to hold me hostage in a state of denial. Completely unaware of the violent battle that was taking place in the unseen realm on my behalf, voices from the podium began to fade as I looked around the room...

I've got to get out of here! Look at this beautiful place; look at these beautiful women! If they knew my secret and what I have done, they would hate me…and rightfully so. I hate me right now! I don't deserve to be in the same room with them. I've got to get out of here with as little interaction as possible.

Taking short, deep breaths to calm my racing heart, I looked at the guests at my table. Some were very close friends. Some, I had just met. We had just finished sharing a wonderful Christmas dinner and fellowship, celebrating the birth of our Savior. We had been educated together in everything concerning parenting verses abortion. We had been presented with a powerful testimony of a gifted young woman whose mother chose life. We had experienced every raw emotion known to women and they had no clue. They had no clue they had just shared an entire evening with someone who chose abortion!

During the final comments, we were being encouraged to visit the pregnancy center and speaker's tables on the way out. As a speaker and founder of a ministry myself, I know how vital the support of others is in keeping a ministry alive. I try to make a conscious effort to support those that have impacted my life. I felt I could approach our speaker's table with confidence if I ignored her pro-life material and focused on her music. But an incredible surge of fear rose at the thought of stopping at the pregnancy center's table. Having to look at pictures of babies' faces, piles of baby gifts, and material on abortion would take more courage than I possessed.

Finally, we were dismissed. I scanned the room for the quickest possible exit. Women were chatting, picking up purses, putting on coats, and getting ready to leave. I was thankful to have survived the evening. An invisible sigh of relief motivated me as I stuffed my silent secret back into its place and grabbed my purse and coat. I had already disassociated myself from the event and was concentrating on getting out of the building with as little trauma as possible. In a few short minutes I would be free of this place, free of this experience, and life would go on as though it had never happened…

After several very short good-byes and Merry Christmas greetings, I entered the lobby, head held high, skillful disassociation and denial leading the way. I scanned the scene, being sure to ignore and completely block out the existence of the pregnancy center's table and the piles of baby gifts stacked all around it. I remembered with a twinge of guilt that the invitation to the party invited us to bring baby items that were to be donated to the pregnancy center. Of course, when I read the invitation, my safe place of ignoring and blocking out potential threats to my emotional sanity kicked in and I conveniently forgot to bring a gift.

One thing I do not do is purposefully put myself through the trauma of shopping in any infant or toy section, period, end of story. I have learned to hold my breath walking past these sections, skillfully using every disassociation tool available to me. I can block out the visual, the cute little booties for tiny little feet, the bibs, the formula and little rattles, and rows and rows of baby food jars. I can block out the noise, people cooing over babies and their incessant giggles. I can block out the images of women with babies and children hanging on to them. I can block it all out, but it is exhausting, it is debilitating, and causes extreme emotional pain that has not been healed to resurface. If at all possible, I avoid the inevitable at all costs. It is simply not worth it. Even after thirty-eight years of developing this skillful disassociation, I was not willing to engage in that trauma battle for this event.

Fear, guilt, shame, and regret stuffed safely back into the recesses of time with my silent secret, I confidently walked over to our speaker's table. I picked up her CDs and spoke briefly to her about what I am comfortable with, prison ministry and how her music would be a blessing to those I serve. Politely, I picked up material about her personal story of being given life because her mother chose adoption rather than abortion. I have no idea why I chose to pick this material up because I had already heard her testimony, but God knew.

As we made small talk through the transaction of purchasing the CD, I could hear the buzz of happy women chatting about whatever women chat about after a Christmas party. Although I was shielded from the pregnancy center's table by the masses leaving the building, I could not continue to ignore and disassociate from its existence because I had this extremely unsettling feeling of being drawn to it.

Oh no! Not on your life! I'm not getting anywhere near that thing! I prepared to sneak out by slipping into the middle of the crowd. I couldn't have been more than five feet from the front door when something completely out of my control happened. Unbelievably, I turned and started walking toward the pregnancy center's table!

WHAT are you doing? That has absolutely NOTHING to do with prison ministry! You're almost out of here! Just a few steps and you'll be able to forget this whole miserable night! Are you CRAZY? What are you going to talk to them about? You KNOW what they're going to talk to you about! My heart and soul screamed at my body, which by this time, had a mind of its own and refused to listen. I was being lured over toward the pregnancy center's table and my body refused to resist! Incredible! *What are you doing? Disassociate! Stop! Run out the front door! Get out of here! Now!*

It was no use. Disassociation's control mysteriously lost its power, giving way to something I would only understand long after I left the building. Incredibly, my body kept moving toward the table.

Within a few seconds I stood in front of the pregnancy center's exhibit table. As baffling as picking up our speaker's personal testimony was, purposefully entering this trauma-producing atmosphere was totally off the chain crazy. Although I have never had an out-of-body experience or known of anyone who has, I have to admit this was a close to one as I could imagine. It was so much more than being present and absent at the same time. It was like I was hovering over myself in disbelief, wanting to run with all that was in me, yet at the same time my body betrayed me with feet invisibly digging into the floor, refusing to budge.

Most of the guests inquiring about the pregnancy center were walking away, making any last attempt at escape impossible. Within seconds, I had made eye contact with one of the representatives and realized I was committed to seeing this thing through…whatever that meant. Walking out the door without talking to her would be extremely rude. At this point I had no other choice! I had to return to full-blown disassociation! Without giving it a second thought, I entered my safe place. I was determined to walk away from this encounter untouched.

Don't look to the left, that's where the piles of baby gifts are. Don't look at the table. They probably have pamphlets about abortion with pictures of babies' faces on them. And whatever you do...don't ask any questions! Just be polite. Tell them you've got to run, it's a long ride home, and get out of here!

The bubbly, charismatic personality of the pregnancy center's representative couldn't penetrate the thick wall of self-preservation I had erected. As she joyfully and with abundant enthusiasm began to share her passion for the mission of the pregnancy center, I found myself slipping farther and farther back into my safe place. I was smiling and nodding my head, hearing every word but hearing nothing.

The words entered my ears but were immediately cast into the abyss of darkness that refused to let me comprehend... wa,wa,wa,blah,blah,blah. I might as well have been Charlie Brown listening to his teacher in Charles Shultz's Charlie Brown's Christmas story. Perfectly poised, present but absent, I politely listened without hearing much of anything. Knowing what I know today, I can say without a doubt that this was disassociation's most blatant, rude exercise of power over me that I have ever experienced.

And no wonder! A heavenly war had been declared against its occupation of my soul!

Fear threatened to overtake me as she motioned for her colleague to join us. Subtle suggestions of disassociation were gaining ground as the other representative approached. *Now there are two of them! Stand tall! Take control! Leave now before it's too late!* I felt myself begin to crumble under the weight of having to talk to two women about pro-life issues. *Will this night ever end?*

These two beautiful women spoke with a kindness I have never heard during a conversation that included abortion as one of three options pregnant women have to choose from. There was no judgment or disdain as they spoke, but a sincere desire to provide those who face crisis pregnancies a safe place to work through their decision-making. Their eyes filled with compassion and care tenderly chipped away at the thick walls of my self-preservation. Soft voices revealed their passion not only for the pregnancy center and its mission, but also for every woman who enters its doors. Although I continued to defend my posture of being absent while present, their Christ-like compassion reminded me of something I had experienced earlier in the evening...the Healing Presence that sustained me through my exposure to what happened to Chloe Renee when I chose abortion.

Suddenly, and without any act of my own will, I found myself reaching for a business card and agreeing to call and schedule a tour of the pregnancy center. I can't even begin to express how utterly unbelievable that was! The same force that lured me over to the table in the first place was in operation again. As I was outwardly agreeing to this most bizarre invitation, the invisible war going on over me and in me escalated. Shouts of *who are you kidding* and *you must be insane* bounced off of each other in the back of my mind. *You can't possibly enter a pregnancy center much less take a tour of it! Get a grip! Don't you know the reason for everything they do is to save babies from abortion!*

What I was considering was unbelievably insane!

Yes...unbelievable, but yet something had hold of me I just couldn't shake. Their smiles, compassion, and the *way* they presented their mission was being used by Divine Providence to keep me from fleeing the scene until this *KAIROS* moment. *KAIROS* is a Greek word and defined as a time when conditions are right for the accomplishment of a crucial action, an opportune and decisive moment.

An *opportune and decisive moment* it was for sure...conditions *were right* for the *accomplishment of a crucial action*. Yet at that moment, we had no idea that we were part of something much bigger than the exchange of a business card and an informative conversation. Thirty-eight years of preparation brought me to this *KAIROS* moment. The time was now. The place was here. With all things in order by Divine Providence, the Healing Presence declared war on disassociation, denial, fear, guilt, shame, and regret.

The moment I reached for their business cards, every warrior in heaven assigned to this battle for my freedom was deployed. Above the pregnancy center's table, a battle cry sounded against every principality and power that would challenge my right to freedom from fear, guilt, shame, and regret over Chloe Renee's death. The business cards that linked us for a split second produced a conduit in the Spirit. This conduit was large enough to carry weapons powerful enough to destroy every disassociation and denial fortress that had been used for decades to hold me hostage to my past.

I had no idea that this battle of monumental proportions was going on around me. To me, this was just another exhausting experience of doing everything I knew how to do in order to survive. I held the business cards loosely in my hand, politely thanked them, and turned to leave. The last thing I remember is walking out the door, breathing a sigh of relief, and holding a couple of business cards that I never intended to look at again.

REST-REFLECT-REFRESH

Let's take some time to rest, reflect, and refresh. I trust you are in your safe place, prayerfully getting ready to engage in sharing some of your story, with pen and paper ready to journal.

As we reflect on the first part of our journey and the Scriptures we shared during chapter 2, *A Single Step*, we were encouraged to face our fears and pursue our abortion recovery because God is with us…

Be strong and of good courage,
do not be afraid, nor be dismayed,
For the Lord your God is with you wherever you go.
(Joshua 1:9)

The Lord is my light and my salvation. Whom shall I fear?
The Lord is the strength of my life;
Of Whom shall I be afraid?
(Psalm 27:1)

I have been very open and honest with you about my emotional state and the thought process I went through the night God invited me to receive healing and wholeness from Chloe Renee's death. At the time, I had no idea what was going on, and was completely unprepared to engage in something that I didn't fully understand. It has been said that we tend to fear what we do not understand.

Denial and disassociation are rooted and grounded in fear... fear of exposure, fear of facing what we have done, fear of what others may think, fear of reliving the emotional pain. You name it; if it is connected to abortion, it causes fear! The fear above all fears for me was facing God. At the beginning of this chapter I shared this with you...

Even though I had taken the first step toward my abortion recovery, I was very timid about including God in my journey. I still held the belief deep in my subconscious that this particular sin was the sin of all sins, and had a very hard time believing I could ever be free from the guilt and shame that surfaced every time I tried to face what I had done. Although I knew I was forgiven by God, when it came to including Him in my abortion recovery, I simply could not lift my guilt and shame-stricken face to look Him in the eye.

As we pause to reflect here, I want to give you the opportunity to meditate on our Scriptures: Joshua 1:9 and Psalm 27:1, and share any fear or apprehension you have about including God in your abortion recovery. I encourage you to take plenty of time to be still and listen to your heart. Talk with God. Write down your thoughts and what you feel He is saying to you. We are not in a hurry.

I'd like to pray for you now...

Lord Jesus, I come to You on behalf of my friend who has shown so much courage by sticking with me while I share my healing journey. Some of the things I've shared may have triggered deep emotional and spiritual wounds that may be extremely painful. She may have been tempted to give up, but she did not. I ask You to give her the strength and courage to press through all her doubts and fears. As I stand beside her now, we lift our empty arms toward You, trusting You with this crucial part of her journey. Please give her the ability to be open and honest with You as she invites You to be her guide. Amen!

Here are some questions to think about that may help get you started. What caused you to pick up *Chloe's Cry*? How long ago did you experience your abortion? What have you been taught about abortion...is it a sin, a moral character flaw, a freedom of choice? Where is God in your life? How do you feel about Him being your guide as you work through the trauma of your abortion experience?

In You O Lord, I put my trust; Let me never be ashamed.
Deliver me in Your righteousness, bow down Your ear to me.
Deliver me speedily, be my rock of refuge,
a fortress of defense to save me.
(Psalm 31:1-2)

As my story unfolds during the Christmas party, the invisible war I had been engaged in since the moment of Chloe Renee's death escalated as denial and disassociation started losing ground. They had stalked and overtaken me at the most vulnerable time in my life. I had willingly let them take charge in order to shield myself from fear, guilt, shame, and regret. These deceptive intruders were being challenged by an unbeatable army, whose Commander in Chief was God Himself!

Everything leading up to and every detail of the Christmas party had been planned before the foundation of the world as a moment in time when conditions were right for the accomplishment of a crucial action. The opportune and decisive moment. This was God's *Kairos* time. He said, "Enough is enough. I am going to set her free, and use her story to set others free. And, I am starting right now."

Let's re-read what I shared earlier about my *Kairos* moment at the Christmas party...

An opportune and decisive moment it was for sure... conditions were right for the accomplishment of a crucial action. Yet at that moment, we had no idea that we were part of something much bigger than the exchange of a business card and an informative conversation. Thirty-eight years of preparation brought me to this KAIROS moment. The time was now. The place was here. With all things in order by Diving Providence, the Healing Presence declared war on disassociation, denial, fear, guilt, shame, and regret.

The moment I reached for their business cards, every warrior in heaven assigned to this battle for my freedom was deployed. Above the pregnancy center's table, a battle cry sounded against every principality and power that would challenge my right to freedom from fear, guilt, shame, and regret over Chloe Renee's death. The business cards that linked us for a split second produced a conduit in the Spirit. This conduit was large enough to carry weapons powerful enough to destroy every disassociation and denial fortress that had been used for decades to hold me hostage to my past.

Let's stop for a second and reflect on what *KAIROS* means...*a time when conditions are right for the accomplishment of a crucial action...the opportune and decisive moment.*

All the events in my life from the time of Chloe Renee's death in 1978 up to and including the night of the Christmas party in 2016 were woven together by Divine Providence to provide the perfect *KAIROS* moment for me. And God shows no favoritism (Acts 10:34). He is forever behind the scenes in every life, working and weaving the perfect tapestry of events

leading up to a *KAIROS* moment for everyone He has created...
INCLUDING YOU!

I believe RIGHT NOW is YOUR KAIROS TIME! THIS is
YOUR KAIROS PLACE! I believe this is the opportune and
decisive moment for you! The moment *you chose* to face fear
head-on and continue your journey, every warrior in heaven
assigned to the battle for your freedom was deployed! A battle
cry sounded over this book and your journal entries against
every principality and power that would challenge your right
to freedom from fear, guilt, shame, and regret over your abortion choice and the death of your child.

*Your choice to pursue recovery by facing fear head-on and
refusing to stop reading Chloe's Cry challenges the right of your
enemies to hold you captive. You have taken a stand against
every principality and power that would challenge your right
to freedom. You have enlisted in the heavenly army to wage
war against fear, guilt, shame, and regret. You are moving
forward in defiant determination. You are fearless because you
trust your heavenly Commander in Chief to protect you during
battle and lead you into victory! Celebrate what God is doing!*

Take a minute to reflect on the events in your life that led up
to this moment in time. What chain of events caused you to pick
up this book? Are you comfortable with God being part of your
abortion recovery journey? Why or why not?

Take time to have a gut-level honest conversation with Him.
Be sure to record your thoughts in whatever you are using for
a journal. Don't hurry through these questions. It is crucial
they are settled before you move on. If during your journaling
process other questions or issues arise, by all means don't move
on until you feel released to do so. Be open to the moving of the
Holy Spirit during this journey and take all the time you need.
He knows best what we can deal with and when.

Before we get back to what happened after I left the
Christmas party, I want to invite you to take a deep breath,
relax, and meditate on the following Scriptures. Be still and ask

God to minister to you as you read and reflect on His desire to guide you into healing and wholeness.

What is He saying specifically *to you about your abortion experience* through these verses?

If we confess our sins, He is faithful and just to forgive us our sins and to cleanse us from all unrighteousness. (1 John 1:9)

He has removed our sins as far from us as the east is from the west. (Psalm 103:12, Life Recovery Bible)

Do not fear, for you will not be ashamed; neither be disgraced, for you will not be put to shame; for you will forget the shame of your youth. (Isaiah 54:4)

Fear not, for I am with you; be not dismayed, for I am your God. I will strengthen you. Yes, I will help you. I will uphold you with My righteous right hand. (Isaiah 41:10)

Be strong and of good courage, do not be afraid, nor be dismayed, for the Lord your God is with you wherever you go. (Joshua 1:9)

The Lord is my light and my salvation; whom shall I fear? The Lord is the strength of my life; of whom shall I be afraid? (Psalm 27:1)

In You Oh Lord, I put my trust. Let me never be ashamed. Deliver me in Your righteousness. Bow down your ear to me. Deliver me speedily, be my rock of refuge, a fortress of defense to save me. (Psalm 31:1-2)

In You Oh Lord, I put my trust. Let me never be put to shame. Deliver me in Your righteousness, and cause me to escape. Incline Your ear to me, and save me. Be my strong refuge, in which I may resort continually. You have given the commandment to save me, for You are my rock and my fortress. (Psalm 71:1-3)

GOD HAS SPOKEN! This is YOUR KAIROS TIME! The heavenly armies are positioned on your behalf! You WILL WALK IN FREEDOM from fear, guilt, shame, and regret. YOU WILL BE HEALED from your abortion and the loss of your child. YOU WILL MAKE PEACE with your past and EXPERIENCE GOD'S HOPE for your future! YOU WILL!

Do not be afraid, stand still and see the salvation of the Lord, which He will accomplish for you today.
(Exodus 14:13)

As we close out this chapter, *Fearless against Fear, War in the Heavens*, I invite you to DECLARE (which means speak out loud) over your life and your abortion experience...

God has spoken to me! This is my KAIROS time! This is my KAIROS place!

God has set things in motion for my deliverance, and His heavenly armies are positioned on my behalf!

I will walk in freedom from fear, guilt, shame, and regret over my abortion and the loss of my child because of what God is doing in my life!

I will be healed from my abortion experience and the loss of my child!

I will make peace with my past and experience God's hope for my future!

Chapter 4

On the Shoulders
of the Great King

*M*y *life is in Your hands...*Lyrics from a song we use during music ministry at the detention center come to mind as I contemplate the events leading up to, during, and shortly after the life-changing Christmas party at Westminster Presbyterian Church.

I am in awe as I remember walking out of that place, taking a deep breath, extremely relieved I had escaped yet another threat of exposure. The cool, crisp December air invited me to relax after surviving the suffocating abortion-filled air I had just left. Oblivious to the intense invisible war that was going on all around me, I numbly walked to my car, unaware I was still holding the business cards in my hand.

That was one unbelievably crazy Christmas party! I've never been so glad to get away from any place in all my life! With a huge sigh of relief, I got into my car, exhausted but hidden safely behind denial's fortress where no one could find me or learn of my silent secret. Inwardly, I smiled. I had survived!

Disassociation reared its proud, ugly head and gloated as I started to pull out of the parking lot, not once looking back. Never been here, never happened. I tucked the events of this evening safely away in my fortress of denial with this most recent pile of guilt and shame, and then automatically dumped the weight of it all on the twenty-two-year-old tramp I had imprisoned years ago. I stashed the business cards in a little cubbyhole in the dash. *Won't ever need these. I'll pitch them out tomorrow.*

As I started the car, I reached for the CD I had purchased earlier. There was a song on it I wanted to listen to on the way home. It was used during our speaker's testimony and moved me to tears when I heard it. I thought it would be a great addition to the music ministry I have in the detention center. I believe music is a universal language that can bridge gaps between any two groups that might otherwise not mingle in the same arena. God used my love for music's place in prison ministry to lure me to her table in spite of my desire to run out of the building as fast as I could.

As I spoke to her about using her music, a connection was made in the Spirit. It was a merging, a marriage. Music became the catalyst to marry prison ministry and abortion recovery deep within the darkness of my experience. This merging, this marriage would bring forth a child who would trumpet the mercy and grace of her Creator, and be used to set others free to experience the same mercy and grace. This child would come forth as *Chloe's Cry*, and would lead many to healing, wholeness, and freedom. This destiny, this child would not be aborted; she would be carried full term. You hold in your hands the product of this merging, this marriage...the unconditional love, mercy, and grace of Chloe Renee's Creator that has the power to set us free.

I quickly unwrapped the CD and prepared to slide it into the player. The invisible war around me escalated and disassociation's proud gloating was challenged. The minute the anointed music filled the car, the merging was sealed. The marriage announced. Although unwilling to completely surrender to the Heavenly King, disassociation had just lost a huge battle in the war for my freedom. God had other plans for the music that stirred my heart. The seed for *Chloe's Cry* had been planted and watered. I was now connected to abortion recovery in the Spirit. It was just a matter of time until destiny's expansion would be revealed. I had no idea what was going on. I had no idea that I was driving on holy ground as I pulled away listening to the music of the gifted woman whose mother chose life.

I arrived home, thankful it was finally over. I had overcome! I had survived! I did not submit to any emotional display that would cause exposure. My secret was still a secret. I carried no fear, guilt, shame, or regret home with me. I had dumped it all on the tramp inside the dungeon before I left. Content with the positive outcome of this most exhausting evening, I went to bed and slept like a baby. Yes, I slept like a baby oblivious to the fact that it had nothing to do with me or my skillful denial and disassociation, but everything to do with the Healing Presence that had declared war on my behalf.

He will not allow your foot to be moved. He who keeps you will not slumber. Behold, He who keeps Israel shall neither slumber nor sleep. (Psalm 121:3-4)

As I peacefully slept, the invisible war of light against darkness raged all around me. The spirits of delusional denial and disassociation were not going to give up their thirty-eight-year occupation of this King's key warrior easily. Every peaceful breath challenged their occupation and chipped away at their fortresses. Huddled in a corner, frantic at the speed in which they were losing ground, they called for reinforcements and an emergency meeting.

This key warrior must not be set free. We must enter her subconscious where she will be vulnerable and unable to fight off our advances. We must not allow her to enlist in the army of light and face her abortion. If she is freed from our clutches, there will be no stopping her. She will take this King's freedom to others. We must engage every known dark spirit of fear, guilt, shame, and regret in battle tonight in order to protect our occupation.

Calling on every subconscious dark memory (whether associated with Chloe Renee's death or not) as reinforcements, they planned on entering my subconscious so that when I woke up I would be worse off than what I was at the beginning of the Christmas party.

When an unclean spirit goes out of a man, he goes through dry places, seeking rest, and finding none, he says, "I will return to this house from which I came." And when he comes, he finds it swept and put in order. Then he goes out and takes with him seven other spirits more wicked than himself, and they enter and dwell there, and the last state of that man is worse than the first. (Luke 11:24-26)

It was no use! Their tactics fell short of the desired outcome! They were stopped cold at the front line, facing the King of the universe. The God of Abraham, Isaac, and Jacob, the God of our Lord Jesus Christ, my Abba Father had already spoken. He declared war on my behalf and said, *"Enough is enough! I am going to set her free. And her story is going to set many others free!"* They could not penetrate the Healing Presence and His army's lines. They could not enter my house and dwell there. My subconscious was no longer subject to their intrusion. He who neither slumbers nor sleeps kept watch in the trenches with the great cloud of witnesses denying the enemies of my soul access to my thoughts or dreams. I awoke refreshed and ready for a new day. I was totally unaware that the King was about to deal a death blow to every illegal occupant, throw them out of my house, and end the entire thirty-eight-year occupation.

The steps of a good man are ordered by the Lord, and He delights in his way. Though he fall, he shall not be utterly cast down. For the Lord upholds him with His hand. (Psalm 37:23-24)

As CEO and founder of Potter's Heart Ministry, I manage the day-to-day operations of the ministry from our home. Every morning around ten o'clock, I travel into town to retrieve the mail from our post office box. The morning after the crazy

Christmas party was no different. I set out on my journey with no other plans than to gather the mail and return home.

My thoughts are not your thoughts, and My ways are not your ways, He says. As the heavens are higher than the earth, so are My ways higher than your ways, and My thoughts than your thoughts. (Isaiah 55:8-9)

My plans of quickly retrieving our mail and heading back home were immediately altered the moment I pulled into the post office parking lot. As the scene unfolds, I'm sure the army of light had to restrain themselves while watching and waiting for the command to deploy. Again, I found myself in one of those *almost out-of-body experiences* I had encountered at the Christmas party the night before. I glanced at the center of my dash where I had stashed the pregnancy center business cards, and without a care in the world, thought the unthinkable... *I should give them a call.*

As word of this independent thought reached the dungeon, all hell broke loose...

The snarling, salivating wolves that guard the deep, dark dungeon where the tormented twenty-two-year-old lived were enraged and beside themselves with fury. *You should give them a call?* Fires of fury erupted, calling the masses to another emergency meeting. Each platoon gathered around their sacred fires and threw logs of fear, guilt, shame, and regret on them. The evil commander in chief of the army of darkness gathered the troops together to issue his orders. Captains of fear guilt, shame, and regret gathered their soldiers in preparation for deployment...

At all costs, I must be stopped from making a connection with the pregnancy center! At all costs, I must be brought back into custody and reminded of their faithfulness in protecting me all these years. At all costs, the army of light must not be allowed access to the dungeon where the tramp lives. The evil commander in chief continued to flame their fury. After all they have done for me, how dare I entertain an independent thought that might challenge the validity of their claims? How dare I entertain an independent thought that might question their occupation of the part of me that I agreed to banish from existence? How dare I face the captains of fear, guilt, shame, and regret, and think a thought independent from their control?

Yes, how dare I?

Flames of darkness shot from the commander's mouth connecting the fires of fury, causing them to erupt into an unquenchable volcano. This volcano hovered over my car, spewing out the soldiers of darkness, the snarling, salivating wolves, engaging them in the invisible war. They climbed all over my car, pounding their paws, violently rocking it in an attempt to intimidate and distract me. Ear-piercing obscenities threatened to shatter the windows as they frantically screamed for reinforcements, trying to get their paws on me. The evil commander of the dark army knew the end of his thirty-eight-year occupation was at stake. Their orders were to stop at nothing in order to prevent me from making a connection with the pregnancy center. Every dark warrior was commissioned to the task. I must be retained and restrained!

Meanwhile, a cross of torture hung high above the volcano produced by the fires of fury. Living, breathing, pulsating, bright red blood poured from every cell of its makeup and shouted... *IT IS FINISHED! IT IS FINISHED! IT IS FINISHED* as its life-giving flow poured over my car. The KAIROS of all KAIROS times for the tortured, battered, and bruised woman banished to the deep, dark dungeon of my tainted past had come. The One whose eyes are like a flame of fire, the One who is clothed with a robe dipped in blood, the One who has a sharp sword coming out of His mouth had arrived on the scene to wage war on the ravenous wolves. And, His army of light, clothed in fine linen, white and clean, followed Him on white horses (Revelation 19:12-15).

There was about to be a miraculous transfer of occupation...

Delusional denial and disassociation, along with the forces of fear, guilt, shame, and regret had been captured by the One whose eyes are like a flame of fire. His army, armed with weapons of warfare created the night before at the Christmas party, surrounded them. They had been shackled and placed in the interrogation room where the One who is clothed with a robe dipped in blood stood. Out of His mouth spewed a sword with truth that penetrated the heart of every lie they had controlled me with for thirty-eight years. Immediately they were stripped of their ability to control my thoughts and actions. They had come face-to-face with the Creator of the universe, the King of all Kings, the Lord Jesus Christ, and He was about to use their own weapons to defeat them and set me free.

Screaming and cursing, delusional denial and disassociation writhed in pain as they were commanded to stand at attention and salute the King of Kings. They were stripped of their dark uniforms, standing naked and exposed to the armies of heaven that had been deployed on my behalf the night before. The heavenly host and great cloud of witnesses cheered loudly, and with great joy...

Glory to Him who is and who was and who is to come, the Almighty! (Revelation 1:8) Let all the earth rejoice! Deliverance has come to the daughter of the great King! And to her it will be granted to be arrayed in fine linen, clean and bright. (Revelation 19:8)

The snarling, salivating wolves of earlier, who threatened my deliverance with a vengeance, were being used by the Almighty to set in motion the chain of events that would lead me out of their bondage and into His freedom. The wolves and their armies of fear, guilt, shame, and regret were no match for this Great King who commanded their obedience. They began cutting themselves, begging death to overtake them rather than be part of helping me gain my freedom. It was no use. They were pawns in His hands and powerless to stop Him...

"Relinquish your control, domination, and intimidation of My daughter, and everything connected to Chloe Renee's death. This is her KAIROS time. This is My KAIROS time! This is your KAIROS time! Things are shaking and shifting. I am doing the shaking. I am doing the shifting! Enough is enough! You will bow to My name, the name above all names and submit to My authority. I am Jesus, Who you defy with your lies and intimidation. I have seen the oppression by which you have oppressed My daughter in the deep, dark recesses of her tainted past. I have come to overthrow your dominion and occupation. I have come to deliver her out of your rule and bring her to Myself in the land that I have purchased for her... to a land void of you and your armies of fear, guilt, shame, and regret. It is a land where I rule with My armies of faith, hope, peace, and joy. This is her inheritance as My beloved child. I, King Jesus, the Lion of the tribe of Judah, have spoken and you shall be no more."

Without a second thought, I found myself reaching for my cell phone and dialing the pregnancy center's number. Again, it was as if I was watching myself from somewhere else. I looked at the phone in disbelief while I dialed the number. As I look back, the Healing Presence that surrounded me the entire time at the Christmas party was in operation in opposition to every evil spirit I had been enslaved to for thirty-eight years. My fingers dialed quickly, my voice spoke without hesitation. I sat in my car talking to the representative, telling her I needed to talk to her and tour the building as soon as possible.

Only someone who has lived the abortion nightmare of fear, guilt, shame, and regret would understand the magnitude of what was going on here. I can only say that God had truly had enough and He was about to deliver me from every evil spirit that had imprisoned me since Chloe Renee's death. Fear, guilt, shame, and regret watched in the background in horror, completely stripped of any power to stop me from making the commitment to tour the pregnancy center.

Wild wailing and ceremonial cries pierced the heavens as they were forced to enter my car with the Healing Presence and His army. Gasping for air, they scratched and clawed at the inside of my windows trying to get out. It was no use. The powerful Healing Presence swallowed up their darkness. One by one, they were no more. I rested in peaceful silence as the last one succumbed to the King of light, and started my car determined to tour the pregnancy center.

During this short but intense battle, the evil commander in chief of the army of darkness shook with rage and increased fury as he watched his power over me disintegrate before his eyes. No matter how violent he got, he could not penetrate the invisible shield that had surrounded me. He thrashed around, spat, and cursed as he watched his savage warriors succumb to the Healing Presence. His fury escalated into a violent frenzy as he realized he was losing a key battle in the war to defend his incarceration of my tortured soul. With an unquenchable rage searching for a place to strike, he retreated to the dungeon where he had left his troops heavily guarding the young twenty-two-year-old who had been left crying out for mercy for thirty-eight years.

What he found turned his rage into an insatiable desire to recapture me and return his dungeon back into what it was created for…his endless, merciless torture of the one who had chosen abortion. *Fear! Guilt! Shame! Regret! Where the hell are you? Where is that tramp?* He slammed the iron gate of the now empty cell with such force that the piles of rubble that had once buried my tortured soul shook as if subjected to an earthquake. Boulders of fear, guilt, shame, and regret tumbled to the ground, disintegrating into a pile of dust as he shouted obscenities. He was mad with rage. Foaming at the mouth, evil daggers flying out of his eyes, he searched the entire dungeon for his troops. There was no one to be found.

In an attempt to reclaim my tortured soul, he returned to the cell to retrieve the soiled wedding gown. His intent was to gather reinforcements and wait until I slept to enter my thoughts and dreams with reminders of my participation in Chloe Renee's death. When he turned the corner in the hall of despair, he was blinded by a bright light. The dim-lit light that had once cast an eerie, evil sense around me no longer hung over the place where I had been imprisoned. The soiled wedding gown had been removed. Fear, guilt, shame, and regret were reduced to dust on the ground. The cell was empty. The heavy, rusted iron gate that was used to imprison me hung wide open. There was no trace of anyone ever being detained there. Swaying freely on its hinges, moving and dancing on the wings of victory, the iron gate mocked everything the dungeon was created for.

The evil taskmaster to whom I had been subjected to for thirty-eight years snarled and spat while turning around with a vengeance and a resolve to stop at nothing in order to find me. His determined pursuit stopped abruptly as his body slammed into an invisible wall. Shaken like a bird that had just slammed into a window, he fell back, landing in the dust that not too long ago was created by his own rage.

Momentarily stunned, his eyes rolled into the back of his head, but he was *not* going to give in to defeat. He grabbed the swinging gate and pulled himself up. He let out a war cry that reverberated throughout the heavens and shook the dungeon. In the distance, he saw the figure of a Man carrying a young woman over His shoulders like a shepherd would carry a wounded sheep. Instead of a filthy, bloodstained rag, she was clothed in a spotless, white wedding gown, and on her head, was a golden crown. Living, breathing, pulsating, bright red blood seeped through the Man's robe, splitting the earth beneath His feet as it dripped to the ground.

In one last, blinded-by-rage attempt to challenge the King of Light, the evil commander of darkness lunged forward only to be knocked back again. The King of Light shouted with the power of Joshua in the battle of Jericho. The earth shook, the dungeon shook, the iron gate which had been secure for thirty-eight years fell off its hinges. The bars of the eternal cell melted. The walls of the dungeon collapsed. The earth opened up and swallowed the one who held the young woman captive in his dark, filthy dungeon for thirty-eight years.

The young woman clothed in a spotless wedding gown clung to the Man whose blood split the earth as He triumphantly carried her out draped upon His shoulders...

The Spirit of the Lord God is upon Me, Because the Lord has anointed Me to preach good tidings to the poor, He has sent Me to heal the brokenhearted, to proclaim liberty to the captives, and the opening of the prison to those who are bound... (Isaiah 61:1)

In slow motion, I gently laid my cell phone down on the passenger seat of my car, started the engine, and pulled out of the post office parking lot. I was no longer the CEO of Potter's Heart Ministry heading home to work. I was the young woman of the dungeon being carried on the shoulders of the Man whose blood split the earth and swallowed up her captor...on her way to take a tour of a pregnancy center.

REST-REFLECT-REFRESH

Let's stop to rest. What I have just shared is pretty intense...I am praying for you now...

Lord, God, Most High, Creator of all that is good, I come to You in all humility and awe of what You have done in my life. As I re-read the words that have been penned by Your Spirit in this chapter titled, "On the Shoulders of the Great King," I can only pause to weep and meditate on the unconditional love You have shown me. I am praying for Your precious child who is reading *Chloe's Cry*, that she may experience this great love as she surrenders her journey to You. I pray and declare in the heavens Your Word over her journey right now. Help her receive it in the deep, dark place where only You know the depths of her brokenness...

For this reason I bow my knees to the Father of our Lord Jesus Christ, from whom the whole family in heaven and earth is named, that He would grant you, according to the riches of His glory, to be strengthened with might through His Spirit in the inner man, that Christ may dwell in your hearts through faith; that you, being rooted and grounded in love, may be able to comprehend with all the saints what is the width and length and depth and height—to know the love of Christ which passes knowledge; that you may be filled with all the fullness of God. Now to Him who is able to do exceedingly abundantly above all that we ask or think, according to the power that works in us, to Him be glory in the church by Christ Jesus to all genera-tions forever and ever. Amen. (Ephesians 3:14-21)

Thank You, Lord, for the promise and power of Your Word over my sister's life and journey toward healing and whole-ness from her abortion. Help her to experience Your great love, trusting You as her tender Shepherd as she walks through the valley of the shadow of her abortion experience. Help her to comprehend the depth of Your love that took You to the cross of Calvary in order to purchase her deliverance and set her free from the clutches of the commander of the army of darkness. Help her receive this light into her darkness...

The Lord is my shepherd. I shall not want. He makes me to lie down in green pastures. He leads me beside the still waters. He restores my soul. He leads me in the paths of righteousness for His name's sake. Yea, though I walk through the valley of the shadow of death, I will fear no evil; for You are with me; Your rod and Your staff, they comfort me. You prepare a table before me in the presence of my enemies. You anoint my head with oil. My cup runs over. Surely goodness and mercy shall follow me all the days of my life, and I will dwell in the house of the Lord forever. (Psalm 23)

It is in You I shall find all I need for this journey! It is in You who carried me out of the deep, dark dungeon on Your brutally beaten shoulders, I shall trust. It is in You I shall walk in newness of life, free from fear, guilt, shame, and regret! It is in You I shall find healing and wholeness from Chloe Renee's death! It is in You my soul rejoices with joy unspeakable!

As the thunder of Your voice and power of Your blood spilt the earth to devour my captor, the valley of the shadow of death had to release me! As You removed my filthy rag and clothed me in a spotless wedding gown, the enemies of my soul were defeated! As You placed the golden crown upon my brow, You anointed my head with oil! As You triumphantly carried me out of the dungeon, You declared to the armies of heaven, the great cloud of witnesses, and the armies of darkness...

Surely goodness and mercy shall follow her all the days of her life and she WILL dwell in My house forever and ever...

I am stricken with the inability to express what is going on inside of me, in the deep, deep recesses of my being. That You willingly allowed Yourself to be publicly stripped and mocked, brutally maimed and murdered, that You endured endless torture in order to purchase my freedom is more than I can bear. Yet, You remind me this is why You came...

It is for this purpose the Son of God was manifested, that He might destroy the works of the devil. (1 John 3:8b)

My victorious King! My Redeemer! My Knight in shining armor! To be given insight as to what You have endured in order to rescue my tortured soul from darkness is sobering. To be unconditionally loved and forgiven after such an unbelievable act of selfishness is beyond my comprehension! To be carried out of thirty-eight years of imprisonment to fear, guilt, shame, and regret gives me reason to shout!

MY CHAINS ARE GONE...I'VE BEEN SET FREE!

In the deep, deep recesses of my healing journey, I hear Chloe Renee's cry as she boldly proclaims from her eternal home with You...

O death where is your sting? O Hades, where is your victory? (1 Corinthians 15:55)

Death has no sting! Hades has no victory! The Man with the blood that split the earth beneath His feet and the voice that commanded the earth to swallow up the one who held me captive is RIGHT HERE, RIGHT NOW, willing to enter your deep, dark dungeon and overthrow your enemy! My dear sister, He offers you the same hope, deliverance, and healing as He did me, RIGHT HERE, RIGHT NOW! Will you let Him scoop you up, place you on His shoulders, and victoriously carry you out of your captivity?

There is an invisible war going on all around anyone who seeks healing and wholeness from an abortion. The enemy of our souls wants to keep us in bondage to fear, guilt, shame, and regret so that we cannot reach our God-given potential and destiny. Once set free from his control, we are empowered to take the message of deliverance to those who are still bound. It is the Healing Presence of the Great Shepherd Who has empowered me to share my story with those who are seeking healing and wholeness from abortion...

Jesus said to them, "Peace to you! As the Father has sent Me, I also send you." (John 20:21)

I want to give you time to find your safe place if you aren't already there. Spend a few minutes in silent reflection on what I shared with you concerning the battle for my freedom in this chapter. Ask the Lord to show you how this same battle has been raging around you as you reflect on your own abortion experience. Prepare your heart by meditating on the Scriptures that are in bold type throughout the chapter. Invite your gentle Shepherd, the same Healing Presence that exposed this battle to me, to share His heart with you as you write out your thoughts. Seek His heart. Listen for His voice. He is tenderly offering Himself to you as your Deliverer. Will you allow Him entrance into the darkest place of your abortion experience? Will you trust Him to lift you up on His shoulders and victoriously carry you out of your captivity?

You may need to re-read this chapter with your journal near to capture your thoughts before they disappear. This is your journal about your personal journey with the Healing Presence of Jesus Christ. This is a personal dialogue between you and your Great Shepherd. Take your time. As with any rest, reflect, refresh exercise we do throughout this journey, if it becomes overwhelming, stop, step back, and take a break.

He will feed His flock like a shepherd; He will gather the lambs with His arm, and carry them in His bosom, and gently lead those who are with young. (Isaiah 40:11)

Chapter 5

Standing on Holy Ground

My cell phone safely laying on the passenger seat and the business cards returned to their cubby hole in the dash, I was on my way to the pregnancy center as calm as if this was something I had done a thousand times before. This sixty-year-old who, from the day of Chloe Renee's death, had become an expert at avoiding anything remotely connected to babies was right now, *on purpose,* making a thirty-minute trip to *intentionally* tour a pregnancy center!

The great cloud of witnesses and the soldiers of the army of light celebrated together as fear, guilt, shame, and regret were nowhere to be found. My car had become a sanctuary of peace, love, and joy as the Great King's Healing Presence saturated every fiber of my being. This tender Shepherd, the great and Mighty King of the army of light who had rescued me from the deep, dark dungeon, was now leading me to the place where I would begin to walk out my freedom.

My first opportunity to experience the power of my deliverance came when I was less than a mile from the center. I had written the directions down on a piece of paper because I had no access to GPS service. I could not find the last street I was instructed to turn on after several attempts at locating it. Not more than twelve hours ago this would have caused me to chuck the whole idea and return to the pit of darkness from where my King had just rescued me!

All I can say is **But God!**...

The moment He carried me out of that deep, dark dungeon on His blood-stained shoulders, something supernatural happened! Events connected to my abortion and Chloe Renee's death no longer haunted me with shame-based accusations, but began to call me with the voice of my tender Shepherd. I felt His Presence gently guiding me to the place where I would begin a healthy, healing process. I knew I was safe. I knew Palmetto Pregnancy Center was the place. I knew today was the day. I was no longer operating from a position of captivity, but operating under the Healing Presence of the One who had carried me out on His shoulders...

No thoughts of backing out and going home entered my mind. The great King of the army of light with His Healing Presence sustained me until I could reach for my phone to contact the center. When I told the receptionist I was lost, she offered to stay on the phone with me until I was in their parking lot. Her voice, the calmness and care that flowed from her mouth, carried with it the same love that lured me to their table the night before. Within minutes I found myself opening the front door to the pregnancy center and boldly walking in.

As the door shut behind me, wailing and gnashing of teeth where the deep, dark dungeon used to stand erupted in a dark chorus of torturous sounds. Every cousin and in-law of the spirits of fear, guilt, shame, and regret from miles around came to the wake. They cried out with horrific hair-curling sounds in vain for their master to come rescue their kin who were engulfed in a volcano. Instead of spewing out the soldiers of darkness as it did earlier over my car, the volcano burned on and on and the snarling, salivating wolves would not die.

A thunderous rumble declared victory in the heavens as the cross of torture with its living, breathing, pulsating bright red blood hovered over me. Its life-giving flow of pure, unconditional love poured over me creating a protective barrier that no demon of darkness could possibly penetrate. Evil spirits of fear, guilt, shame, and regret, who had stalked me from the minute I pulled out of the post office parking lot, trembled and fled as this perfect love engulfed the room.

The great cloud of witnesses and the armies of light stood at attention as the Great King wrapped His arms around me, and placed on me a royal crown. The tortured tramp had been rescued from the dungeon and declared His daughter in the sight of every principality and power. She had been delivered from the kingdom of darkness and welcomed into His kingdom of light. She would wear her royal robe woven with gold and take a tour in this place where, had she still been in captivity, she would have never survived.

Fear, guilt, shame, and regret were truly dealt a death blow as I sat in perfect peace waiting for the bubbly, passionate woman I had met the night before to take me on the tour.

For He has rescued us from the kingdom of darkness and transferred us into the Kingdom of his dear Son, who purchased our freedom and forgave our sins. (Colossians 1:13-14, LRB)

We know how much God loves us, and we have put our trust in his love. God is love, and all who live in love live in God, and God lives in them. And as we live in God, our love grows more perfect. So we will not be afraid on the day of judgment, but we can face him with confidence because we live like Jesus here in this world. Such love has no fear, because perfect love expels all fear. If we are afraid, it is for fear of punishment, and this shows that we have not fully experienced his perfect love. (1 John 4:16-18, LRB)

The royal daughter is all glorious within the palace; her clothing is woven with gold. She shall be brought to the King in robes of many colors... (Psalm 45:13-14a)

As I waited for my tour, the Man whose blood split the earth and triumphantly carried me out of the dungeon knelt before me, placing a basin at my feet. He removed my shoes and set them to the side. He cupped my head in His hands and lifted my chin toward His gaze as He stood. I noticed a filthy, bloodstained garment draped around His waist. Methodically and with precision He removed it from his side and held it out for me to see. I recognized it as the soiled wedding gown that covered me with fear, guilt, shame, and regret for years in the dungeon.

A holy hush overtook the great cloud of witnesses and the armies of light as they hovered over us, preparing for what was to come. The King had chosen this day, this place, this KAIROS time to show me, along with every principality and power known to heaven, what transpired the moment He carried me out of the dungeon on His shoulders.

I had come to trust this Healing Presence, this gentle Shepherd. Without hesitation, I reached for the filthy, blood-stained garment. The chains of fear, guilt, shame, and regret over Chloe Renee's death snapped in two as I looked into the eyes of the One who took this filthy garment and wore it as His own. The moment I touched the garment and our eyes met, the basin that held my feet filled with a warm, soothing substance. A glorious mixture of water and blood flowing from His side poured over the filthy, bloodstained garment of my captivity, washing it clean. He held me close as we watched fear, guilt, shame, and regret fall off the garment into the basin and they were no more. The great cloud of witnesses and the armies of light turned away in reverent silence as they knew the most personal, intimate moment of my deliverance was about to occur.

Tears streamed down my face as the Great King knelt in front of me, preparing to wash my feet. *Who am I that my Lord would wash my feet?* The warm, soothing substance that surrounded my feet came alive the moment His hands lifted my foot to wash it with the newly cleansed garment. The same living, breathing, pulsating, bright red blood that seeped through His robe splitting the earth as He carried me out of the dungeon was living, breathing, and pulsating in the mixture He was using to wash my feet.

How glorious! How wonderful! How awesome is His love for me!

Oblivious to the natural atmosphere surrounding me, I was engulfed in a love that knows no end. The cross of torture that hung over my car earlier was now suspended above this most powerful, KAIROS moment in my life. His hands, while washing, cleansing, and purifying my soul, were at the same time empowering and commissioning my feet to take me to places I would have never gone before...places where He, Himself wanted to go.

This moment the great cloud of witnesses and the armies of light dared not look upon had arrived in glorious splendor announcing a new beginning! This was to be the beginning of something much greater, something more powerful, more intimately connected to the Great King than anything I had ever encountered before. It was to be birthed in the Spirit when His hands touched my feet, when the living, breathing, pulsating blood that surrounded us in the basin united with the blood dripping from the cross of torture that hung above us. It was to be something more beautiful than the English language has words for...

The cleansing towel that had been transformed from the garment of shame danced in the Great King's hands as He lifted my feet out of the glorious mixture to dry them and put my shoes back on. His strong arms lifted me to my feet and held me close. He whispered, *Arise, go over this Jordan. Be strong and of good courage; do not be afraid, nor be dismayed, for I am with you wherever you go. Every place that the sole of your foot will tread upon, I have given you. I will be with you. I will not leave you or forsake you* (*Joshua 1:2-3, 5, 9*).

REST-REFLECT-REFRESH

Are you in your quiet, safe place? If not, I want to encourage you to get there, expecting wonderful things from your Deliverer as we rest and reflect on what was going on in the last few pages of *Chloe's Cry*. Once you are situated, with pen, paper, or journal nearby, take a few minutes to meditate on the following Scriptures. Ask God to reveal what they mean to you and record your thoughts in whatever you are using for a journal.

And when forty years had passed, an Angel of the Lord appeared to him in a flame of fire in a bush, in the wilderness of Mount Sinai. When Moses saw it, he marveled at the sight; and as he drew near to observe, the voice of the Lord came to him, saying, "I am the God of your fathers — the God of Abraham, the God of Isaac, and the God of Jacob." And Moses trembled and dared not look. Then the Lord said to him, "Take your sandals off your feet, for the place where you stand is holy ground. I have surely seen the oppression of My people who are in Egypt; I have heard their groaning and have come down to deliver them. And now come, I will send you to Egypt." (Acts 7:30-34)

After that, He poured water into a basin and began to wash the disciples' feet and to wipe them with the towel with which He was girded. Then He came to Simon Peter and Peter said to Him, "Lord are You washing my feet?" Jesus answered and said to him, "What I am doing you do not understand now, but you will know after this. (John 13:5-7)

So, when He had washed their feet, taken His garments, and sat down again, He said to them, "Do you know what I have done to you? You call Me Teacher and Lord, and you say well, for so I am. If I then, your Lord and Teacher, have washed your feet, you also ought to wash one another's feet. For I have given you an example, that you should do as I have done to you." (John 13:12-15)

In order to write this Rest-Reflect-Refresh section of *Chloe's Cry*, I was compelled to re-read what transpired the day Jesus washed my feet in the waiting room of Palmetto Pregnancy Center. I was brought to tears as the same Healing Presence that surrounded me at the center scooped me up and held me close to His heart. The magnitude of His unconditional love overwhelmed me as I felt His heartbeat and I became undone. I walked around the house praising Jesus for His tender loving care, holding my abortion recovery journal against my heart. As Peter said, so say I, "Why would You, my Lord come to Palmetto Pregnancy Center and wash my feet?" My spirit soared as I heard, "So the Scriptures may be fulfilled in your life..."

The Lord is my Shepherd, I shall not want.
He makes me to lie down in green pastures;
He leads me beside the still waters, He restores my soul.
He leads me in paths of righteousness for His name's sake.
Yea, though I walk through the valley of the shadow of death,
I will fear no evil; for You are with me;
Your rod and Your staff, they comfort me.
You prepare a table before me in the presence of my enemies;
You anoint my head with oil; my cup runs over.
Surely goodness and mercy shall follow me
all the days of my life;
And I will dwell in the house of the Lord forever.
(Psalm 23)

Psalm 23 came to life when the Great King knelt in front of me to wash my feet. I knew without a shadow of a doubt that this tender Shepherd would not leave me or forsake me. I knew I would be able to take the tour and that His goodness and His mercy would follow me every step of the way.

Are you standing on Holy Ground? How do you see Psalm 23 in light of your abortion recovery? Have you considered allowing the Lord to wash your feet? Are you willing to trust Him to walk with you through the valley of the shadow of death of your abortion experience? Journal your thoughts. Share them with someone you trust.

I would encourage you to re-read this short chapter "Standing on Holy Ground." Ask the Lord to reveal to you something about your abortion experience. Do not be in a hurry! Let the comforting truth of today's Refresh Scripture clothe you with peace before moving on...

You will keep him in perfect peace whose mind is stayed on You, because he trusts in You. (Isaiah 26:3)

Chapter 6

Tour or Torture?

"Hey, Lynn!" My tour guide entered the waiting room with the same bubbly, enthusiastic demeanor as she had the night before, immediately putting me at ease. "Would you like to come back to my office and talk before taking the tour?" I answered, "No, I think I'd like to take the tour first." At the time, I had no idea how critical that decision was going to be.

As my tour guide and I engaged in a sisterly embrace, the great cloud of witnesses and the armies of light stood at attention and cheered. The victorious King had used her embrace to shield my heart from what He knew I was going to face as I followed her through the center.

I remember feeling very out of place, yet a surreal sense of belonging hovered over me at the same time. The duality of this experience cannot be taken lightly. Here I was, a post-abortive woman carrying a thirty-eight-year abortion secret into a pregnancy center whose sole purpose for existence is to save babies from abortion! And yet, I was intentionally taking a tour of the place! Unknowingly, I was about to experience one of the greatest miracles of my life!

Because of skilled disassociation and determination on my part to live in my safe place of denial, I was not accustomed to being around anything that had to do with pregnancy, babies, or children. The everyday, natural language of the pregnancy center was foreign to me. I felt as though I had gone to another country with barely a basic understanding of the language. Because I never had children after Chloe Renee's death, prenatal, ultrasound, PT, and a host of other baby terms used during the tour had never been part of my everyday, natural language.

My beautiful tour guide swept through the center with ease, and I followed along as if nothing was out of the ordinary. We moved swiftly though each room while I learned how the center operated. I met some of the staff and was welcomed with the same compassionate enthusiasm my guide had shown me earlier. I was feeling pretty confident about the experience until we stood within eyeshot of a room that caused my heart to race and intense hidden panic to rise.

Something deep within me screamed until I could barely catch my breath. Outwardly, no one would have been the wiser, but the surreal sense of belonging was quickly being swallowed up by dark voices from my tortured past. Although I had been delivered from the dungeon and its tormenting spirits, the evil cousins of fear, guilt, shame, and regret who had claimed territory in the pregnancy center gathered together to challenge my deliverance on their own turf.

As we stood in eyeshot of this particular room, they knew it was their last chance. If they lost this battle, the war would be over. I had come so far and battled so much with the King of Light carrying me on His shoulders that they would have to win this one hands down in order to keep me in bondage. The great cloud of witnesses stood to their feet and the armies of light positioned themselves with the sword of the spirit raised high above their heads as I faced this destiny-determining battle…

Oh no! Don't make me go in there! I can't go in there! Oh! Please! I can't!

My gracious tour guide continued talking. I politely listened while every warrior on both sides of the battle brought out the big boys, the biggest fighter weapons known to their respective armies. This would be the battle to end all battles and decide my destiny…

"Do not be afraid. Stand still, and see the salvation of the Lord, which He will accomplish for you today, for the Egyptians whom you see today, you shall see again no more forever. The Lord will fight for you and you shall hold your peace." (Exodus 14:13-14)

Desperate screams from my tortured past were silenced as I followed her into the room. I was deep into enemy territory and I knew it. Snipers were stationed all around. Evil spirits grabbed my neck and began to squeeze. Gasping for air, I looked at crocheted baby blankets, baby booties, and little baby hats, holding my breath while trying to listen to my tour guide. Little blue and pink things for newborn babies were everywhere, surrounding me in a very, very small, almost closet-sized room. I would have despaired and run out of there had it not been for the cross of torture hanging directly over my head. It hung over me during the whole tour, dripping the living, breathing, pulsating, bright red blood everywhere we went. It now hung directly in the center of the closet-sized room, calling for the King of Light to enter.

I was still gasping for air as the King entered the room. The suffocating spirits tightened their grip in one last murderous attempt to stake claim on my life. The King of Light slowly walked toward me with a beautiful shiny object dangling from His hand. It was the most beautiful necklace I had ever seen. He placed it on my neck and said, "You are My royal daughter. Right here, today, I have set a table before you in the presence of your enemies. As I lead you out of this valley of the shadow of Chloe Renee's death, I will anoint your head with oil and your cup will run over. I will lead you into green meadows of rest. I will walk beside still waters with you as I restore your soul. This is the end of their reign. My goodness and mercy shall follow you all the days of your life. You and Chloe Renee will live together in My house forever along the beach where we will build sandcastles together. Your story will be My trumpet shouting throughout the heavens, declaring war on the captors of my sons and daughters who have been imprisoned by the dark hand of abortion."

The living, breathing, pulsating words of the Lord's Twenty-third Psalm caused lightening from heaven to strike the suffocating spirits. Their hands went up in flames. They screamed and cursed in agony. In a last, very futile attempt to continue holding me captive, they pushed the replay button in my subconscious that contained images of the day of Chloe Renee's death.

They were no match for the Deliverer whose blood split the earth and swallowed up my captor. The King of Light exclaimed with a thunderous shout, "IT IS FINISHED!" Immediately, the flashbacks and tormenting evil spirits disappeared into the living, breathing, pulsating bright red blood of the cross of torture that hung above me in the very, very small, almost closet sized room. The Great King touched my eyes with His nail-scarred hands and triumphantly said, "Tell Me, where are your accusers?"

"I see no one, Mighty King."

"You say rightly, 'I see no one.' For they are no more."

Having disarmed principalities and powers, He made a public spectacle of them, triumphing over them. (Colossians 2:15)

The great cloud of witnesses and armies of light stood at attention with holy respect as the Great King knelt before a golden chest that they knew held my destiny. In His hand were a set of keys, which he held up toward heaven and said, "I am the first and the last. I am He who lives, and was dead, and behold, I am alive forevermore. Amen. And I have the keys of Hades and of Death (Revelation 1:18). This day I release the destiny that has been incarcerated in this golden chest since 1978."

Thunder and lightning declared the power and authority of His words as He unlocked the golden chest. Bright light, too bright for human eyes to gaze upon, shot up from the inside of the chest as He lifted the lid. It almost knocked me to the floor. If the Great King had not touched my eyes earlier, I would have been instantly blinded. Out of the bright light He pulled a garment made of the finest linen in the world and held it up for all to see. Its beauty and majesty were beyond words.

He turned to me and said, "Here, this is for you."

"Oh no! Great King...I could never..."

"Why, My Beloved?"

"Why...it's too white...too pure."

"Beloved, do you not know where this golden chest and fine garment came from?"

"No, Great King, I do not."

He took my hand and placed it on my heart. "My cherished child, My beautiful bride, while you lived in the deep, dark dungeon, I saw every tear you shed. I heard every cry you cried. I felt your fear, your guilt, your shame, and your regret. I wept for you. I agonized over your pain. I never left your side, but you would not call on Me. I waited and waited, and I patiently waited right outside the bars of your dungeon, until you answered My deep calling deep call."

"What is this...Your deep calling deep call...oh Great King?"

"In the deepest part of your dark dungeon, I called you to Myself. I asked you to trust Me enough to let Me in. Is it not there where you experienced the *depth* of My unfailing forgiveness, the *depth* of My unconditional love, and the *depth* of My infinite compassion? Is it not when you allowed Me into your dungeon that you were able to see Me, hear Me, and experience Me in ways you have never known? Is it not in the depth of your darkness, where the depth of the light of My love was able to carry you to freedom?"

"Oh yes, My Great King! Oh yes!"

"The answer to My question lies in the dungeon...the deepest, darkest place of your existence. This is where I found a treasure chest full of pure-white fine linen to clothe you with as I restore you and send you out to help Me restore others. This is deep calling deep...the depths of Me calling the depths of you."

"In the intimacy of the place of your greatest failure, expanded destiny was conceived. Chloe Renee's life and death are not in vain. She is alive and well in the spirit of reconciliation between mother and child, and mother and Me. We will go forth, the three of us into the enemy's camp of those who have been traumatized by abortion, and offer them freedom from their incarceration. This is the victory of the restoration of the broken three-strand cord."

"Oh yes! Great King! Oh yes!"

"My child, My bride. Do you now understand the mystery of the golden chest and the pure-white garment made of the finest linen in the world?"

"Yes! My Great King! Yes, I do!"

As I reached for the glorious garment, the great cloud of witnesses exclaimed, "And to her it was granted to be arrayed in fine linen, clean and bright, for the fine linen is the righteous acts of the saints" (Revelation 19:8)!

I looked at the garment tag and warm tears filled my eyes. The great King held me close as they gently fell on the label. I could barely speak as I looked into His eyes and said, "Oh Great King, it says "Made in USA, October 1978, gently swish in warm water."

He said, "Yes, My Beloved, your sins are washed away. Your filthy, bloodstained rag has been made new. I have turned your dark dungeon into a golden treasure chest."

His blood opened the earth and swallowed my captor. His cross of torture absorbed all the fear, guilt, shame, and regret connected to Chloe Renee's death. His hand, placed on my heart, instantly dissolved the last remaining evil spirit...the spirit of self-loathing. I stood free of anything that would stop me from putting on this glorious garment and following the Great King wherever He would lead me.

My thirty-eight years of captivity had ended. The stains of my sin were washed away. My filthy, bloodstained rag had been removed. I stood before heaven and earth in a spotless white robe made of fine linen with the King of the universe at my side. The great cloud of witnesses bowed to the King of Light and

His army saluted Him as I followed my guide back up to her office, ready and eager to share my abortion story for the first time in thirty-eight years...

And when I passed by you and saw you struggling in your own blood, I said to you in your blood, "Live!" Yes, I said to you, "Live!" Then I washed you in water, yes, I thoroughly washed off your blood, and I anointed you with oil. I clothed you in embroidered cloth and gave you sandals of badger skin; I clothed you with fine linen and covered you with silk. I adorned you with ornaments, put bracelets on your wrist, and a chain on your neck. And I put a jewel in your nose, earrings in your ears, and a beautiful crown on your head. (Ezekiel 16:6, 9-12)

I was free! I was free! I was free! I *wanted* to tell someone my story! I *needed* to tell someone my story! It would happen here! It would happen now! After carrying this silent secret for thirty-eight years, I had no idea how heavy it had become until I sat across from my tour guide, pouring out my heart to her. The same Healing Presence that engulfed our sisterly embrace before we started our tour filled every nook and cranny of her office as thirty-eight years of pent-up tears of grief and loss filled my eyes. Every word, every sentence, every paragraph I shared was like an axe chipping away at the monumental boulder I was carrying. And, oh how exhilarating! Oh, how freeing! The longer I talked, the lighter I felt.

Words I had never spoken to anyone came pouring out without fear, guilt, shame, or regret weighing them down. I was safe. I was loved. I was not judged. She let me talk and talk, even when I'm sure I didn't make much sense. Breathing in the air in the room was like breathing in warm oil that filled my lungs and poured over my broken heart. I was telling my story! Someone was listening and not judging! I heard no preaching. I heard no Scripture. I heard no counseling. I heard nothing but, "I'm so very sorry Lynn, so very sorry." My healing had begun. My story touched her heart. She shared my grief; she shared my pain. She wept with me.

Never in my entire Christian life of twenty-two years have I experienced the reality of Jesus' unconditional love for me more than during the time I spent with this beautiful vessel of the Living God.

Brethren, if a man is overtaken in any trespass, you who are spiritual restore such a one in a spirit of gentleness, considering yourself lest you also be tempted. Bear one another's burdens, and so fulfill the law of Christ. (Galatians 6:1-2)

Her silence, her tears, her tenderhearted, caring presence transformed an everyday business office into holy ground where the Great King would call me deeper into His heart and my healing journey. He knelt before me with a dozen red roses, dripping with His crimson blood, His eyes filled with compassion and care. The great cloud of witnesses and the armies of light bowed with heavenly respect in a moment of silence as He presented the roses to me.

Melodies and music unlike anything I have ever heard saturated the atmosphere with emotional and spiritual healing, setting the stage for what my King was about to do. He took my hand, looked into my tear-filled eyes, and began to sing what would be the first of many love songs He would sing to me as He healed me from Chloe Renee's death...

"Rise up My love, My fair one and come away. For lo, the winter is past, the rain is over and gone. The flowers appear on the earth. The time of singing has come, and the voice of the turtledove is heard in our land. The fig tree puts forth her green figs, and the vines with the tender grapes give a good smell. Rise up my love, my fair one, and come away." (Song of Solomon 2:10-13)

"Oh My dove, in the clefts of the rock, in the secret places of the cliff, Let me see your face, let me hear your voice, for your voice is sweet, and your face is lovely..." (Song of Solomon 2:14)

The call was gentle; the call was deep. He ushered me out of the room and out of the building, riding on the wings of eagles as I set my heart toward His call and my ears to His voice...

My Beloved, My beautiful queen... Do you want to be made well?

REST-REFLECT-REFRESH

As I re-read this latest chapter, "Tour or Torture," there is no other response than for me to stop right now and worship the One who carried me out of the dungeon of darkness on His lacerated, bloody back. I give praise and honor to the One who had compassion on young Lynn Potter while she cried out year after year, living in incarcerated torment. I worship the King who was brutally tortured and murdered so my tormented soul could be set free...

Surely, He has born our griefs and carried our sorrows. (Isaiah 53:4)

That you may proclaim the praises of Him who called you out of darkness into His marvelous light. (1 Peter 2:9b)

I worship the King who came to heal my broken heart, to open my prison door, to comfort me as I mourn Chloe Renee's death. I worship, give praise and honor, to the King who came to exchange the ashes of my life for beauty, to change my mourning into joy, and to give me a garment of praise in exchange for the spirit of heaviness. I worship Him! He is my King! He is my Deliverer! His name is Jesus! King Jesus! He is the King who Isaiah wrote about!

The Spirit of the Lord God is upon Me, because the Lord has anointed Me to preach good tidings to the poor; He has sent Me to heal the brokenhearted, to proclaim liberty to the captives, and the opening of the prison to those who are bound; to proclaim the acceptable year of the Lord, and the day of vengeance of our God; to comfort all who mourn. To console those who mourn in Zion. To give them beauty for ashes, the oil of joy for mourning, the garment of praise for the spirit of heaviness; that they may be called trees of righteousness, the planting of the Lord, that He may be glorified. (Isaiah 61:1-3)

For He made Him, who knew no sin to be sin for us, that we might become the righteousness of God in Him. (2 Corinthians 5:21)

Do you know this Great King? Have you experienced the love that took Him to the cross where He died in your place, became sin for you, and cancelled the debt you owe? Do you know this risen Savior who wants to set you free from a life filled with fear, guilt, shame, and regret over your abortion decision?

As I wrote the dedication page of *Chloe's Cry*, you were on my heart, and you were on my mind. Why? Because you were on the heart of King Jesus, and because you were on His mind. Just to refresh your memory, I wrote, "*I dedicate* Chloe's Cry *first and foremost to my Lord and Savior, Jesus Christ, without whom there would be no abortion recovery for me.*"

I believe with my whole heart that we are fearfully and wonderfully made by a Creator who knows everything about us. We cannot hide anything from Him, or go anywhere where He is not (Psalm 139:14). I believe Chloe Renee was fearfully and wonderfully made, and choosing to end her life was not just a moral failure or choice of convenience. It was the sin of murder, the murder of my innocent child. These are the cold, hard facts of my abortion experience. Thirty-eight years of hiding in the dark dungeon of denial and disassociation could not change them.

There would be no hope of recovering from such a revelation if this was the end of the story. But the night of the Christmas party had been orchestrated by the King of Light before time began to be the place and time where new chapters in my story were going to be written. When King Jesus invaded my dark dungeon of death with His eternal light of life, He pulled out the divine notebook and began to write. *Chloe's Cry* was safely nestled in His heart until such a time as this. You are now reading part of the destiny the Great King released from incarceration the moment He lifted the lid on the golden chest.

The cold, hard facts of your abortion experience, the ending of your child's life, do not have to be the end of your story! God has a plan and a purpose for your reading *Chloe's Cry*, and the most important part of that plan is to draw you closer to His heart without fear, guilt, shame, or regret holding you back. I lived in that paralyzed state for thirty-eight years. My desire is to lead you to the One who is ready and willing to pick up the divine notebook with your name on it, and begin to write.

King Jesus took our sin of abortion on His back when they whipped Him nearly to death and brutally pounded nails into His already beaten body. His sacrifice on our behalf satisfied the debt we owe for all our sin, including ending the lives of our unborn children.

Have you trusted His sacrifice and received His forgiveness? Would you sit at the foot of His cross and present yourself and your abortion experience to Him? His Word says that whoever comes to Him, He will not refuse and that if we confess our sin, He is faithful and just to forgive us of our sin and cleanse us from it all, including our abortions (1 John 1:9, John 6:37).

Will you come to Him today? Will you confess your sin and be washed clean by His sacrifice?

If you are willing…these Scriptures speak of you today!

All that the Father gives Me will come to Me, and the one who comes to Me I will by no means cast out. (John 6:37)

If we confess our sins, He is faithful and just to forgive us our sins and to cleanse us from all unrighteousness. (1 John 1:9)

But as many as received Him, to them He gave the right to become children of God, to those who believe on His name. (John 1:12)

This moment in time, this KAIROS time, is holy ground. Your *safe place* has become every bit as holy as my tour guide's office was when I poured out my heart to her. As we lift our broken hearts, empty arms, and sin to King Jesus today, we can be confident that He will not turn us away. He is here in your safe place, waiting to receive you into His arms, call you His own, and lead you into healing and wholeness from your part in the death of your child.

Let's surrender our lives together! We must surrender it all...the good, the bad, the ugly...all of it...including everything that is attached to the death of our unborn children through abortion.

Let's lift our prayer together...

King Jesus, I confess that I am a sinner, unable to save myself, and I recognize my need for You. I believe You are the Son of God, sent to this world to pay the price for my sin, including my sin of abortion. I believe You were crucified, buried, and rose again and are seated at the right hand of God our Father, praying for me right now. I submit myself, my entire life, and all that is within me to You and Your will. I trust Your Word that tells me that if I come to You, I will not be cast away, and that if I confess my sin, You are faithful and just to forgive me and cleanse me from it all. I believe Your Word says that as I receive You as my Savior and the Leader of my life, I have been given the right to be called Your child. Thank You, Jesus for loving me, saving me, and for paying the price for my sin, including my choice to end the life of my unborn child. Thank You for coming to set me free from my past. I submit my abortion experience to You and trust You as I walk the healing journey You have prepared for me. Amen.

I pray as you surrender your entire life to the Healing Presence of our Lord Jesus Christ, that your eyes will be opened to the great love He has for you, and that you will be confident

He is willing and able to bring you out of your abortion darkness into His marvelous light! I encourage you to meditate on our Scripture for this part of our journey and to journal any thoughts that come to mind before you move on...

Fear not, for I have redeemed you; I have called you by your name; You are mine. When you pass through the water, I will be with you; and through the rivers, they shall not overflow you. When you walk through the fire, you shall not be burned. Nor shall the flame scorch you. For I am the Lord your God, the Holy One of Israel, your Savior. (Isaiah 43:1-3).

I rejoice that Chloe Renee's death is not in vain and that I have been given the awesome opportunity to share the rest of my recovery journey with you...

Come...follow me...and let's see what the Great King has in store...

Chapter 7

Preparation for the Promised Land

"Arise, go over this Jordan. Be strong and of good courage; do not be afraid, nor be dismayed, for I am with you wherever you go. Every place that the sole of your foot will tread upon, I have given you. I will be with you. I will not leave you or forsake you." (from Joshua 1:2, 9, 3, 5)

These words, filled with promise and destiny, were spoken to me only after the Great King had accomplished a mighty work in my life. The personal, intimate washing of my feet had to be accomplished before He could commission me to follow Him into this new chapter He desired to write in Chloe Renee's and my story. He said, "Be strong and of good courage; do not be afraid, nor be dismayed, for I am with you wherever you go."

Not only did He promise to be with me every step of the way, but He also informed me that He had already given me victory…I just had to get up, go, and walk in it! *Every place that the sole of your foot will tread upon, I have given you.* That's past tense! Already happened! Bought and purchased by the living, breathing, pulsating blood that continually flows from the cross of torture above me. My healing, wholeness, and expanded destiny was just across the Jordan!

All I had to do was trust Him, get up, and go!

Something powerful happens when the King of the universe speaks directly into our spirit. His words are full of life and light. They are full of His Spirit and truth. They have the ability to deliver, transform, restore, and empower. Deliverance, transformation, restoration, and empowerment are the four stages of recovery the Great King has planned for those of us who earnestly seek healing and wholeness from abortion.

Then Joshua commanded the officers of the people, saying, "Pass through the camp and command the people, saying, 'Prepare provisions for yourselves, for within three days you will cross over this Jordan, to go in to possess the land which the Lord your God is giving you to possess.'" (Joshua 1:9-11)

The Great King had already accomplished two of the four stages in my recovery as I chose to trust His Healing Presence. I had been delivered from the dungeon at the Christmas party and transformed from a locked-up tramp into a liberated royal daughter at the pregnancy center. Now it was time for stage three…restoration!

It took a few days of solitude and reflection to come to grips with what had just happened. I would never be the same! Within a short twenty-four-hour period, part of me had been resurrected from the dead, and I had truly become a new creation (2 Corinthians 5:17). I was no longer tethered to the ground under the weight of Chloe Renee's death, but was soaring through the heavens on wings of eagles. The dungeon that held me captive was destroyed and the land where it once stood excavated and cleared out. The great cloud of witnesses and the armies of light delighted in their new assignments as they commanded bulldozers and backhoes to clear the land. Restoration called from deep in the land and the Great King smiled as He prepared me for the journey.

* * *

Today's the day. I woke with an insatiable desire to follow my King into the uncharted waters of healing from Chloe Renee's death. *Come My Beloved, today is the day.* He stood before me, His broken, bloody body pouring out a love song as He stretched out His nail-scarred hands toward me…

When you pass through the waters I will be with you; and through the rivers, they shall not overflow you. When you walk through the fire, you shall not be burned, nor shall the flame scorch you. For I am the Lord, your God, the Holy One of Israel, your Savior. (Isaiah 43:2-3)

I am the Lord your God, who has delivered you out of the hands of your enemies. I am the Lord, in your midst. Today is the day you will stand in the middle of this Jordan on dry ground and begin to write stones of remembrance for all generations to read. When they read these stones, they will know that it is I, the Lord your God, who has lead you out of the dungeon and into your promised land. (Based on Joshua 4.)

The room filled with a golden hue as He handed me a beautiful bag covered in radiant colors of the finest linen, and placed around my neck a golden chain, on which hung a golden key.

"Oh, Great King! Is this not the beautiful necklace of the very small closet-sized room filled with baby things from the pregnancy center?"

"Indeed, My Beloved. Yes, indeed it is."

"And, what of this bag, Great King?"

"It is from the golden chest of destiny, of the same room, skillfully crafted for you for such a time as this."

"Whatever shall I use these gifts for, my King?"

"They are for your journey across the Jordan into your promised land."

Perplexed, I looked into the empty bag, and caressed the golden key that hung from the chain.

"Oh! Thank You, Great King, these are beautiful...but I don't understand..."

He grabbed my hand and said...

As you do not know what is the way of the wind, or how the bones grow in the womb of her who is with child, so you do not know the works of God who makes everything. (Ecclesiastes 11:5)

As I pondered this great mystery, I followed Him out of the safety of my home, with childlike trust that He would not take me anywhere I was not prepared to go. He led me to an office supply aisle in a mega discount store where journals of different sizes and colors were scattered all over the shelves. Resisting the temptation to straighten them out, I focused on the task at hand and said, "Great King, what of these piles of journals?"

"Herein lies a hidden treasure that has been missing from the golden chest of the closet-sized room since the day of Chloe Renee's death. Seek, my child, and you will find."

I picked through them until I was drawn to a simple journal with a blue cover. Peace, mixed with joy, flooded my soul as I held it close to my heart. Its exterior was rough to the touch, much like the scars remaining from my years of incarceration in the deep, dark dungeon. The empty pages cried out for *Chloe's Cry* to be written on them. I closed the journal knowing I had made a connection in the Spirit. As I pondered the significance of its exterior color, deep, deep blue, like the clear blue October skies of South Carolina, the great King said...

"Deep calls to deep, My Beloved...this is the one."

"Yes, Great King...this is the one." I said.

A sense of safety, security, and excitement washed over me as the Great King and I prepared to leave. This simple blue journal was going to be my friend, my confidant, and my trusted companion in the days ahead as I followed Him into unchartered waters. Its empty pages, ready to receive my deepest thoughts and emotions, would be used by the King to hold me up and carry me through the healing journey He had prepared for me. I walked toward the checkout lanes with full assurance I was about to make one of the most important purchases of my life.

* * *

"Great King, may I ask You something?"

"Yes, My Beloved?"

"What's the best way to cross this Jordan?"

"One step at a time, My daughter. One step at a time."

"Yes, my King…one step at a time."

"Your journal, covered in deep, deep blue, is the driving force and compass of your journey. As you meditate on My goodness, your deepest thoughts and emotions connected with Chloe Renee's death will surface, needing a place of transparency to be processed. As you put pen to paper, holy dialogue will be birthed as deep calls to deep. I will meet you on the pages of this journal and we will work through your trauma together."

"Oh, my King…I had no idea!" Tears of gratitude filled my eyes at the prospect of such a transparent, intimate experience.

He then presented me a key and a small stone, formed and fashioned from a deep, deep blue lapis lazuli, which I knew was highly sought after, and symbolic of royalty, honor, spirit, and vision. "Place this deep blue key upon your golden chain beside the golden key. It is My promise to restore you to the place of royalty and honor in My kingdom, and release your destiny with My Spirit and My vision. As we walk together step-by-step toward crossing the Jordan into the Promised Land, wear this precious key around your neck as a reminder that I, the Lord your God, have called you to follow Me into freedom. Deep calls to deep is the first key, transparency is the first stone."

"Oh, Great King! This is too marvelous for one such as I to comprehend!"

"Beloved, I knew you before I formed you in your mother's womb. I called you to be healed and whole even before you decided to end Chloe Renee's life. I have rescued you from the clutches of your past and set you free to walk in your destiny. I call you now to share your story with the freeing spirit of transparency so others also may be set free. Transparency is deep calling deep, and deep calling deep is the key that unlocks the mystery of the first step."

"Oh, Great King, what could I say that others have not? I am but one of many."

"Beloved, do not say, 'I have nothing more to say.' For your story shall go everywhere I choose to send it and whatever is in your heart from Me you will speak. I have redeemed you and *Chloe's Cry* for such a time as this. If you remain silent at this time then deliverance for those traumatized by abortion will come from another, and Chloe's death will not produce its intended end-time harvest. Do not be afraid for I am with you to deliver you as you follow Me." (Based on Jeremiah 1:4-8, Esther 4:14, John 12:24)

"Great King?"

"Yes, My Beloved?"

"What of the golden key that came with the golden chain? Whatever is it for?"

To everything there is a season, a time for every purpose under heaven. (Ecclesiastes 3:1)

* * *

The deaths of our children cry out to be recognized, mourned, and vindicated even as the blood of Abel cried out to God in Genesis 4:10. As I continue sharing our story with you, I pray Chloe Renee's death will produce a harvest of life in your personal journey toward healing as you follow me over my Jordan River into my promised land. In order to honor the spirit of transparency, I have chosen not to edit most of the journal entries I will share with you during this portion of our journey. I pray that King Jesus will be able to bring healing and wholeness to your abortion experience through my transparency...

This is the first recorded entry after I *intentionally* followed the Great King with childlike trust to the store where He would introduce me to the journal of my journey...

Journal Entry December 21, 2016

If you would <u>prepare your heart</u> and <u>stretch out your hands toward Him</u>, if iniquity were in your hand, and you put it far away, and would not let wickedness dwell in your tents, then surely you could lift up your face without spot, yes, you could be steadfast and not fear. Because you would forget your misery and remember it as waters that have passed away and your life would be brighter than noonday. Though you were dark, you would be like the morning and you would be secure because there is hope. Yes, you would dig around you, and take your rest in safety. You would also lie down and no one would make you afraid. (Job 11:13-19)

Today I have taken the first official step toward preparing my heart and extending my hands toward Him. I have been contemplating this for several days, but wanted a special journal to be my friend, confidant, and aid through this process. I took the next step toward this uncertain journey by purchasing this journal today and boldly giving it the title, "In honor and memory of Chloe Renee...my daughter."

Now, I must confess to be as so bold to title this journal in this manner is to create life out of death, light out of darkness, and hope out of hopelessness.

This is my story—no—our stories. Chloe Renee's and mine, much of which I cannot remember as the memories are buried beneath the rubble, piles of guilt and shame, years of a numb, distant past. New creation in Christ—old things are gone— behold new things have arrived. Yes, and amen...however? Simple truth, yet buried beneath a living, breathing experience

Chloe's Cry

of mother-daughter oneness screaming to be acknowledged, recognized, and given highest honor of remembrance. How can one go on in the same manner when such an experience has been unearthed from the tomb from which it has been held captive? The tomb of the womb where life once promised to bud, only to be snuffed out by selfish desires and uninformed catastrophic decisions.

It is in the heart of Father God to raise the experience from the depths of guilt and shame—setting the owner of the womb free and introducing her to the occupant who was given life—if for such a brief moment.

There was a life budding—a soul—a person whom Father God formed and fashioned in His likeness within the womb of she who would decide not to choose life.

Years have gone by since that day of decision—so many that all I can remember is that it must have been sometime late 1978 or early 1979. It is now 2016, almost forty years later and the Spirit of the Father who received Chloe Renee into His arms on that day of decision is asking me to follow Him on a journey that will set me free from the guilt and shame.

It all started innocently on December 6, 2016 as I was invited to a Christmas dinner at Westminster Presbyterian Church in Rock Hill, SC. I never turn down the chance to eat and fellowship with this group of several hundred ladies in a decked-out room during the Christmas season. Never in a million years would I have thought this event would change me forever.

INTENTIONAL...this word suggests a deliberate act, a pre-planned, determined, purposeful action on our part toward an expected end. I was *INTENTIONAL* about seeking healing and wholeness from the aftermath of Chloe Renee's death, and that *INTENTIONALITY* empowered me to trust the leading of the Great King with childlike trust. The King's expected end for this part of my journey had been accomplished...the journal of my journey was in my hand, ready to receive the *deep calling deep* dialogue that was about to begin.

Being intentional and trusting the Great King's lead is crucial to our healing!

You may notice that from here on in, I will be referring to my abortion as *Chloe Renee's death*. I found this *intentional action* crucial to my healing. I had to come to grips with the cold, brutal truth that this event was not an abortion...it was the intentional murdering of my child. It was the hardest thing I have ever faced in my life, yet the most freeing. Surely Jesus knew what He was talking about when He said,

You shall know the truth, and the truth shall make you free. (John 8:32)

Referring to that dark day of decision as the day of Chloe Renee's death recognizes her as a living being with a soul who was fearfully and wonderfully made by the God who created her. It gives dignity and honor to her as my daughter and me as her mother. In the midst of the horror of this revelation, there is peace found in the truth that I will see her one day and she will run into my empty arms shouting...

O death, where is your sting? Oh! Hades, where is your victory? (1 Corinthians 15:55)

REST-RFLECT-REFRESH

Read Job 11:13-19a again. How have you prepared your heart for your personal healing journey with the Great King? Have you stretched out your hands and your empty arms to Him in repentance and expectation of His forgiveness? What promises in Job 11:13-19a are ours for being *INTENTIONAL* about repenting of the sin of abortion and receiving His forgiveness?

Being delivered from the dungeon and transformed by the Great King was just the beginning of my journey toward healing and wholeness. In order to heal from the scars left in the aftermath of Chloe Renee's death and move on to the restoration stage, I had to face the facts of what happened to my precious child by my choice at the hand of an abortionist some thirty-eight years ago. The only way I could survive such a traumatic revelation would be by giving the Great King access into the depths of my experience, and allowing His love to miraculously heal the scars. It is now time for me to invite you to do the same.

I trust you are in your safe place, ready for the Great King to speak. Take some time to re-read the notes you have written in your healing journal. Leaf through the beginning pages of this book, looking for the Scriptures in bold, black type. Meditate on the ones that catch your eye and journal your thoughts. This is no time to be in a hurry, or distracted by anything that would prevent you from hearing the voice of the Great King for yourself. Without submitting to this first step of and receiving this first key, your healing will be incomplete at best…

This is where we stop to listen for *deep calling deep…*

King Jesus, we come before You right now and ask Your mercy and grace be upon us as we take this most important, intentional step toward our healing and wholeness. We ask that You would shower us with Your unconditional love, the same love that took You to the cross to bear the sin of our part in the intentional death of our children, and to free us from all the trauma associated to it. We ask that You would honor our transparency and grant us peace.

Great and mighty King, we come boldly into the throne room of Your Presence in response to the cry of the deepest part of Your heart where our stories reside unfinished. We submit to the plan and process You have prepared for us to come to grips with the reality of what happened when we made the decision to submit our bodies to abortion. We present our brokenness to You, our Great King, our Divine Healer, and give You permission to do open-heart surgery in the manner You deem best fit for us. The depths of our pain, sorrow, grief, guilt, and shame only You know, for we have been unable until now to face the truth of our condition. As we lie upon Your spiritual surgical table, we ask You to do a work in us that would bring glory to You and honor the sacrifice You made in order for us to be healed. May the testimony of our lips and the meditation of our hearts be pleasing unto You, oh Lord.

Pour out your thoughts, emotions, struggles, fears, everything deep, deep, deep in the recesses of your experience. This was your child! He or she deserves to be recognized! Do what it takes! Repent, cry, pound pillows, do whatever it takes to allow the Great King access! Deep calls to deep...your healing will be incomplete without responding to deep calling deep!

Take as much time as you need with this portion of our journey. It may take days, weeks, who knows how long to move from this spot. As you allow the Great King access into the depths of your experience, you will have answered His *deep calls deep* call and received your key that unlocks the mystery of the first step...they key of transparency.

Scriptures to meditate on for this part of our journey...

Call to Me, and I will answer you, and show you great and mighty things, which you do not know. (Jeremiah 33:3)

Deep calls to deep. At the sound of Your waterfalls all Your waves and billows have gone over me. The Lord will command His loving-kindness in the daytime, and in the night His song shall be with me — a prayer to the God of my life. (Psalm 42:7-8)

When you pass through the waters, I will be with you; and through the rivers, they shall not overflow you, when you walk through the fire, you shall not be burned, nor shall the flame scorch you. For I am the Lord your God, the Holy One of Israel, your Savior. (Isaiah 43:2-3)

Journal your thoughts.

Chapter 8

Going Back to Move Forward

Journal Entry December 22, 2016

I'm reading Shattered into Beautiful *where today I feel quite a shattered-scattered sense of confusion-purpose-destiny. At sixty years of age and retired from secular work — this full-time ministry has left me disillusioned because 2016 seems to have halted my dreams, a screeching halt — perhaps in the recesses of my mind — a moving backwards instead of forward. This Christmas I find myself in intense pain-loneliness-failure and shame. It is the calling of the Holy Spirit of comfort Who bids me — come My child in your weariness I want to give you rest. We go back to move forward to expansion. The withered hand, the withered tree.*

Again, I find refuge in Job 11:13-18, and journal my thoughts…

There it is — my promises if I move forward in going back with Jesus, Spirit of love and comfort, His love, His forgiveness, and His assurance. That this is the journey He has set before me. I am preparing my heart by meditating on this very personal invitation of Job. I am stretching my hands — my empty hands toward Him, along with my empty womb and heart. I suppose, my heart is not empty, but at this moment in time, full of self-loathing, regret, shame, and guilt. In the midst of this darkness, however, I read on in Job 11 to verses 18 and 19a ...

Yes, you would dig around you and take your rest in safety. You would also lie down, and no one would make you afraid. Even as I read Job 11, the accuser of the brethren is actively trying to distract me and distance my heart—the deep place where rivers of living water reside—this is the space where Chloe Renee's memory is. Here is the place of promise ...

Though you were dark, you would be like the morning (Job 11:17b). This is the place—the depths of the womb turned into a tomb—where the light and hope of the Gospel of Jesus Christ must be released to set me free ...

The Spirit of the Lord God is upon Me because the Lord has anointed Me to preach good tidings to the poor. He has sent me to heal the brokenhearted, to proclaim liberty to the captives, and the opening of the prison to those who are bound. To proclaim the acceptable year of the Lord and the day of vengeance of our God. To comfort all who mourn. To console those who mourn in Zion. To give them beauty for ashes. The oil of joy for mourning. The garment of praise for the spirit of heaviness. That they shall be called trees of righteousness, the planting of the Lord, that He may be glorified. (Isaiah 61:1-3)

I may be called a tree of righteousness! Wow! I don't mind saying I am nervous, to the point of nausea, fearful, hiding as if it were from Jesus. I cannot ever remember hiding in this much shame. Surely it is coming to His Light shame shall be cast away in the light of His beauty and His cross. This is the shame He took in my place. This is the deepest part of my shame— the Love that would wear this is something I cannot grasp right now. I must look to His Word on shame. Guilt I can deal with—guilt I can comprehend hanging on the cross—somehow guilty—yes, I am—He buried the guilt.

The shame, however, is so internal, so intense, it is what causes me to hide—to attempt to hide—but I know there is no hiding. Shame is so much different than guilt—guilt to me is something I admit—take it to the cross—receive forgiveness— and walk away guiltless. Shame, however, is a different matter altogether. Shame is so deep, so intense, its tentacles attach to every molecule of who I am. Shame stops me from approaching the cross at the deepest part of my need. I will pause here to watch a documentary, **Life After Abortion.** *Just for the record, I feel sick in my stomach. THANK YOU, JESUS. YOU ARE WITH ME...*

"Yes, My Beloved, you speak truth, I am with you. Did I not promise never to leave your side? Why, Beloved, do you hide your face from My love? Why is your soul cast down?"
"Oh! Great King, I do not know..."

O, my dove, in the clefts of the rock, in the secret places of the cliff, let me see your face, let me hear your voice; for your voice is sweet, and your face is lovely. (Song of Solomon 2:14)

"Great King! Your love song is sweet to the taste! I am engulfed in Your love! My hope is in You, my King! I speak to my soul in response to Your love...

Why are you cast down, O my soul! And why are you disquieted within me? Hope in God! For I shall yet praise Him! The help of my countenance and my God! (Psalm 43:5)

The King cradles me in His arms, breathing peace into my soul as the videos of *Life After Abortion* transform my shame into His acceptance. I am at peace writing in my journal...

A beautiful time listening to other women tell their stories—a safe place—I am believing healing has begun—to know I'm not alone in the darkness of guilt and shame. These are beautiful women...
I'm reading **Shattered Into Beauty** *by Jeannie Scott Smith. Something is striking me—she speaks about seeing in a church bulletin the need for volunteers at a place called Piedmont*

Women's Center—AMAZING. I spent ten days at Piedmont hospital this June 2016—in the woman's center—part of the hospital. This woman's center she is speaking of is a pregnancy medical clinic caring for women with unplanned pregnancies. She says, "I didn't know much about this ministry, but I knew God wanted me there."

So—it seems to me as I meditate on the Christmas dinner at Westminster—the <u>huge</u> ultrasound that breathed on my heart, and the women I stopped to see on the way out—I remember stopping at their table thinking this is irrelevant to my life— little did I know it was a divine appointment, unlike any other and none will ever be.

A crossroads, a place of reflection, direction, restoration, awaits me as I continue pursuing this journey as He is knitting it—weaving it into what is already planted into Potter's Heart Ministry. The Potter's <u>HEART</u>—the mending of the deepest wound a woman can endure—the intentional choice to take her child's life. I see a new "TAB" on the Potter's Heart Ministry website. "Abortion Recovery." To God be the glory! Great things He has done!

Since this journey began December 6, 2016, and I have committed to walk this way—Abortion Recovery has been knit into my heart—not only for myself, but for those who God gives me within His call of prison ministry. It is a birthing, Chloe Renee. Budding—new birth. A call of destiny. The right thing. The right path. Her voice shall be heard, her life honored, and my destiny experienced. Chloe Renee—yes. Potter's Heart Ministry. The Lord bless you...

A song fills the air as the mulberry trees blow in the breeze. Surely the Great King prepares to speak? Let my heart prepare for His word! A drum roll of determined destiny reverberates through the atmosphere. The Great King must have something important to accomplish today. I sit and wait. Anticipation escalates even as the drums call attention to the heavenly host and the great cloud of witnesses. It is a day of declaration, I can only surmise, for the rumble increases to almost bone-shaking heights.

I set my heart toward the eastern sky where the Great King delights in revealing Himself. Until the day He splits it open for all to see, I watch and wait in the Spirit for His personal, intimate *deep calling deep* dialogue with me...

Your lips, O my spouse, drip as the honeycomb; honey and milk are under your tongue; and the fragrance of your garments is like the fragrance of Lebanon. (Song of Solomon 4:11)

"Whatever do You mean by this, Great King?"

The righteous shall flourish like a palm tree, He shall grow like a cedar in Lebanon. Those who are planted in the house of the Lord shall flourish in the courts of our God. They shall bear fruit in old age; they shall be fresh and flourishing to declare that the Lord is upright. He is my rock, and there is no unrighteousness in Him. (Psalm 92:12-15)

"My King, my Great King! My soul sings at the waterfall of Your refreshment! I drink in Your words as a nomad at an oasis in the desert. Please give me, oh Great King, the interpretation of these refreshing words, and I will seek the thirsty and give them drink."

"Beloved, My Beloved. As it was in the days of old, fragrant oil extracted from a majestic cedar mixed with hyssop cleansed the leper's house, so shall it be in this day. The fragrant oil extracted from your royal garment mixed with the hyssop of My suffering shall cleanse the leprosy of abortion in My house. As it was when I walked the earth, so shall it be today. I will reach out My nail-scarred hands to all My post-abortive children, touch their leprosy, and declare them clean before all principalities and powers which are in heaven, on the earth, and beneath the earth. Thus, darkness and light alike will know that I am the Lord, Your God, who has redeemed you and set you free to walk in the destiny I preordained for you. This is the mystery of the fragrance of Lebanon and the call of the honey-comb" (from Leviticus 14:49-51).

"Oh, Great King! These words are Spirit, and they are life! Surely *deep calls to deep* and I am changed! My cup runs over! Surely You heard the cry of my heart…

Purge me with hyssop, and I shall be clean, wash me, and I shall be whiter than snow. (Psalm 51:7)

Note: For more information on anointing oils, cedar, and hyssop, and their biblical significance, please see "Love Unlimited" at love-unlimited.org

REST-REFLECT-REFRESH

Guilt, shame, and self-loathing play a huge part in hindering our recovery. As you can see by my last journal entry, I was struggling back and forth between knowing I am forgiven to succumbing to the darkness surrounding the day of Chloe Renee's death. Journaling my thoughts presented a path toward restoration, as again, it was the truth that set me free.

The invisible, insidious lie that no other Christian woman had ever, or would ever, think of ending the life of her unborn child caused me the most shame. My head knew this to be a lie, but my heart was so shattered that it did not have the strength to reject it. *Life After Abortion* was just what I needed to move me from the place of guilt and shame into believing something beautiful could come from the tragedy of Chloe Renee's death.

When I could see, hear, and experience through visual media the stories of other beautiful, Christian women who did not choose life for their unborn children, a whole new world of acceptance opened up for me…

I thought… I'm not alone, I'm not the only one! I don't have to hate myself anymore for what I've done! There are others, thousands of others just like me, who need healing!

There is a whole community of women with a safe place of refuge where I am permitted to grieve Chloe Renee's death without judgment or rancor. I was no longer alone, left to the self-loathing spirit that wanted to destroy me. The lid on the golden chest opened wider. Expanded destiny was released. Jesus was healing me from me.

Until I watched *Life After Abortion*, I was still bound by a spirit of self-loathing. The spirit of self-loathing is a destiny-defying spirit whose sole purpose for existence is to eternally incarcerate us in a deep, dark dungeon with its recorder spirits guarding us. These recorder spirits push the replay button every time we answer the Great King's call to freedom, accusing us of being unworthy of His mercy and grace. Their strategy is to continuously remind us of our tainted past, exploiting the fear, guilt, shame, and regret that's attached to it. Their perverted passion is to watch us crawl back into our self-inflicted prison, where they start the whole process over again, and to prevent us from living out our God-ordained destinies.

The beauty of the cross of torture, however, and the power of the blood that was poured out on our behalf, is that the spirit of self-loathing loses its power the minute we accept the reality of who we are in Christ. At the KAIROS time, ordained by the Great King, the cross of torture with its powerful blood enters the dark dungeon in the Person of Jesus Christ and sets its captive free. Jesus said…

I am the way, the truth and the life…you will know the truth and the truth shall make you free. (John 8:32, 36)

Let's take a minute to reflect on something I shared with you earlier from my personal thoughts in our chapter, "A Single Step." I believe you will agree that these thoughts validate my position concerning the incessant, murderous agenda of the spirit of self-loathing…

Who am I that I should be set free? Who am I that I should walk in newness of life, healed, whole, and forgiven? Who am I that I should hope? These degrading accusations surfaced the moment I chose to be intentional about seeking healing and wholeness from my abortion. It is too much! I cannot go there! I cannot face what I have done! Intense fear and disgust rose together at the thought of facing the deserted, wounded part of me that I had left behind and imprisoned in darkness. I walked away from her years ago hoping she would cease to exist for I felt she had no right to live...

Can you hear the torturous slander of this evil, conniving spirit? Do you see the crippling effect it could have on our ability to walk in our God-ordained destinies? Can you taste the bitter herb of debilitating defeat as I came into agreement with the lies of darkness?

O wretched man (woman) that I am! Who will deliver me from this body of death? I thank God—through Jesus Christ our Lord! (Romans 7:24-25)

But God! But God! But God! Thank You, Great King, King Jesus, for Your tender mercy and grace toward me! You, who saw me lying in my own blood and came to rescue me! Thank You a million times a million! (See Ezekiel 16.)

As we draw near to the Great King, resist the incessant lies of self-loathing, and accept the truths of who we are in Him, this degrading, destiny-defying spirit must go! Amen!

Blessed be the God and Father of our Lord Jesus Christ, who has blessed us with every spiritual blessing in the heavenly places in Christ, just as He chose us in Him before the foundation of the world, that we should be holy and without blame before Him in love, having predestined us to adoption as sons by Jesus Christ to Himself, according to the good pleasure of His will, to the praise of the glory of His grace by which He made us accepted in the Beloved. (Ephesians 1:3-6)

Chapter 9

The Great Exchange

Journal Entry December, 26, 2016

*W*ell, *it has been several days since my last journal entry. There are several reasons. First, Christmas is upon us and gone. This year, so bittersweet as we put our tree up—yet another reminder of childlessness. Amazing this year, the first year that the blatant exposure hits me square in the forehead—absolutely no gifts under the tree—no children—no grandchildren. Never before have my eyes seen such a void. There is true peace, however, as the Christ Child has given me peace on earth, good will toward men. It is in this season of uncertainty about this post-abortive healing journey that my heart is certain that this will be the most freeing time of my life—filled with the great exchange—my sin for His righteousness—my fear for His love—perfect love casts out fear—my sorrows for His joy—my shame for His acceptance. To walk free of shame—to embrace children—especially infants free of guilt—until December 6, 2016 was only a fleeting thought in a fairy tale written for someone else. Surely, the Spirit of the Lord has begun a work in me that only He can direct and complete, setting me free of thirty-eight years of bondage to self-loathing and rejection of myself.*

The love and compassion of this gentle Spirit of the Man of sorrows, connecting me to His agape love overwhelms me to the point of coming undone. Isaiah 53 jumps in the womb as something to meditate on as it has a meaning so deep, so pure, so holy, so liberating — there are no words in the English language powerful enough, eloquent enough, or sufficient to describe the transforming power of the revelation of His suffering for my choice to abort Chloe Renee. He was despised so I no longer have the right to despise myself. He was rejected in my place. I can receive His acceptance. He was a man of sorrows and acquainted with grief. I hid my face from Him — the deep, deep face of guilt and shame for who I believed I am — a murderer of my own child. Surely, He has born my grief and carried my sorrows. He was wounded for this abortion choice. He was bruised for this murder. The chastisement for my peace was upon Him, and by His stripes, I am healed. My Prince of Peace — Shalom — wholeness. By His stripes I am made whole.

If you would prepare your heart and stretch out your hands... my withered hand... hidden behind my back... The secret — stretch out the secret toward Him... the withered hand... the shame...

And He said to the man, "Stretch out your hand." And he stretched it out and it was restored as whole as the other. (Matthew 12:13)

The Great King replied, "Beloved, what is in your other hand, and why do you clutch it so?"

"Great King, it is the deep blue stone You gave me after we bought my journal! I'm holding on to it tightly because I don't want to lose it! It makes me feel safe. It reminds me I won't ever be alone no matter where this journey takes me. I thought You might want me to do something with it, so I was waiting for Your instruction."

"You are wise to wait for instruction. You are wise to move when I say move, and be still when I say be still. One of the virtues of the deep blue stone is wisdom, born out of your relationship with Me. You have carried it well and learned from it. You may put it into the bag made of fine linen, for I have another stone to give you. The mystery of the bag made of fine linen is that it is the carrier of all you need for your journey. Transparency is the first stone. True wisdom, which is born of our *deep calling deep dialogue,* will guide you in its proper use." The Great King reached into His heart and brought forth a crimson sapphire that seemed to breathe in the light of His breath. Of all the precious stones on this earth, there would be none to compare...

"Oh! Great King, the beauty of this stone! Whatever have I done to deserve such a gift?"

"It is for the mystery of the Great Exchange that I hand you this stone. It is nothing you have done, for there is no price you could have paid to acquire such a treasure. I freely give to you what you do not deserve, and receive from you what I do not."

Hidden underneath the dazzling crimson sapphire was a key of the same composition. Lifting my hand, He placed it in my palm. "This crimson key that unlocks the mystery of the Great Exchange of My sacrifice, I give to you. Not as religion gives you, but as our *deep calling deep* relationship gives. Receive the Great Exchange...

For He made Him who knew no sin to be sin for us, that we might become the righteousness of God in Him. **(2 Corinthians 5:21)**

"Oh! Great King! You have already shown me much of this Great Exchange! How I adore You! What shall I do with this stone and key?"

"Place the crimson key on your golden key chain beside the deep blue key, and carry the crimson stone with you until we meet at heaven's shores."

"Yes! Great King! I shall heartily do as You command!"

The great cloud of witnesses and the heavenly hosts shouted with joy, "Let heaven and earth rejoice! Wisdom and revelation has come to the daughter of the Great King!"

Journal Entry December 27, 2016

I will meet with one of the directors of Palmetto Pregnancy Center this morning to share my journey to healing and wholeness in Christ thus far. There is a lightness in my heart that is new—an expectation of hope—destiny—purpose—new direction—or expanded direction I should say...

The Great King broke out into song and the heavens shook as He scooped me up in His arms, spinning me around like a parasol above His head...

Be merry, all ye witnesses of the Great Exchange! Be merry, all ye heavenly hosts! Prepare the trumpets! Sound the alarm! Let the heavens rejoice! Let the moon and stars dance! Let the sun smile with radiant joy! Let the seas roar, and all its fullness! Let the fields be joyful and all that is in it! Let the trees clap their hands! For, I the Great King, have come to judge the dungeon with My righteousness. I have exchanged its dark destiny for the destiny of light! My daughter who was dead, has come alive, she was lost, and now she is found! Rejoice all that I have created, for today My daughter walks away from the destiny of darkness, and into her destiny of Light! Rejoice! Rejoice! Rejoice and be glad! And, again I say, rejoice! (From Luke 15:24, Psalm 96:11-13, Isaiah 55:12)

"Oh! Great King, I am dizzy with delight! Put me down or truly I will spin into oblivion!"

"Beloved, Beloved!" He laughed as we spun to the ground, the soft green pasture receiving us.

Today you shall go out with joy and be led out with peace. The mountains and the hills shall break forth into singing before you, and all the trees of the field shall clap their hands. (Isaiah 55:12)

"Beloved, where is your crimson stone?"

"Right here, safe in my hand, Great King."

"Place it in the bag covered in the finest linen beside the deep blue stone."

"With joy, I shall do as You say! With joy!"

He reached into the heavens where clouds danced around the sun in response to His vibrant song of triumph, and brought forth a glistening green emerald of unmeasurable quality. He held it out for me to see.

"My Beloved! What do you see?"

"Oh! Great King! I see mountains and hills beautiful as the Swiss Alps…they are singing! The trees upon the mountains are clapping! Oh! Great King! This is too glorious for one such as I to experience! First You tell me, then You show me! How marvelous are Your ways!"

"Oh! Great King! I see fields, and fields, and fields scarred and barren from great fires of death. The inhabitants lay shriveled up, bodies of skin and bones and sunken eyes. Tell me, Great King, where are these fields? They are crying! They are dying! I must go to them! Oh! Great King! They are in agony! Look! They are weeping and crying out, even as I was in the deep, dark dungeon. My heart breaks for the inhabitants of these barren fields. There is no water, no food, no light, and no hope. They don't even know they are dying! Great King, I must know this way that I have never gone before! Lead me and I will follow."

Your neck is like the tower of David, built for an armory, on which hang a thousand bucklers, all shields of mighty men. (Song of Solomon 4:4)

"Whatever do You mean a neck like the tower of David? Such words are a mystery to me."

He reached into His heart and brought forth a key, which was fashioned out of the glistening emerald stone. He gave it to me and said…

Enlarge the place of your tent and let them stretch out the curtains of your dwellings. Do not spare. Lengthen your cords and strengthen your stakes. For you shall expand to the right and to the left. And your descendants will inherit the nations and make the desolate cities inhabited. Do not fear for you will not be ashamed, neither be disgraced for you will not be put to shame, for you will forget the shame of your youth. (Isaiah 54:2-4)

Sing O barren, you who have not borne! Break forth into singing and cry aloud. You who have not labored with child! For more are the children of the desolate than the children of the married woman, says the Lord." (Isaiah 54:1)

"Beloved, herein is the mystery of the glistening green emerald. The broken neck of the deep, dark, dungeon restored to nobility and strength carries a warrior bride into the fields burned with fires of death. The Great Exchange of destiny is the key that unlocks the mystery of the glistening green emerald. Follow Me, and I will lead you to the fields crying in the wilderness."

"Oh! Great King! My heart breaks for the inhabitants of the fields! There is no water, no food, no light, and no hope! Great King, I must know the way! Lead me and I will follow."

The Great King disappeared into the clouds from which He brought forth the emerald stone and key, and I was left to ponder the mystery…

Journal Entry December 27 Continuation

Stretch out the curtains of my dwellings — moving our tent pegs, written by Garris Elkins[1]… This is a time for expansion. I am about to move my people (Lynn Potter) into a new experience with My presence. I need them (Me — Lynn Potter) to be mobile and ready to move with Me. The tent of My presence is

---

[1] Garris Elkins, "Moving Our Tent Pegs," *Prophetic Horizons*, March 8, 2011, www.prophetichorizons.com.

expanding. Pull up the tent pegs that lie before you, but leave the tent pegs of your history intact. My expansion plan includes both your past and your future. Look ahead. Get ready. Expect movement. Expansion in all things is upon you...

The meeting with Palmetto Pregnancy Center director was awesome! So much moving around in my head, my heart, my gut. It is all too crazy to even imagine... this tapestry unfolding before my eyes. To sit in a public place and talk about abortion—my abortion—so openly without shame is a testimony to so much, I don't know where to begin—well, yes—and you shall know the truth and the truth shall set you free.

* * *

Journal Entry New Year's Eve, December 31, 2016

Today is New Year's Eve, 2016. I am filled with hope for 2017. I developed an ache behind my right leg causing concern. I place my health and life in His hands today. Contemplating going to see about it. Jesus Calling Dec. 31 says: Receive My Peace.

As I continue to journey into wholeness, I call on my Prince of Peace who never leaves me. As I open my heart to receive healing, I receive His peace. My Healer, my Redeemer lives!

For unto me a child is born,
Unto me a Son is given,
And the government will be upon His shoulder,
And His name will be called
Wonderful, Counselor, Mighty God,
Everlasting Father, Prince of Peace.
(From Isaiah 9:6)

Peace like a river flows—great peace in the midst of trial and uncertainty...And He showed me a pure river of water of life, clear as crystal, proceeding from the throne of God and of the Lamb. In the middle of its street, and on either side of the river, was the tree of life, which bore twelve fruits, each tree yielding its fruit every month. The leaves of the tree were for the healing of the nations. (Revelation 22:1-2)

Though you were dark, you would be like the morning. (Job 11:17b)

But we have this treasure in earthen vessels, that the excellence of the power may be of God and not of us. (2 Corinthians 4:7)

The reading of 2 Corinthians chapters 3 and 4 in the eyes of abortion recovery opened eyes of hope for me—removing the wall of separation—the wall of denial and shame—what a call! What a thing to look forward to! What a hope, what a joy! To receive this hope, this joy from my Prince of Peace, my Counselor, my Mighty God, my Everlasting Father!

The Great King tapped on the door of my heart and said, "Beloved, there is something I must give you for your journey. Would you join me at My banqueting table? There we will commune and I shall instruct you in the way you should go, just as you have asked of Me."

"Oh my! Yes, Great King! I delight in Your invitations! I shall be there at once!"

The aroma of fresh bread baking led me to an elegant table set for two where a crystal goblet filled with red wine and an empty crystal plate added mystery to my invitation. I smiled as I remembered Him saying, "It is the glory of God to conceal a matter, but the glory of kings is to search out a matter." Bright light, like none I had ever seen before, filled the dining room as He entered. In His hand, He carried a basket woven with strips of fresh-cut cedar, which was a delight to breathe in.

He sat across from me and placed a golden scroll tied with a golden cord on the crystal plate and placed the basket to the side. "Today, Beloved, we shall share the wine as I hand you this scroll. Father, as we drink this cup together, I commend this journey of our beloved daughter to You, and bless this scroll, in which lies the sustenance for her journey."

"Great King, where is the bread that caused such a pleasing aroma to lead me to the table?"

"Beloved, I am the bread of life. My words, they are truth and they are life. They will sustain you through the valleys and great divide of this journey." He handed me the golden scroll, and said, "Take...eat."

The scroll was warm to the touch, its parchment soft like the oil of aloe. As I untied the golden cord, the Great King said, "Beloved, herein lies your right of passage. It is the parchment of the Great Exchange. It carries all the power and authority you need for your journey. It is to be presented at every check-point where fear, guilt, shame, and regret stand guard. They will have no power to send you back to your place of origin, for they will be blinded by the light of the truths that are written in the living, breathing, pulsating bright red blood that flows from My cross of torture. Read, eat, and be strengthened. For, tomorrow you shall face the greatest divide on your way to the Promised Land."

I wept with joy as warm oil from the words written in His living, breathing, pulsating bright red blood flowed into the depth of my suffering over Chloe Renee's death...

RITE OF PASSAGE
GRANTED BY THE KING OF THE UNIVERSE
BY THE AUTHORITY OF HIS PASSION...
THE HOLDER OF THIS SCROLL IS EXEMPT
FROM ANY DEBT
AND MUST BE PERMITTED PASSAGE

My sin for His righteousness.
My fear for His love.
My sorrow for His joy.
My shame for His acceptance.
He was despised so I no longer have the right to despise myself.

He was rejected in my place, so I may receive His acceptance.
He was a Man of sorrows and acquainted with grief.
He has borne my grief and carried my sorrows.
He was wounded for my abortion choice.
He was bruised for this murder.
The chastisement for my peace was upon Him.
By His stripes I am healed.
He has paid the price for the Great Exchange for me: a destiny of darkness for a destiny of light!

THE DEBT HAS BEEN PAID IN FULL
FOR THE HOLDER OF THIS SCROLL…

REST-REFLECT-REFRESH

Wow! What an adventure! What a story! What an awesome King! Let's take a minute to reflect on the *Great Exchange* Jesus offers to those of us who have experienced the trauma of abortion and are walking this healing journey with Him.

Take some time to read and meditate on Isaiah 53, the entire chapter. It is called the prophecy of *The Suffering Servant*, and where much of my journal entry for *The Great Exchange* originated. I encourage you to write your own *Great Exchange* as you read. The *Great Exchange* truths contained in my Rite of Passage are what I use to combat the dark voices of fear, guilt, shame, and regret when they challenge my deliverance.

THE GREAT EXCHANGE, OUR RITE OF PASSAGE, BOUGHT AND PAID FOR BY THE GREAT KING!

Take some time to meditate on our Scriptures for *The Great Exchange*. Journal your thoughts.

For He made Him who knew no sin to be sin for us, that we might become the righteousness of God in Him. (2 Corinthians 5:21)

He is despised and rejected by men, a Man of sorrows and acquainted with grief. And we hid, as it were, our faces from Him; He was despised and we did not esteem Him. Surely, He has borne our griefs and carried our sorrows; yet we esteemed Him stricken, smitten by God, and afflicted. But He was wounded for our transgressions, He was bruised for our iniquities. The chastisement for our peace was upon Him, and by His stripes we are healed. (Isaiah 53:3-5)

Chapter 10

The Holy of Holies

I did as I was instructed…I took and I ate the golden scroll with the golden cord…

Every cell in my body, rejuvenated by the living, breathing, life-giving words of the golden scroll with the golden cord grabbed instruments of praise, forming an orchestra that no one could number…declaring, even as Mary did the moment Destiny jumped in her womb…

My soul magnifies the Lord, and my spirit has rejoiced in God my Savior, for He has regarded the lowly state of His maidservant; for behold, henceforth all generations will call me blessed, for He who is mighty has done great things for me, and Holy is His name. And His mercy is on those who fear Him from generation to generation. (Luke 1:46-50)

The Great King stood and walked around the table reaching His hand toward me. "Beloved," He said, "may I have this next dance?"

Again, He picked me up and spun me around like a parasol above His head. I exclaimed with sheer delight…

Your words were found and I ate them! And Your Word was to me the joy and rejoicing of my heart! For I am called by Your name, oh Great King! (From Jeremiah 15:16)

"Remember, Beloved, although this way will be hard for you to travel..."

When you pass through the water, I will be with you and through the rivers, they shall not overflow you. When you walk through the fire, you shall not be burned, nor shall the flame scorch you. For I am the Lord your God, The Holy One of Israel, your Savior. (Isaiah 43:2-3)

"As I have said before, I say again, tomorrow you will face the great divide in your journey toward the Promised Land. Fear not, for I will be with you every step of the way. From here on in, you must revere the *Great Exchange* and hold it close to your heart."

"The truth of the *Great Exchange* shall not depart from your mouth and you shall meditate on it day and night, so that all that is written in it will become part of your DNA. For then your way will be prosperous and then you will have great success. Destiny awaits those who eat the words of *The Great Exchange* and believe them. As I have said before, so I say again, "Be strong and of good courage, For I, your Great King, am with you wherever you go." (From Jeremiah 1:8-9)

Journal Entry January 1, 2017

Read a Facebook post—Leave the broken, irreversible past in God's hands and step out into the invincible future with Him. Oswald Chambers. Today I will fellowship with "The Body" church as I enter 2017. I feel the need to be there. I am seeking direction and wisdom in an unfamiliar place with an open heart. My heart is heavy in the midst of hope, for my sweet, sweet Stacey has lost her beautiful Candyce Skye before birth. She is clinging to comfort in Jesus. This triggers remorse

112

and detachment protection. I know this recovery journey is pure and Holy Spirit driven. It is my journey with Him and that makes me feel safe...

For I know the plans I have for you, to prosper you and not to harm you, plans to give you a hope and a future. (Jeremiah 29:11)

It's amazing how Scripture read through intense grief, denial, fear, shame, or remorse can come to life as a life raft thrown to a drowning soul. In the midst of intense regret — the Word of God becomes the only anchor — steadfast truth to grasp onto when crying out in the darkness. This will be my song — our song, Chloe Renee. My Jesus, as tears threaten, I cannot go this alone. Candyce Skye's death has touched me deep, deep. Deep — a place of darkness so dark without the anchor — the steadfast sureness that I am forgiven as Your Word clearly states — I could not go on with this journey. This wound is so, so very deep, so huge and unimaginable, so threatening, loud, so in my face...I cannot bear it without the grace of the blood of Christ. I need help. I need hope. I am a sixty-year-old woman, childless...ever mindful — of no children, no grandchildren. I have been awakened from a deep, deep, sleep — a numb comatose amnesia — too painful to bear alone. Shame and guilt are constant companions. There is no turning back — no way of returning to sleep. There is only going forward with His promise...

I know the plans I have for you. Plans to prosper you and not to harm you. Plans to give you hope and a future. (Jeremiah 29:11)

As I prepare for the journey toward wholeness — I hold on to this anchor...Awake you who sleep. Arise from the dead. And Christ will give you light. (Ephesians 5:14)

* * *

New Year's Day, 2017 will forever be etched into the recesses of my mind, separated from the rest of my experience behind a veil that shields the *Holy of Holies* from any defiling agents.

I tremble with holy fear, searching for words concerning this part of my journey that will respect and honor the lives of those traumatized by the passing of Candyce Skye, while at the same time, declare the delivering power of the Great King in my life. I will use the term *sleeping* instead of *stillborn* as this is how Stacey refers to her precious Candyce Skye's arrival.

I dedicate this portion of my story to all who were in the delivery room with Stacey on January 1, 2017. Although you knew nothing about me, you granted me access into one of the darkest moments of your lives. Only the Great King knows how far-reaching this part of my journey and your trust will go.

Let the words of my mouth and the meditations of my heart be acceptable in Your sight, O Lord, my strength and my Redeemer. (Psalm 19:14)

The great cloud of witnesses and the armies of light prepared a candlelight vigil, hours before Stacey and her family arrived. They were in the delivery room, positioned to offer their hands as invisible buckets to catch the waterfall of tears as they were sure to fall. The nurses and staff solemnly and compassionately moved through the delivery room, preparing it for their arrival.

This vibrant, young woman of twenty-five was expecting to deliver a beautiful, bouncing baby girl on January 5, 2017. On December 31, New Year's Eve, tragic news fell upon this young mother and her family as they were informed that there was no longer a heartbeat, and their precious bundle had passed away in utero. Pitocen had been administered earlier in the morning, and the full-term baby waiting to be delivered would be delivered sleeping. I thought by the time I had arrived to the hospital the young mother and her family would have already had the opportunity to gaze upon their sleeping princess and begin their mourning process.

I entered the hospital unsure of myself, but, believing this to be a divine appointment, I approached the check-in desk, waiting to be given access to her room. Little did I know how powerfully freeing the next few hours were going to be. The revelation of Chloe Renee's death and my hand in it was still an open wound, deep, raw, and in need of much healing. It had only been about four weeks since the Christmas party and the exposure of my thirty-eight-year-old secret. The Great King had instructed the heavenly hosts to form a barrier around me so I could proceed to the young woman's room without anxiety or distress.

I calmly walked through the halls of the hospital toward the delivery room until I came upon a nurse's station where I had to stop and state my purpose. From there, I was escorted to a room across the hall from the delivery room where Stacey's friends quietly waited. The sleeping child had not been born yet. As I sat by the young mother's friends, a sense of peace washed over me as I realized the Great King had provided me extra support for what I would be experiencing in the not-too-distant future. After a few brief introductions, we silently kept vigil.

I stared at the delivery room door with deep, deep sadness, as darkness covered my thoughts. I cried silently for Stacey, who desperately wanted and loved this child. I wept for Chloe Renee who was never born. I wept for Candice Skye who would be born lifeless. I wept for the woman who chose life. I wept for the woman who didn't. I wept for two mothers whose stories were as far as the east is from the west, yet the outcome was just the same…

Our silent vigil was interrupted as agonized screams from Candyce Skye's grandmother announced her arrival behind the delivery room door. Suddenly, the door that separated us from the source of her anguish burst open as she fled the room and collapsed on the hallway floor in front of us. Her cries, defying her need for oxygen, reached through the ceiling into the second and third heavens, and kept on going until they reached the ears of the One who had just now welcomed Candyce Skye into

His Presence. After being helped to her feet, she fled into the room we once occupied wailing, disorientated, and distressed.

A voice was heard in Ramah, lamentation and bitter weeping, Rachel weeping for her children, refusing to be comforted for her children, because they are no more. (Jeremiah 31:15)

A nurse came out of the delivery room to offer us access. We silently filed in, my head bowed toward the floor, partly in reverential prayer, and partly giving myself a little more time to process what I was about to see. Eight pounds, twenty-one inches of heavenly beauty lay lifeless, cradled in her mother's arms on a birthing bed, and a room filled with grieving women is what I saw when I lifted my head.

Tender weeping from all corners of the room and soft voices comforting one another filled the air as the young mother motioned for me to come close. A deluge of emotion churned deep inside me as I walked toward the bed. Gut-wrenching, raw emotion from the depths of Chloe Renee's death were contained only by the Healing Presence that surrounded me. No one in the room except the young mother knew me, and no one, including the young mother, knew of my choice to end Chloe Renee's life thirty-eight years ago. How could I stand here in this room and grieve with this family? How could I legitimately look upon this heartbroken mother and her lifeless child and offer any type of ministry after what I had done? Deep calls out to deep...

"Deep answers deep, Beloved. How quickly you forgot the parasol twirl and the Divine Dance of yesterday. The sustenance, the answers to these tough questions, and the courage to move into what will set you free is in the parchment of the *Great Exchange.*"

"Oh yes. Great King. My Rite of Passage. I ate and it was freedom for my soul."

"Yes. And for such a time as this, My Beloved. Step onto the bridge that spans the great divide built by the parchment of My Word that you have eaten. Move freely throughout this room, and minister in My love. When arms reach out to you, receive what they hold. The key to the mystery of the great divide is in the receiving."

"Yes. My King. But how will I know of this great freedom? How will I recognize this receiving?"

"You will know, Beloved...you will know."

A bright light shone in the midst of the anguish-driven questions where the King's deep calling deep answered the cries of my heart.

"Beloved...the answers are within you..."

The cross of torture that faithfully hung above me from the moment I walked into the Christmas party until now was lit up by His Healing Presence in the depths of my being where my anguished cries originated. Every promise of *the Great Exchange* written on my Rite of Passage flowed down the sides of the cross of torture as the living, breathing, pulsating, bright red blood formed words that I could read. Upon the cross of torture hung a brutally beaten body that no man or woman could recognize...

Fear not, My Beloved. I am always with you. I will never leave you. Be at peace. Your Rite of Passage was paid for by My blood and has been presented to the principalities and powers in this place. Your cries have been heard. You no longer need to spend your energy fighting them. I have spoken from the cross of torture from which My blood eternally flows. They have been cast out of here. Spend My energy within you to minister in this place. Mourn with those who mourn. As the Father has sent Me, so send I you...

Immediately, perfect peace washed over me as I gazed upon Candyce Skye and her mother. Although there would be no movement from the beautiful child in response to her mother's love, I could sense the mother-daughter bonding the two of them enjoyed during Stacey's pregnancy. I leaned over and hugged her, gently brushing my hand through her hair. With tear-filled eyes threatening to spill over, I told her how beautiful her little Candyce Skye was.

"Hey everybody! This is Ms. Potts. She goes to the church I was baptized in." Although startled by her abrupt response to my approach, I immediately recognized it as both a coping mechanism for her and an open door for me. I was met with polite nods and thank-you-for-coming greetings as I moved around the room, offering silent hugs to the grieving women.

As I watched this grief-stricken young mother share her sleeping princess with the other women in the room, I can truly say I entered a sphere of existence that is otherworldly. There are no words in the English language to adequately describe what I witnessed, felt, and experienced from this moment on. I tremble as Paul did when he wrote…

And I know such a man — whether in the body or out of the body I do not know, God knows — how he was caught up into Paradise and heard inexpressible words, which it is not lawful for a man to utter. Of such a one I will boast, yet of myself I will not boast except in my infirmities. (2 Corinthians 12:3-5)

The hospital room ceased being a hospital room. It had become an intimate, personal place of refuge for those longing to bond with Candyce Skye before she would be taken away for burial. They walked with her and talked to her. They cradled her and rocked her. They softly sang love songs to her. They wrapped her tiny little fingers around their own, tenderly brushed her nose and forehead saying, "Look, she's perfect… look…she only has a little bruise above one eye." Their tears fell on her lifeless body. I had entered *The Holy of Holies*.

Without realizing what was happening I had become one with them as I watched them cradle her beautiful, lifeless body in their arms. The longer I witnessed their tender engagements, the more I bonded to their experience, and my place in the divine tapestry began to change. I was being transformed from a spectator to a participant in this most *Holy of Holies* encounter.

I had entered their pain, their grief, and their sorrow, and it had entered me.

It was in this place of refuge that the great cloud of witnesses, the heavenly hosts, and the Great King had come to honor the daughters of two women whose stories were as far from the east is to the west. It was in this place that by Divine Providence, our *Holy of Holies* would unite as one…

"Would you like to hold her?"

The Great King had said, "When arms reach out to you, receive what they hold. The key to the mystery of the great divide is in the receiving." The great cloud of witnesses and the heavenly hosts stood by waiting. They knew how critical my answer would be to my being able to cross the great divide. They, along with the Great King, waited in anticipation for my response…

"I would be honored." I said. I opened my empty arms to receive the precious, eight-pound, twenty-one-inch, lifeless bundle I had been watching these precious women cradle, hug, sing, and weep over. My tears dripped on the beautifully crafted, crocheted cap and blanket she was wrapped in. Through blurry eyes I kissed her forehead and wrapped her little fingers around mine. "You are beautiful, Candyce Skye, you are so beautiful," I said.

The rest of the women gathered around me. They sang over her and talked to her while I cradled her in my arms. They kissed her forehead, touched her lips, and held her hand. They played with her little cap and blanket. Our tears mixed together and fell on her lifeless body with the angelic face whose eyes would never open…they wept with me…we wept as one.

Every word on the golden scroll with the golden chord came alive within me as I looked upon heaven's beauty for the last time. Surely, I have seen the face of God, my Redeemer who would trust me with holding His precious creation in my arms. The same arms that refused the opportunity to hold Chloe Renee so long ago. Surely, I have seen the redemption of my sin. Without a doubt, I was standing on holy ground, inside the very depths of the Great King's heart, in the Holiest of Holies prepared especially for me before the foundation of the world. Surely, but surely, I have seen the face of God in this sleeping beauty…

My soul magnifies the Lord, and my spirit has rejoiced in God my Savior, for He has regarded the lowly state of His maidservant; for behold, henceforth all generations will call me blessed, for He who is mighty has done great things for me, and Holy is His name. And His mercy is on those who fear Him from generation to generation. (Luke 1:46-50)

Sensing my time with this precious family was about to come to a close, I released Candyce Skye into their loving care and returned to Stacey's bed. As I kissed her on her forehead, our eyes met and something holy, divine, and too sacred for words transpired. I was overcome by emotions that I never knew existed and right now, am unable to express. They belong only to this time and place of sacred reverence in the Holiest of Holies where anger, rage, unanswered questions, and unimaginable grief were permitted a voice without restraint.

It would be days before the Great King would reveal to me what transpired in that moment. I grabbed Stacey's hand one last time and prepared to leave. I moved around the room, with one last hug of condolence for each one present. Every hug brought me closer to their Holiest of Holies where I sensed angels ministering to their broken hearts (Hebrews 1:13-15).

I sensed it was time to leave the young mother and her grieving family in the very capable hands of the servants of the One who carried me out of the dungeon. The great cloud of witnesses and the armies of light would keep their servant's vigil, catching every tear that fell long after I left the building. The Great King escorted me through the halls where His Healing Presence provided me a safe haven to begin processing what I had just witnessed and encountered in Delivery Room #2 on January 1, 2017…

Weep with those who weep---bear one another's burdens, thus fulfilling the law of Christ...

"Oh, Great King...for what reason have I been summoned to this place of anguish?"

"Beloved, I conceal and I reveal. Listen with your heart and not your head. Not too many days from now you will understand that you have conquered the mystery of the great divide in the receiving. It was in the weeping with those who weep and cradling their loss as your own that the bridge over the great divide was built. It was in the receiving you activated Ruby Red and moved one step closer to crossing over the great divide into your promised land."

"Oh, Great King! Your mysteries forever call me to Your heart! Deep calls to deep! My heart bursts with mysteries yet to be revealed! What is this Ruby Red you speak of? Why are my arms so heavy? I *must* trust you as a child with no knowledge!"

"Yes, Beloved. This is the promise of security. Childlike trust shall guide you safely to the other side of the great divide. This day, in the sharing, bearing, and receiving, you have been granted permission from the Highest Court to grieve the loss of your precious Chloe Renee. Go in peace and cross this great divide, get to know your daughter, and lay her to rest. This is the destiny of the mystery of the heavy arms...to cradle the Promised Land forever free."

"Yes, my King, I shall trust You with this mystery as I have seen You face-to-face in the secret place of the sharing, bearing, and receiving. I delight in learning the mysteries of Your heart in the deep, deep places of the Holiest of Holies where You openly teach me Your ways."

"Beloved, stretch forth your bag covered in the finest linen, for Ruby Red will guarantee you safe passage. Prepare your golden chain to receive the key to the crossing of the great divide. The mystery that causes your heart to swell, the mystery of the heavy arms, shall be to you an anchor in the raging sea, a lighthouse in the storm, and a shelter from the rain. For in a few days, you must cross the highest mountain and through stormy seas to access the bridge that spans the great divide."

"Great King, I should tremble as a leaf holding on through a hurricane if I did not know You are with me always! You say Ruby Red shall guarantee me safe passage across the highest mountain and through the stormy seas. Ruby is the stone of my birth, is it not?"

"Yes, Beloved, it is. Just as Ruby Red's Rite of Passage was in the receiving, her destiny is in the releasing. Receive her crimson stone and key today. Hold them tight as you climb the highest mountain, face the stormy seas, and embrace the revelation of the mystery of the heavy arms."

"Oh! Great King! Although I am a child and lack understanding, I delight in receiving the gift of safe passage in the Ruby Red and her destiny in the mystery that is yet to be revealed. My trust is in You alone. For You alone, hold the revelation of all mysteries in the palms of Your hands."

The Great King escorted me out of the building with His nail-scarred hands held high. All of creation was silenced by His gesture and my tongue would cease to move for hours. The chatter and noise of everyday life had been silenced by the King of Kings and Lord of Lords in honor and memory of His two precious daughters, Candyce Skye and Chloe Renee.

"Great King? May I ask the purpose of these beautiful, precious stones I carry?"

"Beloved, the mystery of the stones is in the memorial. As your fathers crossed the Jordan, so shall you cross this great divide, receiving stones of remembrance along the way. When others say, 'Whatever are these stones for?' you shall answer, 'I crossed over this great divide, for the Great King caused the mountains to become as flat lands, and the roaring seas to be as still waters.' These stones shall be a sign and memorial in the land of promise for you, and all who read *Chloe's Cry*, that by My mighty hand, you have made safe passage" (Based on Joshua 4).

I walked to my truck pondering the mysteries I carried inside the bag covered in fine linen, with my right hand clutching the keys that hung from the golden chain...

REST-REFLECT-REFRESH

I have just shared with you the most intimate, pivotal part of my journey. This is where my deliverance was tested to the extreme. I was sixty years old and had never, and I mean never, ever, cradled a baby in my arms. This happened less than one month after I faced my thirty-eight-year-old secret head-on and allowed the Great King to rescue me from the dungeon!

These words, like the words on my Rite of Passage, have become part of my DNA...

My soul magnifies the Lord, and my spirit has rejoiced in God my Savior, for He has regarded the lowly state of His maid-servant; for behold, henceforth all generations will call me blessed, for He who is mighty has done great things for me, and Holy is His name. And His mercy is on those who fear him from generation to generation. (Luke 1:46-50)

As we stop to rest, I want to encourage you to take some time to meditate on the Great King's love for you and what He has been doing for you during your abortion recovery. I believe He has walked you through at least one intimate, pivotal part of your journey, and I would ask you to become creative in your expression of gratitude toward Him. If you are an artist, paint, draw, or sketch Him something. A musician? Write Him a song. A sculptor? Sculpt Him something! A poet? Write Him a poem! You get it! Whatever gifts He has given you, use them to create a representation of your gratefulness for what He has done! You hold in your hands mine! When you are finished...meditate on, and make Luke 1:46-50 part of your DNA!

My soul magnifies the Lord, and my spirit has rejoiced in God my Savior, for He has regarded the lowly state of His maid-servant; for behold, henceforth all generations will call me blessed, for He who is mighty has done great things for me, and Holy is His name. And His mercy is on those who fear him from generation to generation. (Luke 1:46-50)

The following chapter, "Reflections," will contain much of my personal journal entries during the days immediately following Candyce Skye's death and the impact it had on my healing journey. I will be sharing with you some of the deep, raw feelings I expressed until the Great King presented me a question. My answer to His question would be the deciding factor of whether or not I would be successful in crossing over the great divide and into my land of promise.

At times, the entries may contain thoughts that seem to ramble on without sense of order, but it was the freedom to be transparently raw with myself and the Great King that helped me move forward toward healing from Chloe Renee's death. I trust my transparency will free you to express your deepest raw emotions to this Great King, where true lasting healing is found.

I encourage you to spend time meditating on my thoughts and not rush through "Reflections," as I believe the Great King wants to meet you in places you have feared to go. Allow your creative gifts to come forth and be part of your healing journey. The release of your deep, raw feelings through creative expression will become stones of remembrance for years to come. Even as I typed my personal journal entries into the DNA of *Chloe's Cry*, I received additional healing and wholeness from the Great King. I believe that gut-level honesty is what it takes to set us free...

And you shall know the truth and the truth shall make you free. If the Son makes you free, you shall be free indeed. (John 8:32, 36)

It is in humble gratitude to my Great King, and for His glory, that I share "Reflections" with you...

Chapter 11

Reflections

Journal Entry January 2, 2017

I'm not sure where to start today. So much revelation coming, it is hard to comprehend in the natural what the Spirit is intent on accomplishing. New Year's Day 2017 is without a doubt a testament to the faithfulness of God to make Himself known to the hungry soul seeking Him.

It is so sacred, so holy, that I tremble to give account of unbearable sorrow fallen on a human heart. To be summoned to such a place is beyond all my natural understanding, so with the Holy Spirit's understanding and grace-filled knowledge, I attempt to recapture these events, looking at them from some other dimension or place known only in the heart of God. Great distress stirs as my mind recalls sights, sounds, emotions, and people in the room. Time stands still for me somewhere deep, deep, deep where things take forever to process. I believe this is mercy on the part of God our Father, for He knows the extent of what we can handle.

Journal Entry January 3, 2017

Still not able to put words down on paper the tremendous emotions and holy atmosphere surrounding this life-changing encounter with life/death all at the same time. The beauty, the tragedy, the surreal moments in time as mother, grandmother, great grandmother, aunt, cousin, friend (me), cradled, held, sang over, spoke to, loved, and shared this bundle of life/death, beauty/tragedy — too holy for words ... really.

Journal Entry January 4, 2017

Little Candyce Skye — white, pure, sincere, sheltering, opening doors already to share Chloe Renee. Still reluctant to share, but when opportunity arises in an atmosphere where I feel safe comes along, the hesitance is short lived. Mixed deep, strong emotions are tied in my being between Candyce Skye and Chloe Renee. Both given by God, both in Jesus' arms, but two totally different circumstances. Candyce Skye's memorial service is in two days. I will go. Unsure of what I will feel, but I'm willing to go. This is a place where I feel so vulnerable, but yet at such peace. I cannot but help believe I am walking this way in God's plan and purpose. Too many things falling in place for me to think otherwise. Just yesterday, out of the blue, one of the ladies that sat at the Christmas party table this past December shared her abortion experience with me. Neither one of us knew of each other's secret. I'm uncertain of the road ahead, moving slowly, one step at a time, in obedience of what I sense the Lord stirring in my spirit. Speak to me Lord ...

Journal Entry January 6, 2017

The scenes are almost too much to bear — the inner turmoil of reality sitting in a room where shortened life — the reality of life without the mother's child too hard to witness and be part of without shutting down again. Two persons wept in the room with the tiny casket, stuffed animals, candles, and grief.

A friend, a mother all wrapped up in one soul—one who knows all too well the loss of future joy. The difference—the one who is grieving this day—was not self-induced grief—This was NOT her CHOICE.

"Oh, Great King, comfort me in my time of need, for grief threatens to devour me…"

Let not your heart be troubled; you believe in God, believe also in Me. In My Father's house are many mansions, if it were not so, I would have told you. I go to prepare a place for you. (John 14:1-2)

I will not leave you as orphans. I will come to you. (John 14:18)

There is a place for me in our Father's house! A murderer of the unborn—a place in our Father's house! There is a place for me! I am overwhelmed at the prospect that all my stains are washed away…And to her is was granted to be arrayed in fine linen, clean and bright, for the fine linen is the righteous acts of the saints (Revelation 19:8). Grace like rain…Hallelujah grace like rain falls down on me. All my stains are washed away…A vivid memory of an episode of MASH…Loretta Switt in a wedding gown covered in blood, white soldiers walk slowly, silently past her into eternity. Now with understanding in the Spirit's revelation why I HATED that episode—the visual, the blood—oh the blood on the wedding gown! Oh! The red stains… Oh! Hallelujah my stains—all my stains are washed away!

Journal Entry January 7, 2017

Speak to me Lord! I sit quietly…They cried to You, and were delivered; They trusted in You, and were not ashamed (Psalm 22:5.) I'm trusting all my stains are washed away. I'm trusting even this stain of abortion—the blood on my wedding gown is washed away and You have placed on me a pure white gown, ready for the wedding supper of the Lamb. All my stains are washed away! The Lord has heard the voice of my weeping! The Lord has heard my supplication! The Lord will receive my prayer. Let all my enemies be ashamed and greatly troubled. Let them turn back and be ashamed suddenly (Psalm 6:8b-10).

I fear I have returned to numb again. The passing of Candyce Skye, holding her, attending her memorial—many shed tears, true, tender tears at the loss of a child. Deep, deep scars of remorse overshadowing reality. I have been to the cross in my heart and in my mind, but deep, deep in my soul, I cannot find the ability to attach myself personally to Chloe Renee. Candyce Skye was safe. I could grieve as one weeping with those who weep. As I saw her tiny little body lying in a coffin no bigger than a suitcase, the loss too great to bear. Sitting right behind her mamma—the grief too strong. Like a boulder bearing down on a heart that cannot enter time past and choose another way.

I have yet to go to the cross specifically for the pardon so readily available to me and I am truly puzzled by this. I do suspect, that for me, the general thoughts and truth—that all my stains are washed away is an abstract detached truth, so at this present time—I walk by faith—not by sight or healed at any emotional level. The horror of what happened inside my body is too great of a burden to walk—to carry up Calvary's Hill. That's why my Jesus carried it for me.

Oh, to be able to come together in one piece, void of separation—wholeness, unashamed even of the shame. Guilt is easily—or should I say easier to lay at the cross, for guilt is something much lighter than shame. For me, guilt is a fact—something I can carry on a plate—outside of myself and lay it down—plate and all at the cross's foot. Shame on the other hand, presents a greater attachment to me as it is a defining fact, or shame on you. So, guilt stays at the cross where I know it belongs. Shame however leaves with me as I have carried, buried, and housed it for so long that it has attached itself to my identity. I must go to the place of the event, attach myself and together in wholeness of agony, find myself at the foot of my loving Jesus, and allow Him to embrace me. He of course has already said, "It is finished."

"Why the hesitancy, Beloved? Why are you not moving forward with Ruby Red?"

So, there is this thing about permission — permission to grieve — perhaps at the cross. I will receive this gift. I am stuck at this phase. Being near Candyce Skye opened a safe passage to grief. The loss of a child. The loss of a niece, a grandchild, a great grandchild, a cousin. All-encompassing safe place to grieve with those who grieve. Sorrow beyond comprehension was given permission in those holy moments to surface from the deep — bringing me a glimpse of healing. The question I hear in my spirit...Do you want to be made well?

Now a certain man was there who had an infirmity of thirty-eight years. When Jesus saw him lying there, and knew that he already had been in that condition a long time, He said to him, "Do you want to be made well?" (John 5:5-6)

The Spirit asks me, "Do you want to be set free — to take up your bed and walk?" It is a choice. At first this would seem to be an absurd question, but light is shining in the darkness. Me — a twenty-two-year-old young woman cowering in the corner of a dark room engulfed in fear because of guilt and shame...do you want to be made well? That is a question I do ponder and know it is well founded. A question I ask myself. Why would I hesitate to jump and answer YES? I believe it is the demonic strongholds of guilt and shame that act like scar tissue in the bowls — cutting off blood flow, restricting the natural process of elimination of poisonous life-threatening toxins...

Journal Entry January 9, 2017

God is our refuge and strength, a very present help in trouble. Therefore, we will not fear, even though the earth be removed, and though the mountains be carried into the midst of the sea; though its waters roar and be troubled, though the mountains shake with its swelling, there is a river whose streams shall make glad the city of God. (Psalm 46:1-4a)

Yes, I am ready. I want to be made whole. I am ready to face my fears, the truth, the facts, the reality. Thirty-eight years! Yes, I want to be made well! Secretly and silently, spirit-to-spirit groanings — prayer without words — royal daughter to Abba longs to know who my baby girl was. What were the gifts and talents Abba created her with? How could I possibly know who she would have become? What she might have done? Gone on to be?

This was the hesitancy — to be made whole myself without ever knowing my daughter. How could I be made whole other-wise? A journey to wholeness for me would have had to include her reality, her substance, her God-breathed personality. As I wept with Stacey over Candyce Skye, I now realize the intense bonding and understanding of her grief. To see her daughter but never hear her cry, laugh, run, and play in the snow... all the delights of motherhood stripped from her in an instant. This is the protection of denial. If it didn't really happen, I haven't lost anything. The horror of the reality and life-long results is too much to bear without the aid of my precious Savior, the comfort of the Holy Spirit, and the power of the cross to cleanse and restore. If we confess our sins, He is faithful and just to forgive us our sins and to cleanse us from all unrighteousness (1 John 1:9).

All my stains are washed away — why don't I feel it? I believe the Spirit answers... Just as Candyce Skye's mother delayed bringing forth her sleeping daughter, you have carried your sleeping daughter thirty-eight years. The moment you deliver her — you must prepare to return her to Your Father until such time when you will be united again. This is your hesitancy to move forward. The name you have chosen gives you a glimpse of your daughter. You are blessed in the Spirit to carry her now with understanding, to embrace her name you embrace who she was and is. She lived and continues to live. I have prepared your heart. I have healed your self-inflicted wound. Receive her

as your own. Her name — Chloe — means first shoot of plants in
spring, new growth, green shoot, fresh blooming, tender shoot.
Renee — means reborn, born again, rebirth...

"Oh! Great King! I was blind but now I see! Chloe Renee! Chloe Renee! Oh! What a beautiful name! Oh! What glorious destiny yet to be revealed! Oh! What rapture of my heart! This surely is the mystery of the receiving. I sense the way over the bridge is in Ruby Red."

"You say right, My Beloved! It is in the receiving of Ruby Red you shall cross. You have been brought to the bridge over the great divide for such as time as this. The tender shoot of Chloe Renee's release will bring healing and wholeness to many. Strength for the journey over the bridge is in Ruby Red. You have said to the Keeper of the bridge, 'Yes! I want to be made well!' "

"Whoever is the Keeper of the bridge, Great King?"

"It is I, My Beloved, it is I. I delight in being the Keeper of the bridge! I know your heart's desire is to be made well. The mystery of cradling the land of promise is in crossing the bridge. The journey over the bridge begins in the receiving, and ends in the releasing."

"But, oh, Great King, the mystery of the releasing is too much to bear. My heart cries out with uncontrollable sobs at the prospect of holding my precious Chloe Renee, close only to let her go. However will I be able to do this?"

"Strength is in the knowing and in the knowing you will find strength. The destiny of the tender shoot is first to die, then to sprout and bring forth life. To everything there is a season, a time for every purpose under heaven. Be still and know that I am God. It is in the power of Ruby Red, the receiving and releasing, you will cross the great divide and cradle the land of promise."

"I believe Your promises, Great King, and receive Your words with joy!"

"Make provisions for yourself, for you will receive your tender green shoot that must be laid to rest so that others may heal. You will not cross this great divide alone. Receiving Ruby Red and carrying her to this place of decision has given you access to all whom I command."

We walked toward the bridge and stood at the edge. I trembled at its length, height, and width. It was extremely narrow, and had no railings to keep me from falling to my death into a rugged gorge below. I could NEVER, EVER cross this bridge!

The Great King became very agitated by this latest attack against the healing journey He had prepared for me. Fire shot out of His eyes toward every demon of anxiety and fear. Thunder and lightning erupted from the heavens as He roared against them...

The Lord also will roar from Zion, and utter His voice from Jerusalem. The heavens and earth will shake, But the Lord will be a shelter for His people, and the strength of the children of Israel. (Joel 3:16)

Every demon that tried to stop me at the edge of the bridge scrambled to cross over, only to fall to their deaths in the same manner they had prepared for me. The heavens opened as a scroll, and I saw a company of angels, too numerous to count, and too large to measure. They proceeded to the bridge where they began to form a living, breathing fortress on either side of the bridge. No longer did I need to fear falling to my death into the jagged gorge miles below! The Great King had roared! All of heaven and earth stood and took notice. Great hope and peace washed over me as I looked upon this sight that I did not understand.

The massive company of angels turned toward the east, which caused me to do the same. Two beautiful beings, clothed in white, came out of the eastern sky with rainbows covering their glowing bodies. They carried golden bowls, which emitted a golden hue unlike anything I have ever seen before. Their height surpassed that of the tallest sequoia, and with great respect, I trembled at their sight.

"Fear not, Beloved, these are the archangels *HOPE* and *PEACE*. They will be stationed at each end of the bridge, protecting you from anxiety and distress as you journey toward cradling the land of promise. The bowls they carry hold the treasures of destiny, which were contained in the golden chest I unlocked for you at the pregnancy center. *HOPE* will be your rear guard as you cross the great divide. *PEACE* will be forever in your view as you make passage. Once you cross the great divide, they will accompany you as you lay Chloe Renee to rest. You will know you have passed over when you are able to lay your precious daughter to rest, trusting Me with her care. This is the mystery of the receiving, releasing, and the great divide."

REST-REFLECT-REFRESH

As you reflect on my journal entries, what, if anything in my story can you relate to? Journal your thoughts, and meditate on the following verse…

Now a certain man was there who had an infirmity of thirty-eight years. When Jesus saw him lying there, and knew that he already had been in that condition a long time, He said to him, "Do you want to be made well?" (John 5:5-6)

I kept Chloe Renee's death a secret for thirty-eight years. When I read John 5:5-6, I cried out from the depths of where she was stripped of her life and said, "Yes! I want to be made well!" I had no idea what that meant at the time, but the Great King did! Crossing the great divide into my land of promise was filled with a mixture of every emotion known to a woman, yet the end result was beautifully stable. Trusting the Great King with my painful, yet healing journey brought forth *Chloe's Cry*, and the desire to start an abortion recovery group. Only the Great King could take what the enemy meant for harm to bring healing to myself and many others!

But as for you, you meant evil against me, but God meant it for good, in order to bring it about as it is this day, to save many people alive. (Genesis 50:20)

Chloe's Cry has been written with you and your child in mind. My desire is to bring you to my bridge over the great divide, and offer you my story with transparency and truth. I am writing to you from the position of victory, where I know Chloe Renee is safely in the loving care of the Great King, and at the same time restored to her rightful place of honor in my heart.

The Great King desires to offer you the same opportunity to cross the great divide and enter into your land of promise. Will you let Him? How many years have you been carrying this burden? Do you want to be made well? Will you answer, "YES!"? No matter where you are in your healing journey, take time to pour out your heart to the Great King in creative expression before you move on!

Now a certain man was there who had an infirmity of thirty-eight years. When Jesus saw him lying there, and knew that he already had been in that condition a long time, He said to him, "Do you want to be made well?" (John 5:5-6)

I humbly submit the raw, inner me to you as the Great King begins to introduce me to my daughter...

Chapter 12

Names of Honor

"Oh, Great King! I loathe myself. Where is the courage and strength Ruby Red's safe passage promised? I cannot bear the weight of the truth! How will I ever face her?"

"Beloved, we have come here for such a time as this. Write what you feel, for I will heal many though your words. Speak to the mountain and it will fall. Speak to the sea and it will be still. Speak the truth and it will not only set you free, but all who read your words."

He is taking me to Chloe Renee. He holds me tenderly. His focus is totally on me.

Journal Entries January 11-16, 2017

Surreal emotions tied to the sentencing to death of Dylan Roof who was convicted of murdering nine people in a Charleston, SC church in cold blood in December 2016. Amid the horror of his actions and lack of remorse, I cannot but think of the millions of defenseless unborn children who succumb to the unbelievable torture in their murders. This is a step-by-step journey to my own healing as I now add the word "murder" to the list of words that bring up intense feelings of guilt and shame. This, too, I must lay at the cross. I must allow His healing hands to touch the places I am unwilling or cannot go. Does this torture I put myself through bring about any positive result? Of course not. Why do I walk this path of disconnect from myself at twenty-two years of age and sixty? It is the horror of this truth that should set me free I cannot bring to the plate. It sickens me. I cannot eat this truth.

Oh, Chloe Renee…how will I ever face you?

So, as I write, I come to realize it is me that sickens me. I cannot come to terms with me. My present stage in life is sixty years old — no children living, no grandchildren. It is as if at sixty I have been forced to recognize the reality that my twenty-two-year-old selfish self has deprived me of so much. Can I loathe myself as the world looks upon Dylan Roof with utter contempt? He has no right to live. My only relief as I read about his death sentence was to find out what Sister Helen Prejean's reply was. She said that even Dylan Roof should not be executed. Just a glimpse of relief. A seed of hope for me. I need not execute myself. I cannot disassociate myself with me. His healing hand. His healing touch is what I need. His hand, the only hand that can weave the tapestry of my life together, so that together we can expand His kingdom. He brings me to His Word in full force… What I have called clean, do not despise…

Now, that's a paraphrase… in my spirit He said He would bring to my remembrance all that He taught me. Much of what I have preached to inmates for over nineteen years is coming back to me to bring healing to my own pain…

The Lord is my Shepherd I shall not want. He makes me to lie down in green pastures. He leads me beside the still waters. He restores my soul. He leads me in the paths of righteousness for His name's sake. Yea, though I walk through the valley of the shadow of death, I fear no evil. For You are with me. Your rod and Your staff, they comfort me. You prepare a table before me in the presence of my enemies. You anoint my head with oil. My cup runs over. Surely, goodness and mercy shall follow me all the days of my life. And I will dwell in the house of the Lord forever. (Psalm 23)

There is so much truth in Psalm 23 in connection to abortion. Of course, I never saw it before. As I asked the Lord to speak to me today before I picked up this pen to write, I could not imagine the journey He wants to take me. As I meditate on Psalm 23, His healing hands are skillfully weaving my shattered soul back together. His words to Joshua come to mind even as I take His out-stretched healing hand. "I do not despise you, I died for you." He says, "Arise and go over this Jordan. Have I not said to you, be strong and of good courage, do not be afraid, nor be dismayed, for the Lord your God is with you wherever you go?" He says, "Lynn, prepare provisions for yourself. For within three days you will cross over this Jordan to go in to possess the land which I am giving you to possess." He says, "Lynn, I am giving you rest and giving you this land." Joshua 1:1-13 is the action put to Psalm 23.

I am not alone in this abortion recovery journey. He is with me wherever He takes me. He is setting this table of truth before me in the presence of fear, guilt, shame, and regret. Though I walk through the valley of the shadow of death, I will not fear because He is leading me. I do not walk alone. I can go now. I can face it now. His promise is...Lynn, I am giving you rest and I am giving you this land. Rest is your inheritance. I purchased it with My own blood. Rest is what you long for. Rest in My embrace. This is my hope for healing, for wholeness...

It is He who is walking with me. It is He who carries me in His bosom. What could be a safer place than in the bosom of the One who created me? He carries me in His bosom and gently leads me. He is taking me to Chloe Renee...He reassures me of His care and sings over me...

He will gather me in His arms, carry me close to His bosom, gently lead me to Chloe Renee, and wipe my tears when we arrive.

Of this I am sure, Ruby Red has not forsaken me...in this Great Shepherd...I will trust...

REST-REFLECT-REFRESH

I was in a parking lot one afternoon getting ready to start my car and head home after doing a little grocery shopping when the name *Chloe Renee* dropped into my spirit...*Chloe Renee.* I sat for a few minutes and thought, *Chloe Renee?* The sound of her name was like warm oil pouring through every broken place in my being. In the depths of my heart, I knew it was the name chosen by heaven for my daughter. Names are very important to the Great King as they are given in accordance to the character of the holder. The Great King was inviting me to get to know my daughter! Was I willing to go to this place of pain in order to be made well?

It was one thing to face the facts of my abortion, another thing to admit that it was the murder of my innocent child, but to give her a name, and face the reality of what that meant turned my whole world upside down. I knew in my heart of hearts I would never cross the great divide and into the land of promise if I stopped short of getting to know my daughter and laying her to rest. I realized that solving the mystery of the highest mountain and the raging seas was in receiving Chloe Renee from the Great King and releasing her back to Him.

By dropping her name into my spirit, He offered me the first step toward getting to know her. The Great King continued to whisper her name into the depths of my brokenness until the dormant seed of motherhood began to sprout. *Chloe Renee* — tenderly spoke over and over — stirred something deep within that caused me to want to get to know this tender shoot in spite of all the pain it may cause. Yes! I want to be made well! Yes! I am desperate to know my daughter!

Immediately, I started searching for the meanings of her name, as I knew they would answer my questions of what she would have been like. I wept with joy as I learned of the high calling on her life in the name the Great King had chosen for her. It was in my *intentional* response to His offer that I moved forward to bonding with her and toward the bridge over the great divide.

Coming to this place of bonding with Chloe Renee was very difficult for me, but necessary if I ever had any hope of recovering from her death once I came out of thirty-eight years of silence. It would be eight months of getting to know her before I was able to lay her to rest and release her to the Great King through a beautiful memorial service.

Have you given your unborn child a name? If so, I encourage you to be creative in honoring him or her with whatever creative gifts you have been given. Write a poem, a song, paint a picture, write a short story. At the very least write the name out as many times as you need to feel his or her presence without experiencing guilt or shame. If you have not had opportunity to give your unborn child a name, I encourage you to seek the Great King for the name He would have you choose before moving on. Our first step in crossing the great divide is to name our unborn children in order to honor and celebrate their short lives before we lay them to rest and release them from our hearts back to the heart of the Great King.

Keep in mind as you do, we are created as individuals with different capacities for different things. My story is just that... my story. Your time frame most likely will not be the same as mine. Only move on from this portion of *Chloe's Cry* after you have been able to name your unborn child. Once your child has been named, do a name search as I did and get to know the characteristics of your child. Journal your thoughts and reactions to what you learn and experience. I will be sharing some of mine in the next chapter...

Chapter 13

Road to Reconciliation

"Beloved, it is time to cross the great divide. Chloe Renee is waiting for you…"

Journal Entry January 16, 2017

I am preparing to go. I am ready, but hesitant for once I get there, I will have to let go, say goodbye. I trust His love to carry me through. I am excited to go which seems very strange. There must be something beautiful there for me. I have such a peace now I cannot put to words. I am wrapped in His arms and do not have to walk this path alone. There is no other I wish to travel with. His rod and His staff, they comfort me. My sin… oh the bliss of this glorious thought…my sin not in part, but the whole is nailed to the cross, and I bear it no more. Praise the Lord, Praise the Lord, oh my soul. It is well, it is well, it is well with my soul.

Surely, He has born my grief, and carried my sorrow… He was wounded for my abortion. He was bruised for Chloe Renee's death. The chastisement for my peace was upon Him and by His stripes, I am healed (from Isaiah 53:4-5). There is a knowing deep, deep in the place where I must go that all is well.

I am His lamb. His total attention is on me. The crowd behind Him is of no concern right now. I am His and He is mine.

Jesus wants to carry me to the place where destruction became too personal to be. He wants to deliver me from the evils which obstruct reception of His power to heal and set me free from bondage and knit me back together. He wants to introduce me to Chloe Renee...allow me to begin to grieve... while receiving His and her forgiveness.

The part of me that has been destroyed, He seeks to make whole.

He tenderly holds me in His arms, steadies my emotions, loves me unconditionally, prepares my heart, showers me with His forgiveness, breaths strength, His strength into my being, holds me close. I am hesitant but not as hesitant as even a few days ago. I took a big step yesterday; I chose to watch a Steelers game. I chose to identify with Pittsburgh — the place of my birth and Chloe Renee's death.

A song I don't recall while writing this came on during a commercial and it took me back to the time when Chloe Renee was still alive in my womb. It made me uncomfortable, but not overwhelming. I cannot escape the fact that Pittsburgh holds a lot of traumatic memories for me, but facing those memories being held and carried in my loving Shepherd's arms is what is going to set me free.

I must see Him as He sees me or I cannot go there. I must know I am safe in His arms. I must know He was there in 1978 although I turned away from Him. I must know what He says is true... though you were dark, you would be like the morning (Job 11:17b).

It is in the knowing that I am safe. It is in the knowing that I am secure. It is in the knowing that my Lord will enable me to go to this place of long ago to be reconciled to Chloe Renee and myself. It is there where a threefold cord cannot be broken, where I will be reunited with Chloe Renee and myself, where tears will be permitted, grieving celebrated as the pathway to wholeness, where our Deliverer, Savior, Abba Father will hold us both in His care, and allow me to heal, to hold you, and be at peace until I see both of you face-to-face...

The Great King, who has me on His shoulders, leans down to let me slide off. We stand at the edge of the bridge over the great divide. Angelic hosts line each side of the narrow bridge, while archangels HOPE and PEACE are stationed behind us, waiting for the Great King's command.

"HOPE, you who guard the entrance to the bridge over the great divide, extend your wings as a covering that we may pass under. You shall be our rear guard as we cross this bridge, for with very step we take, the bridge will dissolve behind us. You, hosts of heaven, who line the sides of the bridge, be ever mindful of My Beloved, for she has never passed this way before. Grant her safe passage by guarding the edges of this narrow bridge that spans the distance over the jagged gorge below. PEACE, you who stand guard at the entrance to the land of promise, I give you charge over the colors of healing. When the waterfalls of sorrow flow, release the colors of promise to comfort. I will carry her over this great divide and all of heaven and earth will witness the glory of the Great King. Prepare your stations. Our journey has begun."

"Oh! Great King? What of this beautiful rainbow I see in the distance?"

"The rainbow will be for a sign to you that when you shed tears in the light of My presence, your tears will be as the cleansing, purifying, and cradling of the land of promise. It is in your tears that you will cradle the land of promise. Your tears are holy in My sight. I will catch every one that falls. Fear not as you move forward. This rainbow of tears will be as a crown placed upon your head. You will weep freely, My daughter, for the Keeper of the bridge gives you permission, and Chloe Renee waits to greet you in the arms of the Keeper of the Stars."

I hold Ruby Red tight in anticipation of needing her strength for this journey ahead...

Journal Entry January 16, 2017 Continued

Where do we go now, Lord? The details are few. The memories blotted out, concealed, buried. Her address at conception was in Trafford. She had a family! Her home was a singlewide, two-bedroom mobile home nestled in the woods. Not much of a place for a toddler to play in — the lots were quite small. Chloe Renee's house sat on the edge of a hill that made her Grandma nervous! We always wondered if it would fall over the edge during high winds. So, I think I'm going to rewrite this, Chloe, and write it to you. The more I write your name — the more peace comes to me. Our Abba Father is surely holding me. My heart is beating with anticipation and joy at sharing these things with you. Dear Chloe...

I really hope Jesus introduced you to Candyce Skye when she got there. I hope you are showing her around and preparing a place for me and her mom, Stacey. I just wanted to let you know you have a family here, and some have come to where you are. I'm not sure if your father is still here, but I believe your aunt is, but your grandma, pap pap, grandmas G & W, and great aunt, well, they are all where you are. Your Grandma J is still here. Uncle B is in your neighborhood too. He left us two years ago. Your Aunt B is still here but lives far away from me. I know everyone would have loved you rotten — as they say here in the South. I originally was going to give you the name Melissa Lynn, which I actually used for several years in secret. No one really but me and Jesus knew you by that name, until just a few weeks ago. Now...Here's where it gets tough, Chloe Renee...

I feel the roadblock coming. I will pause here to refresh. A living child with an address, a family, and a name snuffed out before leaving her place of development. Abused in the very place where nurturing and love should have resided. Yes, it's easy, Chloe Renee, to speak of what was rightfully yours, until reality hits that I chose to deny you all of it....

Forgive me, Chloe Renee.. Forgive me, Jesus. Forgive me, Lynn. Forgive me, everybody for denying you Chloe Renee.

Tears of remorse of what could have been. Jesus is here. He is comforting me. Chloe Renee is with Him. Chloe Renee, how will I ever forgive myself?

I am crawling, slowly crawling out of denial. Thirty-eight years is a long time to deny the existence of a human being developing inside of you. There is intense pain associated with writing to you Chloe — to becoming that intimate with a reality, subdued, hidden, and locked away for so long. Recent memories of holding sleeping Candyce Skye whose body I held, but whose soul was in the arms of Jesus are all too close to this journey toward you, Chloe Renee.

We held Candyce Skye, we talked to her, we sang over her. She was with us, but she was not. She was in fact with Jesus. Is the pain and anguish Stacey faces frightening to me? For surely when Jesus shows me Chloe Renee my world will crumble!

Unless a grain of wheat falls to the ground and dies, it remains alone, but if it dies, it produces much grain (John 12:24). These two precious seeds have gone on but their seeds are producing much life. The very thing I fear is what is setting me free. It is in the embrace, the tender look, the compassionate aura of this picture... the spotless, white lamb in contrast to the bloodied body of my Redeemer that anointed my eyes with eye salve, that I might see the truth that sets me free... Speak to me, Lord!

REST-REFLECT-REFRESH

As you can tell from my journal entries, emotions were not stable during this part of my journey, nor would they fit into any formula for abortion recovery. As I stated in our last resting session, we are unique individuals created by God to process things in unique and individual ways. As we stop to rest and reflect, I encourage you to take some time to explore the feelings you have toward bonding with your unborn child and find a way to release them in a positive, healthy way. Whether it be in writing, painting, sculpting, singing, or whatever manner of creative expression fits your individual journey, use this time to recognize and release those feelings.

Before you move on, I encourage you to write a letter to your unborn child. If this seems frightening or at any way intimidating, perhaps starting with a short note would be advisable. Tell him or her about their families, where they were conceived, and anything else you would like them to know. Perhaps re-reading my journal entries will help if you find yourself stuck and don't know where to begin. Reach into the recesses of your heart where your unborn child still resides, and you will be amazed how much you want to bond and share life with them!

When I started writing to Chloe Renee, the reality of her personhood, her special place in the heart of her Creator, and the longing I had to hold her close became a source of great peace and comfort as my journey progressed. The Great King used this bonding process to enable me to move forward. The magnitude of the miracle that was unfolding in my life astounds and humbles me more than you could ever know. All I can say is, the Great King reigns! His mercy endures forever and is new every morning! Great is His faithfulness to all generations! Great is His mighty, powerful name! Great is His kindness to heal and restore!

I will be writing to Chloe Renee in one form or another until I pass from this life into the next, where I will see her face-to-face and hold her in my arms. I encourage you to start sharing your life with your unborn child and begin bonding with him or her right now. Allow the Great King to lead you into your own bonding process, and experience His kindness to heal and restore you. May He grant you hope and peace as you step out in faith and begin bonding with your unborn child.

May He bless you as you take this important step toward crossing the great divide...

The Lord bless you and keep you,
The Lord make His face shine upon you,
And be gracious to you, The Lord lift up His
Countenance upon you, and give you peace...
(Numbers 6:24-26)

Chapter 14

Recognizing My Need

Journal Entry January 24, 2017

*C*hloe Renee, today I really feel like talking to you! I'm asking Jesus what you look like, what your personality is like, what your gifts and talents are, and all things beautiful He created in you. I went to get eggs from the chicken coop just a little bit ago. The dogs love to follow me to the coop. Our female gets so excited like it's the journey of a lifetime — trotting happily toward the door. Yes, Chloe Renee, you are an adventurous, happy person. Small things, simple things make you smile. You are easygoing and love to laugh. You are tenderhearted and soft, caring, and compassionate. You are playful and a carefree lover of life.

"Oh! Yes! Thank You Great King! Playful, carefree, and a lover of life…that's my Chloe Renee!"

Journal Entry January 25, 2017

It's moving from abstract knowledge and understanding to reality. I know now why we bury this deep and disassociate from reality — the pain is too much to bear. Being part of a group — if ever so abstract — has helped me come this far. I now believe I'm not the only one in the world that has snuffed out the life of their child. I keep thinking of Stacey and Candyce Skye — it is too much. The Holy Spirit says, "Come to the foot of the cross. It is the only place of hope."

Oh! Great King! The stormy seas and this highest mountain built with millions of thoughts would surely stop me from crossing this great divide if You had not given me Ruby Red!"

"Beloved, though you are tossed and afflicted and not comforted, I will lay your stones with colorful gems, and all your walls of precious stones. Chloe Renee shall be taught by Me, and great shall be her peace. You shall rise from the ashes of your thoughts and cross this great divide and cradle your land of promise. I have spoken. It shall be so" (from Isaiah 54:11).

The Great King knelt at my feet and looked up into my face. His eyes dripped golden tears in response to my pain, and He sang me a love song…

Wrap your empty arms around Me, and lean into My chest…
Hear the heart that beats and breaks for you,
When you cannot find your rest.
My child, the tears you shed are gold, you'll see,
For when they mix with Mine, they'll set you free.
So, wrap your empty arms around Me,
and lean into My chest…
Hear My heart that beats and breaks for you,
And you will find your rest…

By Lynn Potter

I sobbed uncontrollably at the depth of His love in the midst of my anguish. I was crumbling under the weight of grief and sorrow, brought on by the reality of what Chloe Renee and I had missed in life. The great cloud of witnesses and the heavenly hosts stood behind the angels on either side of the bridge, waiting to see what the Great King would do. As my tears fell in

His presence, a rainbow appeared over my head confirming the word He recently proclaimed as we stood at the entrance to the bridge over the great divide. Magnificent colors danced around me, engulfing me in their beauty. At the Great King's command, the stormy sea calmed and every torturous thought ceased its aggravated assault. I now stood tall in the King's glory with the beauty of His rainbow's promise dancing all around me.

"Great King! What is this I see in the distance? It appears the angels on the east side of the edge of the bridge are separating. Whatever could this mean?"

"Beloved, they are making room for the holder of your tears to rise from the bottom of the jagged gorge below at the command of Ruby Red. Come, let us take our leave and journey toward this sight that has caught your eye. Open your bag covered in the finest linen to receive the mystery of Samaria and the stones of tears I give to you this day."

I did as the Great King instructed. He pulled from His chest two beautifully crafted tear-shaped golden stones and placed them gently into my bag. "Beloved," He said, "receive the mystery of Samaria and the stones of tears hewn from the cries of the cross of torture." Immediately my eyes were opened to their meaning. How magnificent is this love that would share my sorrow! "Oh! Great King! Are these not some of the golden tears you shed while you sang to me?"

"Indeed, My Beloved, indeed."

"But what of the mystery of Samaria?"

He left Judea and departed again to Galilee. But He needed to go through Samaria. So, He came to a city of Samaria which is called Sychar, near the plot of ground that Jacob gave to his son Joseph. (John 4:3-5)

"Beloved, the mystery of Samaria lies in the oneness of two resting at the sight of the holder of your tears."

"But, Great King! These golden tears are heavy in my bag, too heavy for me to carry." I struggled to lift the bag to show Him. "Would You help me?"

A fresh waterfall of tears flowed down His cheeks onto the ground, forming a golden path in front of us. "Beloved, I have waited thirty-eight years to hear this! It is in the yoke of oneness that the journey toward the land of promise brings forth new life out of death. It is in your admission of need that the great divide loses its power over you. You shall conquer it with the golden tears in our oneness of sorrow."

"Oh! Great King! How shall I ever understand Your words?"

Come unto Me, all you who labor and are heavy laden, and I will give you rest. Take My yoke upon you and learn from Me, for I am gentle and lowly in heart, and you will find rest for your souls. For My yoke is easy and my burden is light. (Matthew 11:28-30)

"Great King? Is there not a key for the mystery of Samaria and the golden tears for me to place on my golden chain?"

"You have learned the way of the journey toward cradling the land of promise well. The key to the mystery of Samaria and the golden tears is in your oneness with Me. This key cannot be put on a chain for it is formed and fashioned in your heart's response to the cries of the longings of My heart. The tear-shaped stones will be for a remembrance for generations to come as they read of your safe passage over the great divide. Watch over them. See that no one steals them from you."

"However shall I carry them over the great divide? They are too heavy!"

"Beloved, pick your bag up and receive the mystery of the yoke of oneness. You shall see that the golden tears have become light in response to your admission of need."

"Oh! Great King! Your mysteries are so intriguing, so exciting, so freeing! I delight in learning of them! They are music to my ears and salve to my eyes! They give me courage and strength to move forward into the vast unknown!"

Tears of joy poured down my cheeks and onto the ground where the Great King's had formed the golden path. The bridge shook as our tears mixed. "Fear not, My Beloved. Come...let us drink of this mystery together."

REST-REFLECT-REFRESH

Many times, we endure the aftermath of traumatic events through the eyes of despair because we feel as though we are alone in our struggle. Because choosing abortion carries with it mountains of guilt and shame, we need someone willing to share our journey without judgment or condemnation. Although the Great King had shown me kindness through the beautiful women He placed in my path, when it came to sharing my deepest grief and sorrow, He became my ultimate sojourner.

The day the Great King unveiled the mystery of Samaria and His golden tears, I no longer feared moving on toward bonding with Chloe Renee and releasing her back to Him. It was in the reality of His love and care for both of us that I was able to hold on to Ruby Red's childlike trust and follow Him across the bridge to lay her to rest. As I embraced this revelation for myself, I was reminded of the two most comforting words in all of Scripture...

Jesus wept. (John 11:35)

Just as Jesus wept at the tomb of His friend Lazarus, He longs to weep with us at the tomb of our womb where our children were taken before their time. And, just as He called forth Lazarus from the grave, He longs to call forth our children from the tomb of our silent secrets.

Will you answer the cry of His heart as I did? Will you take hold of Ruby Red, the childlike trust that is required to continue this healing journey? Would you say yes to sharing your tears with the Great King and allowing them to form a golden path for you to cross your own great divide?

I encourage you to take some time to meditate on the following verses in the account of Jesus at the tomb of Lazarus.

Envision Him weeping with you over the death of your child. Allow Him to comfort you and wrap His arms around you as you continue to bond with your child. This is a special time of bonding with Him as well. Journal your thoughts before we move on. Be creative in your response to His love and care for both you and your child.

Therefore, when Jesus saw her weeping, and the Jews who came with her weeping, He groaned in the spirit and was troubled. And He said, "Where have you laid him?" They said to Him, "Lord, come and see." (John 11:33-34)

Jesus wept. (John 11:35)

Then the Jews said, "See how He loved him!" (John 11:36)

After you have spent time bonding with your child and the Great King, follow me as He reveals the Mystery of Samaria...

Chapter 15

A Mother's Heart

*H*e left Judea and departed again to Galilee. But He needed
to go through Samaria. So, He came to a city of Samaria
which is called Sychar, near the plot of ground that Jacob gave
to his son Joseph. Now Jacob's well was there. Jesus, therefore
being wearied from His journey, sat thus by the well. It was
about the sixth hour. (John 4:3-6)

Journal Entry January 21, 2017

Water from the well met me before I stepped out of bed.
Chloe Renee is so real to me, and knowing of her existence does
not carry guilt, shame, remorse, or trauma for me today. There
is an inner peace, a healthy longing and desire when I think
of her, when I whisper her name. My thoughts of her are being
transformed from abstract to reality. Light surely is shining in
darkness. Surely the Lord has visited me at the well! But He
needed to go through Samaria (John 4:4).

He needed to go through MY HOME TOWN and stop at MY
HOUSE! There He found me searching for water! Here, at my
house, He spoke to me about living water. I awoke this morning
with a childhood song I remember from Sunday school...

Chloe Renee's death is not in vain...Behold I say to you, lift up your eyes and look at the harvest fields, for they are already white for harvest (from John 4:35).

Oh! Great King! Who am I that You would visit me? I declare with Zacharias…Blessed is the Lord God of Israel, for He has visited and redeemed His people (Luke 1:68)! Your mercy and compassion are like no other! You are the Lord who heals me! I rejoice in Your salvation that has come to Your maidservant! Glory to Your name in heaven and on earth! Chloe Renee's death is not in vain! You have declared it! Yes! Oh! Great King! I will lift up my eyes and look at the harvest fields all around me! I will go where You send me to declare *Chloe's Cry* to the ends of the earth for Your glory! May the meditations of my heart and the words of my mouth be acceptable unto You, oh Lord! May *Chloe's Cry* trumpet the power of the cross of torture and the everlasting, redeeming blood that continually flows from it! Yes, and amen!

Journal Entry January 30, 2017

It has been several days since I've had quiet reflection time. In the meantime—The Right-to-Life march has transpired. It is really hard to put into words the emotions, thoughts, and reactions my heart went through. Now I have a face, I have a part, I have Chloe Renee to defend. It is the most bizarre, crazy thing I could have ever imagined. I suppose it is all the unborn Chloe Renees that my heart defends…A MOTHER'S HEART! LYNN POTTER HAS A MOTHER'S HEART! REVELATION— DIVINE—REVELATION! I AM SAFE AND CAN BE TRUSTED WITH A CHILD BECAUSE I HAVE A MOTHER'S HEART! Serve Him with a loyal heart and with a willing mind (1 Chronicles 28:9b). A mother's heart is a loyal heart.

"Oh! Great King! How can I ever thank You for this revelation? How can I ever express to You what is in this mother's heart? Oh! Glorious King! Your mercy at the well is beyond measure! I shall sing of Your goodness and mercy in all Your house as gold and silver refined in the fire!"

Moreover, because I have set my affection on the house of my God, I have given to the house of my God, over and above all that I have prepared for the Holy House, my own special treasure of gold and silver. (1 Chronicles 29:3)

"Beloved, before I formed you in the womb, I knew you. I knew the decision you were going to make concerning Chloe Renee. I set you apart for such a time as this to declare My mercy to all who are traumatized by abortion. You say well that Chloe Renee's death is not in vain! For yes and amen, her death will produce life! Together with the mystery of Samaria and the golden tears, we shall offer freedom to many."

I counsel you to buy from Me gold refined in the fire, that you may be rich, and white garments, that you may be clothed, that the shame of your nakedness may not be revealed and anoint your eyes with eye salve that you may see. (Revelation 3:18)

"Oh! Great King! You gave me a mother's heart when You created me! Fear, guilt, shame, and regret convinced me that I had no right to that part of who I am because of what I had done! They are liars and sons of the great liar! Oh! How glorious is this revelation! Oh! How freeing and liberating! I am being knit back together in a place where I thought the tear was so deep that restoration would be impossible! A mother's heart! Oh! I have a mother's heart!"

The great cloud of witnesses and the armies of light bowed as He reached into His chest and brought forth a golden case filled with heavenly salve. Their silent reverence for the moment caused me to anticipate with joy what He was about to do. He cupped my cheeks and lifted my face toward heaven. "Whatever is this vision I see?" I said.

"You shall understand not too many days from now. Receive what the mystery of Samaria and the golden tears have to offer..." He placed His hands upon my eyes and began to sing...

"Comfort, yes comfort My People!" Says your God. "Speak comfort to Jerusalem, and cry out to her. That her warfare is ended, that her iniquity is pardoned; for she has received from the Lord's hand double for all her sins." (Isaiah 40:1-2)

"Oh! Great King! The healing salve upon my eyes gives me permission to grieve as any mother would grieve the death of her child! Oh! The tears of grief! The tears of joy! Oh! The tears mixing together becoming golden tears, refined in fire, that I may become rich with the blessing of motherhood! Oh! Great King! That the nakedness of my silent secret would be covered with the white gown You purchased for me on the cross of torture! Oh! Thank You Mighty King for this salve upon my eyes that I might see the way across this great divide into the land of promise! Thank You! Thank You! Mighty, Mighty, Great King! I can't thank You enough!" A waterfall of tears fell at my feet in response to the Great King's touch. I leaned into Him as He stood behind me, offering His support. Warm, wet tears flowed over my shoulders.

"Oh! Mighty King! You are weeping?"

"It is for the mystery of Samaria and the golden tears that I weep. Look, Beloved! The holder of your tears which held you captive in the dungeon has been cast into the jagged gorge below. He has been swallowed up in the oneness of our sorrow. No longer will you be weighed down by the unshed tears of your captivity. I release you now to grieve the loss of Chloe Renee and in the grieving, you shall find her. Today, receive the gift of grieving in the rainbow of My love."

As PEACE, the keeper of the healing colors, released their essence, the Great King placed His hand on my heart. The rainbow of His love penetrated the jagged gorge of my shattered mother's heart as He sang words of life into my destiny...

O you afflicted one, tossed with tempest, and not comforted. Behold, I will lay your stones with colorful gems. And lay your foundations with sapphires. I will make your pinnacles of rubies, your gates of crystal, and all your walls of precious stones. All your children shall be taught by the Lord, and great shall be the peace of your children. (Isaiah 54:11-13)

"Great King? Whatever does this love song mean?"

"Beloved, the mystery of the mother's heart and the great divide is hidden in the vision and the love song. Not too many days from now, you will cradle their meaning. It will be in the land of promise that the great divide will be conquered and the eye salve will have completed its task."

Journal Entry January 30, 2017

I truly believe Jesus has met me at the well. He has helped me forgive myself and He has introduced me to Chloe Renee. This is the first step toward healing my mother's heart—stop punishing myself. I was born with a mother's heart. I was born with a daughter's heart. Both have been shattered. Both are being healed. I have a mother's heart that was given to me when God formed me in my mother's womb.

"Comfort, yes comfort My people," says your God. "Speak comfort to Jerusalem and cry out to her. That her warfare is ended. That her iniquity is pardoned. For she has received from the Lord's hand double for all her sins. (Isaiah 40:1) As a mother comforts her child, so will I comfort you." (Isaiah 66:13, NIV)

Jesus called a little child to Him, set him in the midst of them and said, "Assuredly, I say to you, unless you are converted and become as little children, you will by no means enter the kingdom of heaven. Therefore, whoever humbles himself as this little child is the greatest in the kingdom of heaven. Whoever receives one little child like this in My name receives Me. (Matthew 18:2-5)

I opened my bag woven in fine linen and tenderly fondled its contents. "Great King! Look at the beautiful gifts You have given me for my journey!" I held them up one by one for Him to see. "Oh! How I cherish the lapis lazuli, the stone of transparency where deep has called me to deep! She has given me the gift of facing the truth...truth that is setting me free! Oh! How I honor the crimson sapphire whose beauty was purchased on the cross of torture! I carry my Rite of Passage because of her! Oh! How my heart swells with gratitude as I gaze upon the glistening green emerald of the great exchange! She reminds me I have been brought out of the deep, dark dungeon into Your marvelous light..."

"But, oh, Great King! Look! My Redeemer, my Shepherd, my Healer! The splendor of this one, the Ruby Red! For without her, the lapis lazuli, the crimson sapphire, or the glistening emerald would never be able to help me over the great divide! Look! She's Ruby Red! Yes! She's childlike trust that believes You are who You say You are, that You will do what You say You will do, and that I am safe in Your care. Yes! Without Ruby Red I would still be on the dark side of the great divide! Thank You, Great King for these, Your precious gifts!"

"Beloved...the wisdom you have received from the mysteries of the keys and stones will guide you across the remainder of this great divide and usher you into the land of promise. The keeper of your tears has been defeated and your grief healing process has begun. Because you hold Ruby Red in such high esteem, you shall trample on serpents and scorpions that are strategically stationed on your path by the king of darkness. He has ordered them to stop you from grieving your loss."

I fell at His feet and began to weep. Uncontrollable tears of grief flowed like a healing river from the wells of deep calling deep, washing the dust off His feet and cleansing my soul...

And behold, a woman in the city who was a sinner, when she knew that Jesus sat at the table in the Pharisee's house, brought an alabaster flask of fragrant oil, and stood at His feet behind Him weeping; and she began to wash His feet with her tears, and wiped them with the hair of her head and she kissed His feet and anointed them with the fragrant oil. (Luke 7:37-38)

Behold, I give you the authority to trample on serpents and scorpions, and over all the power of the enemy, and nothing shall by any means hurt you. (Luke 10:19)

"Oh! Great King! Ruby Red says I need to receive the gift of grieving the loss of Chloe Renee right now! I need to stretch out my empty arms and allow You to place Chloe Renee in them. I must enter my own Holiest of Holies and embrace my precious daughter just as I did Candyce Skye! I must to talk to her, walk with her, sing over her, and listen for Your voice as I begin the healing process of grieving her loss. Ruby Red tells me You have wept with me all the years I was locked up in the dark dungeon while waiting for me to embrace her childlike trust. She tells me You never stopped calling me through the deep, deep blue lapis lazuli of transparency. She reminds me of the torture You endured that purchased my Rite of Passage over this great divide. She invites me to sing and dance with joy in praise of the Great Exchange that sets me free! She brings me to Your feet and positions me to receive everything You endured for me!"

"I see now that You never left my side! Oh! How marvelous is Your patience and Your tender loving care! You have met me at the well of my sorrow and mixed Your golden tears with mine! I have embraced Ruby Red at the place of my deepest sorrow and received Your permission to grieve the greatest loss of my life. This knowledge is too wonderful for me!"

"This is the mystery of Samaria and the golden tears…is it not, oh, Great King? All the gifts of the keys and stones activated by Ruby Red!"

"Yes, it is, Beloved…indeed it is. Are you ready to follow Ruby Red and receive Chloe Renee? Are you ready to trust Me as you lay her to rest and begin your grieving process? Are you ready, My Beloved, to cross over the deepest, most treacherous part of this great divide in order to enter your land of promise?"

"Oh! Great King! How could I not trust You after all You have brought me through? How could I throw away Ruby Red at this most critical time in my journey? My mother's heart longs to hold Chloe Renee just as I held Candyce Skye. I shall hold tight to Ruby Red, my King!"

"Beloved, it is Ruby Red, your childlike trust that has opened the heavens above you and shown you things that you could have never understood. She has given you wisdom beyond your years and the ability to pursue your healing journey without knowing where it would take you. You have gained strength through your transparency and your willingness to receive the Great Exchange and your Rite of Passage. You have faced the giants of fear, guilt, shame, and regret head on with Ruby Red, and she has caused you to stand your ground and walk in victory. She is born of My heart, My suffering, My sacrifice, and My victory, and has brought you to My feet for such a time as this…"

"It is time for you to cradle Chloe Renee, lay her to rest, and walk in newness of life and purpose. This part of your journey will require you to hold tight to the keys and stones you have received with Ruby Red leading the way. This way will be difficult, but you will not walk alone…"

"Great King?"

"Yes, My Beloved?"

"Truly, I trust you, I do. But, Great King…this is such a hard path…"

"Beloved, I see your shattered heart. I hear the cries of your soul. I know the sorrow you face. Come, let us sit for a while. There is something I want you to see." As we sat, a vision appeared before us.

"Whatever is this, Great King?"

"It is the land of promise that awaits you on the other side of this great divide."

"Oh! Great King! But my vision is blurred!"

"Beloved, it is for clarity of the vision of the Promised Land that you sit at my feet today. It is for clarity of the vision that you will find the courage to continue on this most difficult part of your journey. It is for clarity of the vision that you will complete the journey that will birth the delivering power of your victory in *Chloe's Cry*."

"Beloved, it is for clarity of the vision I rescued you from the deep, dark dungeon."

REST-REFLECT-REFRESH

This was the most exciting, yet frightening part of my healing journey, as I was faced with the decision of trusting everything I learned from following the Great King. He had brought me so far, but was I ready for this deep, deep healing to occur? I had received some healing and was truly grateful for all that had transpired, but to intentionally subject myself to such pain and sorrow seemed sadistic to me.

Yet, I knew in my heart of hearts that there would be no other way over this great divide, nor any lasting healing without allowing myself to grieve. I had no other choice but to embrace Ruby Red and follow the Great King on His path for me. He was firm in His assessment of what I would be facing, but at the same time, He reminded me that I would not be alone. His comfort and faithfulness since the moment He carried me out of the dungeon gave me the ability to trust Him to carry me the rest of the way.

How about you, dear friend? Are you ready to embrace your child in preparation for your own grieving process? Take some time to meditate on this and journal your thoughts.

Whoever receives one little child like this in My name receives Me. (Matthew 18:5)

A mother's heart grieves like no other at the loss of her child. It is a beautiful thing for those of us who have caused the deaths of our children through abortion to allow ourselves to grieve.

Was I ready to handle this part of my journey? Absolutely not! Not on my own! I didn't even believe I had the *right* to grieve until the Great King openly gave me permission!

I wasn't even sure what this type of grieving was supposed to look like. Candyce Skye's death and her mother's grief still haunted my thoughts. How could I possibly permit myself to grieve over something I *chose* to do? I even felt guilty about accepting the Great King's permission to grieve! But above all this, the fact that I had just begun to bond with the daughter I would never hold somehow made me feel as though I was resurrecting her from the dead only to have to bury her again. It would have been overwhelming had I not experienced the oneness at the well in Samaria with the Great King of the golden tears.

The Great King had more than my healing in mind. It isn't about what I did. It isn't about what I had just witnessed. It's not even about my guilt or innocence or even my grief. It is about honoring Him as the creator of all life, including mine and Chloe Renee's. It is about honoring His sacrifice and trumpeting what He has done for me. It is about Chloe Renee, her life, her death, and honoring what the Great King has in store for her destiny. I had no right not to accept His offer! I had no right to deny myself permission to grieve! I had no right to deny Chloe Renee the honor and dignity of being my daughter and being respectfully laid to rest!

I fought any dark thoughts with the assurance of Ruby Red and that the Great King had my best interests in mind. I trusted Him when He said no weapon formed against me could prosper as long as I followed Him over the great divide. Trusting Him until the day I laid her to rest was the key to crossing the great divide and cradling my destiny in the land of promise.

There is a Samaria for you. There is a well for you. It is here! It is now! The Great King wants to meet you right here, right now, to give you His permission to grieve the loss of your child. He paid the price for your sin of abortion and shed His blood so that you may be released from the heaviness of the unshed tears of your captivity. He says, "In your grieving you shall find your child. Today, receive the gift of grieving in the rainbow of My love. You shall not weep alone. I weep with you at this place today. This is the mystery of Samaria and the golden tears."

The Great King placed His hand on my open heart and I received His rainbow of love. I received His permission to grieve, which enabled me to allow myself to grieve. If you want to receive this life-changing gift today, hold your hand on your heart. Allow Him to sing His love song to you…

Wrap your empty arms around Me, and lean into My chest...
Hear the heart that beats and breaks for you,
When you cannot find your rest.
My child, the tears you shed are gold, you'll see,
For when they mix with Mine, they'll set you free.
So, wrap your empty arms around Me,
and lean into My chest...
Hear My heart that beats and breaks for you,
And you will find your rest...

By Lynn Potter

Journal your thoughts. Create something for the Great King and your child in response to His love song and share it with Him! He wants to be invited into every part of your journey!

Chapter 16

The King's Highway

The Great King reached for my hand and lifted me to my feet. "Come, Beloved. We shall take our leave from here and journey toward your land of promise." As He spoke, I saw what looked like a rainbow of colors rising from the jagged gorge below. They appeared to be dancing all around the armies of light who had formed the railing on each side of the bridge. "Great King, how do these healing colors come from such a deep, dark place?"

"Beloved, it was in your receiving the gift of grieving and the oneness of our sorrow that cast the holder of your tears back into the gorge. His hard-shelled exterior exploded at the command of Ruby Red releasing every tear of your incarceration. Once united with My golden tears, they were transformed into the beautiful healing colors that you now see. This is the power of the mystery of Samaria in the oneness of sorrow. Come…follow Me…"

As He led me to the east side of the bridge, the armies of light separated long enough for me to look over the edge. I could not believe what I saw! "Whatever is going on down there?" I said. "Oh! Great King! The gorge is not as deep, nor as jagged as it once was!"

"My sweet daughter, My beloved queen, mother of Chloe Renee! You have walked this long, hard path, trusting the words and mysteries I have given you. You have invited Me into the deep, dark places of this great divide, this jagged gorge, into the very depths of your brokenness. Every time you received one of My keys, one of My stones, one of My mysteries, the armies of light and the great cloud of witnesses poured heavenly oil over the cracks and jagged places. Wherever the oil was poured, healing colors were created and pushed the holder of your tears toward the surface where he was exposed for who he was. His exposure to the light of My love through My golden tears transformed your tears into healing colors and cast him into the abyss. He has lost his power over you forever!"

"I say to you today that these tears of incarceration have been transformed into tears of deliverance and joy! I have spoken in the presence of the great cloud of witnesses and My heavenly host! And so, it shall be! This is the clarity of the vision in the land on the other side of the great divide...that your tears will usher in your destiny and your story will proclaim the power of My love to the masses."

"Oh! Great King! How can I ever thank You enough for the gift of Ruby Red and the keys and stones that You have given me? Oh! How I delight in Your mysteries! I know I shall be able to go on! I know I shall be able to face anything that tries to stop me from cradling my destiny in the land of promise! Oh! Great King! Your love and compassion, they fail not...great is Your faithfulness! I sing and shout with the psalmist of many days past..."

Those who sow in tears shall reap in joy. He who continually goes forth weeping, bearing seed for sowing, shall doubtless come again with rejoicing, bringing his sheaves with him. (Psalm 126:5-6)

"Come, Beloved. We must journey on. There is great deliverance as you embrace the healing colors of the released tears of incarceration. Prepare for your journey. Hold fast to all you have received from Me. Take hold of My hand. You shall cradle Chloe Renee not too many days from now. But first, you must receive from the Visions of Life and the Doors of Destiny…"

Fear not, for I have redeemed you. I have called you by your name. You are Mine. When You pass through the waters, I will be with you, and through the rivers, they shall not overflow you. When you walk through the fire, you shall not be burned, nor shall the flame scorch you. For I am the Lord you God, the Holy One of Israel, your Savior. (Isaiah 43:1-3a)

Warm, crimson blood seeping from His rough, carpenter hands reassured me of His faithfulness as we walked along in silence. The sweet-smelling aroma of an early spring morning filled my nostrils as I breathed in the same air He exhaled. Hand in hand, heart to heart, no words were necessary. I was safe. I was at peace. I was with the Deliverer who had promised me nothing but good should I trust Him through the rest of my journey. With excited anticipation and uncontained curiosity, I broke the silence…

"Whatever are the Visions of Life and the Doors of Destiny, Great King?"

"It is in the understanding of the Visions of Life that unlocks the doors to cradling Chloe Renee and your destiny." He said. He pulled a shepherd's rod from the middle of His chest and began writing in the thick dust that had settled on the bridge…

Get wisdom! Get understanding! Do not forget, nor turn away from the words of my mouth. Do not forsake her, and she will preserve you. Love her, and she will keep you. Wisdom is the principal thing. Therefore, get wisdom. And in all your getting, get understanding. Exalt her, and she will promote you. She will bring you honor when you embrace her. She will place on your head an ornament of grace, a crown of glory she will deliver to you. (Proverbs 4: 5-9)

"Whatever does this mystery mean, Great King?"

"Patience, My Beloved. Patience. You shall know soon enough!"

Directly in front of us a door slowly appeared through a thick cloud. I dared not look at the sight for fear I would be blinded. "Oh! Great King! What is this sight in front of me that I cannot look upon?"

"Beloved, this is the entrance to the Visions of Life which holds the Doors of Destiny. Come near! Fear not! Receive the salve of light so that you may see and the canister of hope that you may know the way." I shielded my eyes and followed the sound of His voice until I stood in front of Him. The same warm crimson blood that comforted me as we walked soothed my eyes as He placed His hands upon them. The same sweet-smelling aroma of a warm spring morning filled my nostrils as He gently whispered, "Receive the salve of light and the canister of hope."

"Oh! Great King! Warm tears mixed with the warm crimson blood dripped upon the canister as He placed it in my open hand.

"Receive the canister of hope," He said.

The canister was small but beautiful to behold. Its lid was covered with all the gems of my journey…emeralds, sapphires, lapis lazuli, and rubies. As I opened the lid, a bright light too beautiful for words captured the healing colors that surrounded me and danced to His voice. Immediately I was taken back to the glorious place of deliverance in the pregnancy center where the golden chest containing my destiny was opened and the cross of torture hung above me.

"Beloved," He said, "this canister of hope was in the golden chest all along, waiting for such a time as this to be opened. You had to travel this far in order for its contents to be able to fulfill their part in your journey. Herein lies the mystery of the Visions of Life and the Doors of Destiny."

"What shall I do with this canister of hope, Great King?"

"Place it in your bag woven with fine linen where the stones of your journey have rested. You will need the canister once we enter the Visions of Life. Come…let's take our leave and go."

As the Great King finished speaking, He placed the shepherd's rod back into His chest and took my hand again. I looked, and behold, the sight I saw was magnificent, glorious, spectacular…

Before us a golden door hung from the heavens with the archangels in charge of my journey standing on either side. They held giant golden trumpets to their mouths in preparation of announcing our arrival. The bridge we had been walking on was swallowed up by a golden street, which moved and expanded with the sound of our feet as if it were in concert responding to a master conductor. As I reached down to touch it, waves of the Great King's heartbeat met my hand. I was no longer walking over a dust-ridden bridge spanning a deadly deep, jagged gorge! I was walking with the Great King on streets of gold toward a door that hung suspended in air by the heavens themselves! Oh! How glorious! Oh! How wonderful! The King and I walking toward this great sight that only moments ago I could not turn my face toward. Wherever will I be going? Whatever is beyond that door?

The intensity of what was going on escalated the closer we got to the door. Hearing, seeing, smelling, touching, and feeling became otherworldly. The golden streets not only responded to our feet, but now they were responding to the heartbeat of the Great King. *Boom! Boom! Boom!* With every beat, the street erupted and subsided in perfect rhythm, causing a spectacular ripple as it met the glory of His countenance. The salve of light was doing its job. I could see the heartbeat of the Great King as we walked toward the golden door that hung suspended in the heavens. *Thump! Thump! Thump!* The heart of the Great King sped up in anticipation of escorting me into the Visions of Life where the Doors of Destiny awaited us.

"Oh! Great King! The streets are marching to the beat of Your heart! My feet are dancing with them! Oh! How glorious is it for me to dance to the beat of Your heart! How great is Your love toward me that I would experience this thing on the King's highway! The streets…oh…look! They are smiling! They are honored to have You walking their path! Great King! This is the most amazing thing…" I stopped and held my head down.

"Beloved, what is it? Why has your countenance turned so quickly?"

"Oh! Great King! I should like to know what my heartbeat feels like and be able to dance to it. Would it be too much to ask the Great King to speak to the streets of gold and ask that I could feel my heartbeat as I travel?"

He cupped my checks in His hands and said, "Beloved, My sweet Beloved. Do you not know? Do you not see? This journey is not yours alone. These streets are not Mine alone. There is only one heartbeat the streets of gold can respond to. It is the heartbeat of the mystery of Samaria and the golden tears that cause them to dance and smile! It is the oneness of sorrow that they rejoice and roll themselves out from the door of the Visions of Life for us to travel on! Yes, Beloved! When you feel the heartbeat of the golden streets under your feet, you are feeling the heartbeat of the oneness of our joined sorrow over the death of your precious Chloe Renee! Rejoice! Oh! Mother of Chloe Renee! Rejoice! Oh! Beloved of the Great King! The streets of gold celebrate the oneness of sorrow and our upcoming entrance into the Visions of Life!"

"Come…let us not delay…the door is eager to open for us!"

REST-REFLECT-REFRESH

There is a saying that goes something like this…I'm not where I want to be…but I thank God, I'm not where I used to be! This is very true as we embark on abortion recovery. No matter where we are in our journey, we need to celebrate that we are not where we were when we started!

IT IS TIME TO CELEBRATE!

This would be a great time to go back over the Scriptures that are written in dark, bold type in *Chloe's Cry* and use them to create a letter to the Great King and your child. As you meditate on the Scriptures, let the Spirit of God minister to you. Ask

Him to open your eyes to what He has already accomplished in you and also what He has in store for you as you continue to seek healing and wholeness from your abortion. Take your time with this Rest-Reflect-Refresh session. It can be a source of great strength and courage for you as we move on!

At this point in my recovery, I was ecstatic to find that the jagged, deep gorge of my heart was not as jagged and deep as it was when I set out on this journey. I was able to comfortably discuss Chloe Renee and my abortion experience with several trusted friends and ladies at the pregnancy center. I had come to grips with the fact that abortion was not a choice of my convenience, but the intentional ending of my daughter's life. I was even strong enough to admit that my abortion was the murder of an innocent child. I had come to recognize that as I faced the facts of what I had done and brought them to the light before myself, God, and a few trusted sojourners, I was well on my way to recovery. I had received everything the Great King had to offer and was anticipating great things ahead…As I looked into the jagged gorge that was dramatically changed from what it was, I realized…IT WAS TIME TO CELEBRATE!

CELEBRATE WHAT HE HAS DONE!
CELEBRATE WHAT HE IS DOING!
CELEBRATE WHAT HE IS GOING TO DO!
CELEBRATE, COME ON LET'S CELEBRATE!

Throughout my entire journey, I knew there was something much bigger than my healing in store as I said yes to the Great King on the dark side of the great divide. I had no idea that what you have in your hands now as *Chloe's Cry* was on the other side as I entered my land of promise. It was in walking through the Doors of Destiny that I received clarity of the Visions of Life and where *Chloe's Cry* fit in. Declare with me, "Look at what the Lord has done!"

I waited patiently for the Lord and He inclined to me
And heard my cry.
He also brought me up out of a horrible pit,
Out of the miry clay,
And set my feet upon a rock,
and established my steps.
He has put a new song in my mouth —
Praise to our God.
Many will see it and fear,
And will trust in the Lord.
(Psalm 40:1-3)

I invite you to join me as I walk through the Doors of Destiny…

Chapter 17

Visions of Life:
Doors of Destiny

Journal Entry March 3, 2017

*C*hloe is becoming more real and dear to me every minute of every day as I follow Jesus into this unchartered water. I cannot describe the peace I feel right now as I contemplate her existence. Being able to hold the tiny one at Palmetto Pregnancy Center two days ago was unbelievable reality of tenderness. I believe this tenderness stems from the tenderness of Christ in me — my hope of redemption, forgiveness, and healing. I believe Chloe Renee is with Him, safe and secure, waiting for me. His peace has swallowed up death, guilt, and shame. I stand in awe of His merciful tenderness toward me. When I look back upon the events since that Christmas dinner, I just have to be amazed to know these events were planned out all before the foundation of the world. What a mighty God I serve!*

Journal Entry March 4, 2017

Chloe Renee has become an expression of Your love to me. As I meditate on the events in my most recent days since

December 2016, I am in awe of Your infinite bigness, Your infinite wisdom, truth, understanding, and compassion—Your oneness with me—in the darkest of places deep within my soul where You have shined the light of Your mercy and grace. This is the foundation of my trust—faith in what You say and do is always for my good.

This gift of wholeness brought on by this gift of trust in You always wanting the best for me—this gift of faith in You as a good Father with the inherent spirit of compassion and caring which draws me under Your protective wings has brought me to the place of rest in knowing Chloe was alive, Chloe is alive in You, and Chloe was and still is a part of my life—no longer is her memory, entombed and buried under the piles of guilt and shame I allowed the enemy to pour upon my soul. She is alive and well in my heart, for she lives in You and You live in me! You are alive forever more. I rejoice in this freedom to acknowledge her. Amen.

* * *

"Oh! Great King! I am able to see more clearly the closer we get to the golden door! It looks like there is something hanging on it. Perhaps a parchment of some sort?"

"Yes, Beloved. Indeed, it is. The golden door is the gateway to the Visions of Life and the Doors of Destiny. Come, let us prepare for the sounding of the trumpets and the unveiling of the Daughters of Destiny."

His strong arms became as wings covering me as He sang with authority and power...

Lift up your heads, O you gates! And be lifted up, you everlasting doors! And the King of glory shall come in. Who is this King of glory? The Lord strong and mighty, The Lord mighty in battle. Lift up your heads, O you gates! Lift up, you everlasting doors! And the King of glory shall come in. (Psalm 24:7-9)

Lightning and thunder erupted as the trumpets of the archangels standing guard on each side of the golden door repeated the command of the Great King. *Lift up your heads, O you gates! And be lifted up, you everlasting doors!* The magnificent golden door jumped and swayed.

I would have been struck dead had it not been for the outstretched wings of the Great King protecting me. *Who is this King of glory?* The power of their sound shook the golden street on which the golden door rested, proclaiming the authority by which they were commissioned.

The Lord strong and mighty, The Lord mighty in battle!

"Come, Beloved. The trumpets have prepared the golden door for our arrival. I am the Lord, strong and mighty, The Lord mighty in battle. I speak to the heavenly golden door on your behalf in the midst of the greatest battle you will face on the other side of its hinges…"

Lift up your heads, O you gates! And be lifted up, you everlasting doors! Prepare yourselves for I, the King of glory, and My beloved shall pass through your gates…

As we neared the door, my heart rate escalated and my breathing became labored. High-energy anticipation was birthed through the mighty sounds of the heavenly trumpets and the response of the golden street beneath me. Everything seemed to respond with extraordinary exuberance to the command of the Great King. Who is this King that even the molecules of the universe would explode with passion at the sound of His voice?

"Beloved, all your questions will be answered one day. But for now, I instruct you to remove the ruby-red key from your golden chain and the ruby-red stone from your bag woven in fine linen. This stone and key has served you well and will permit your entrance into the Visions of Life through the golden door. Herein you shall be given the opportunity to reach for the stars while you walk though the most difficult portion of your journey over the great divide."

"Oh! Great King! Should I be ready for such an adventure? Surely I could not pass this way without Ruby Red and You by my side!"

"You say well, My Beloved. This journey has been hard, but you have gained strength by carrying Ruby Red and allowing her to activate all the other keys and stones given from My hand into yours. Read now what you could not see from afar...the parchment which hangs on the golden door for all who suffer at the dark hand of abortion..."

O you afflicted one, tossed with tempest, and not comforted,
Behold, I will lay your stones with colorful gems,
and lay your foundations with sapphires.
I will make your pinnacles of rubies, your gates of crystal,
and all your children shall be taught by the Lord,
and great shall be the peace of your children. (Isaiah 54:11-13)

"Oh! Great King! If it were not for receiving the keys and the stones from You, this parchment for the abortion afflicted would make no sense! But today I celebrate the gifts You have given me and I believe everything written on this parchment is for me! Oh! Great King! I am starting to understand many things I could not just days ago!"

Images began to appear as I read the words of Isaiah on the golden door. "What am I seeing here behind the words of the parchment? It is as though the gold in this door has become a mirror. There are men and women, of all ages, races, and creeds standing in the distance behind me on the dark side of the great divide."

I turned to look and saw a multitude chained to the ground with wide tape over their mouths. They stood in puddles of water with their heads hanging low. "Who are these, Great King? Why are they chained there weeping?"

"Beloved, many are called but few respond. You are one of millions that I have called to take this journey toward healing and wholeness from the dark hand of abortion. These are those who have not been able to embrace Ruby Red and trust Me with their brokenness. They stand in the distance holding on to fear, guilt, shame, and regret. Many of them have been there for decades. Not too long ago, you stood among them."

I wept for the captives of the dark dungeon chained to the ground.

"Oh! Great King! What a tragedy! How I wish I could help them!"

"One day you will, My Beloved. One day you will…"

Awestruck, I watched as the golden door became as a scroll and rolled itself up into the heavens, exposing thousands upon thousands of wooden doors lined up as far as I could see from the east to the west.

"Whatever are these doors, O Great King?"

"To every soul chained and tortured by the dark hand of abortion a door belongs; to every life a destiny awaits. All are called to the door. Some come. Some do not. This day you have entered through the golden door by the parchment of My cross of torture to seek out and to pass through your door."

"But, Great King. I do not understand. Some of these doors have parchments hanging on them and some do not. Whatever does this mean?"

"Beloved, not all who are called come through the golden door. Those who do not embrace Ruby Red never make it this far. They stay in the crowd you saw in the mirror. The doors that are void of parchments wait for their owners to embrace Ruby Red and allow Me to unchain them from the dark hand of abortion. But you, Beloved, have answered the call to freedom and are very near to crossing over the great divide."

"Oh! Great King! How great are Your mercies toward those of us who have suffered at the hands of such a decision! How kind You are to invite us into the Visions of Life and through the Door of Destiny to experience the healing balm of the permission to grieve! How great is Your love for us that You would pay the ultimate price for our freedom and hand us the key that would unlock the doors to our destiny!"

"I am ready now, Great King, to walk through my door. I know Chloe Renee is on the other side. I know I will see her and have to let her go. This has been made clear in the journey set before me. She is part of me, and I of her. I understand I must celebrate her life before I can lay her to rest and want to bond with her before doing so. I trust You to allow only what You know will benefit me as I *intentionally* walk through this door not knowing what I will experience on the other side. I *choose* to embrace Ruby Red and trust You to hold me up no matter what. But oh, Great King? How will I ever find the door that belongs to me?"

"Beloved, this is the sign of your door of destiny. Follow the golden street until it stops."

"What then shall I do?"

"I say the same to you as I said to My servant Joshua…"

"Pass through the camp and command the people saying, 'Prepare provisions for yourselves for in three days you will cross over this Jordan, to go in to possess the land which the Lord your God is giving you to possess.' " *(Joshua 1:11)*

"Beloved, you must be prepared to present your Rite of Passage, for fear, guilt, shame, and regret have been strategically stationed around your door to temp you to retreat. There is a nail which is covered in the blood of the cross of torture on the door. Hang your Rite of Passage on it. The evil spirits that would try to stop you will be consumed by the flowing blood. Then, locate the lock. It will be directly under your name where the blood from the cross of torture flows. Use your ruby-red key to unlock the door."

"I shall do as You say, Great King!"

"My wings shall cover you as you journey toward the door. My love song of protection shall guard your heart and mind as you walk the streets of gold toward your destiny. Listen only to My promise and you will arrive without incident to hang your Rite of Passage and unlock the door to your destiny…

Thus says the Lord, who makes a way in the sea and a path through the mighty waters...Do not remember the former things, nor consider the things of old. Behold, I will do a new thing. Now it shall spring forth; shall you not know it? I will even make a road in the wilderness and rivers in the desert. The beast of the field will honor Me. The jackals and the ostriches. Because I give waters in the wilderness and rivers in the desert, to give drink to My people, My chosen. This people I have formed for Myself, they shall declare My praise. (Isaiah 43:16, 18-21)

"Oh! Yes! Great and Mighty King! I desire to walk the path You have prepared for me through this rough sea and mighty ocean that lies before me! I thirst and long to drink of the water You provide in this wilderness! I choose to know the new thing and the new way You are preparing for me! I am so grateful the beasts of my journey have been made to bow to Your power and honor You by releasing me from their judgment! I shout with joy that You have formed Chloe Renee and me for Yourself and that we will declare Your praises to anyone who will listen! I rejoice in the knowledge and wisdom I have gained on this journey, for the precious keys and stones I have been given, and the path You have set before me!"

"I walk in confidence on this living, breathing, pulsating street of gold that responds to Your heartbeat concerning Chloe Renee and me. I dance on this street of gold knowing You are for me and not against me. I dance to the sound of Your love and compassion that has kept me safe this far. I dance with joy knowing that whatever I face on the other side of this door will ultimately be for my good and the glory of Your sacrifice which has brought forth my freedom! I sing with all that is within me because Chloe Renee and I have been chosen by You for such a time as this and with such a story to tell! Oh! I delight in dancing and singing with David…"

Because You have been my help, therefore in the shadow of Your wings I will rejoice. My soul follows close behind You. Your right hand upholds me. (Psalm 63:7-8)

"Yes, and amen, Great King! I see the end of the golden street up ahead. Again, my vision is clouded. For what reason is that?"

"Beloved, it is so that you may see through the tears of your heart. That they may comfort you as you face the door that separates you from the path that ends the great divide and ushers in the land of promise. Tears of joy and tears of sorrow are in abundance in the wells of your experience, waiting for their release on the other side of the door."

I take a deep breath and say, "I am ready, Great King, as I feel the protection of Your wings all around me. I have my parchment ready and my ruby-red key is in my right hand. What are the sounds I hear from the other side of the door, Great King? My heart will surely burst if I must wait another minute!"

"Beloved, destiny's door has waited thirty-eight years for this moment. The land behind it and its occupants are making last minute preparations for the unveiling of the Daughters of Destiny. All must be perfect and in place. It is the chance of a lifetime for many daughters and those who have crossed this way before long to celebrate and grieve with you. These are your fellow sojourners. You will be among those with the understanding and wisdom of the journey over the great divide. This is a company that only those who have suffered at the dark hand of abortion can walk among. We shall enter when the seas hear My voice and the day becomes night."

"I do not understand, Great King."

"You shall understand, My Beloved, in due time as everything unfolds before you."

"There is a song in my heart, Great King, that I wish to sing to Chloe Renee before I meet her. Will she be able to hear me?"

"I know this song quite well, My Beloved. She is in your heart, so I suspect so."

"I would like to sing it after I hang my Rite of Passage on the door but before I use Ruby Red to unlock it."

"Yes, My Beloved. It shall be as you wish. The archangels, the great cloud of witnesses, and the heavens wait patiently to hear you sing for the first time to your daughter…"

An ocean of emotion washed over me as I approached the door. My daughter, whom I had chosen to end her life, was somewhere on the other side of this door and I was about to see her, talk to her, sing over her, and touch her. The only way I could continue without completely falling apart was to speak to her through the song that was in my heart. Warm tears freely flowed, dripping on the golden street, causing it to weep with me. Although the Great King stepped back to give me space, His wings of protection continued to cover me. I placed the hand that held the ruby-red key upon my heart and softly sang into the keyhole…

Chloe Renee? This is your Mommy…

I hope that you can hear me, I have something I need to say.
It's part of the Great King's journey,
that's brought me here today…

I gazed upon a lifeless form, and held it in my hand.
An eight-week-old fetus it was called, a model with no name.
My tears fell on its precious face,
as my hands caressed its head.
Oh, Chloe Renee, you came to life, no longer were you dead.
Your tiny eyes, they opened, they were squinting in the light.
Your arms and legs, they moved around,
replaying my darkest night.

My heart cried out in anguish,
My soul in great despair.
Oh, Chloe Renee, you came to life
The loss, I could not bear…

This tiny model, this lifeless form,
Spoke deep within my heart,
"Mommy, I forgive you,
There's a place we'll never part.

"It's where the King and I reside
You know His Word is true.
We live and breathe in this beautiful place,
Just waiting here for you.

"So, Mommy leave the lifeless form
And very soon you'll see.
When you follow the Great King's lead,
He'll bring you straight to me!"

I listened to you in my heart
And gently laid it down
With tear-filled eyes I walked away
And followed the path unknown.

So, now I stand at the wooden door,
That shuts me off from you.
Will you forgive me, my little one,
And help me to walk through?

My heart, it says you hear me. My heart, it says you're free.
My heart, it says you're patiently waiting there for me...
With forgiveness in your hand, and a song within your soul,
You're calling my heart to conquer fear and open up the door...

By Lynn Potter

With every word, every line, every thought sung through the keyhole, the bonding with Chloe Renee intensified into the deepest place of my being, the place where she was prematurely torn from my body. It was a miracle among the greatest ever recorded. For me, it was the miracle of all miracles. Here, standing below my Rite of Passage with the living, breathing, pulsating, bright red blood of the cross of torture flowing, I could truly say that fear, guilt, shame, and regret had no place. My soul began bonding with my daughter and what I have known all along in my head was coming to fruition in my heart. Chloe Renee was, is, and always will be part of me, and I of her. I could *feel* her on the other side of the door longing to see me, to touch me, to say something to me. I had no idea what the Great King was talking about when He told me the land and its occupants were preparing for my arrival, but the time was getting very near for me to find out.

Oh! Chloe Renee! Very shortly I will be given the chance to touch you, to celebrate you, to honor your life and death with dignity and respect. There is so much I want to say to you. I am not sure how much time we are going to have, but I believe the Great King will give us just what we need. His faithfulness to me throughout this entire journey is more than I could ever have known to ask or think. You know Him much better than I, for you have been in His manifested presence for thirty-eight years. I suspect you could tell me a thing or two! Oh! Chloe Renee! I shall see you momentarily in the Visions of Life as I pass through this, my Door of Destiny!

Surely, my precious Chloe Renee, miracles are birthed when the blood of the cross washes over a tender love song sung by a grieving mother to a daughter she has never known.

Warm spring rains falling from the heavens in response to such tenderness almost melted the wooden door that separated me from my daughter, washing me, cleansing me, preparing me. The Great King moved toward me in reverential silence and placed His hand on my shoulder. I lifted my left hand and placed it upon His. As I looked into His eyes, we both nodded *yes*. Without a word, together we guided Ruby Red into the keyhole that had just transmitted my love song into the atmosphere where Chloe Renee waited for me…

REST-REFLECT-REFRESH

Whew! This is an incredible journey…is it not? I am on the brink of entering the Visions of Life, having no idea what is on the other side of this door of destiny, and you, my treasured friend, have being given a front-row seat! You will be reading this experience right off the press, as they say. It will be fresh. It will be raw. It will be present and happening as my fingers hit the keyboard on my computer. What do you think of that? It is the most exhilarating, yet frightening thing I have ever done in my life! I will be not only sharing bits and pieces of my journal with you, but actually writing it as the Great King unfolds this part of my journey.

I believe standing at this door of destiny is the most critical part of our journey toward healing and wholeness from the aftermath of our abortion experience. It is here we are faced with the reality of never being able to live life on this earth with our children. It is here we learn they are in fact, alive and well with destiny and purpose in a realm of existence we have only been able to read about in the Scriptures.

It is here we are given the opportunity to receive our children from the Great King in order to lay them to rest with dignity and honor and return them back to Him. It is here that the childlike trust we have learned to rely on will be tested to its limit as the evil spirits of fear, guilt, shame, and regret would try their best to resurrect themselves every step of the way.

I had come too far in my journey for any of their nonsense! They were no match for this mother who desired more than anything to pass through her door of destiny and receive her daughter from the Great King! This mother who had never held an infant, held a full-term, eight-pound little girl born sleeping only a few weeks after her thirty-eight-year silence was broken! This mother, who received the King's keys and stones and put them into practice, was not about to turn around and head back to the dark side of the great divide! Anxiety caused by the anticipation of grief and sorrow was not even enough to make me turn back!

My daughter deserved more! My daughter deserved the love of a mother that would pass through any storm to bring honor and dignity to her life and death! I was determined to be the mother that I was unable and unwilling to be thirty-eight years ago! I would walk through this door with my head held high and my heart opened to any emotion that any mother would experience at the death of her child! I WANTED to experience the grieving process! I NEEDED to experience the grieving process! I would not choose the easy way out this time! I would NOT! The Great King promised me that in the receiving and releasing I would cradle my land of promise! I trusted His words. He had not let me down...ever!

Understanding and wisdom were held in the keys and stones that the Great King had given me. They were my companions all along, but kept silent until I stood at the door of destiny and sang to my daughter through its keyhole. Understanding and wisdom are in the heart of the Great King and will follow us through the wooden door. Great is His faithfulness. I have no doubt that what I see and experience on the other side will bring me peace and hope.

As I prepare for what is behind my door of destiny, I would like to invite you to do the same...

Would you allow the Great King to lead you to your door of destiny? Would you trust His words when He says, "In the receiving and releasing of your child, you will cradle your land of promise"? Are you willing to risk what you may experience on the other side of your door of destiny in order to honor and bring dignity to your son or daughter's life and death?

Take some time to meditate on these few questions and journal your thoughts. Perhaps it would be a good idea to meditate on the Scriptures that the Great King gave me as I wrote this chapter. While you are meditating on the Scriptures, journal your thoughts and reactions to the words as you contemplate their significance to your own abortion experience...

Lift up your heads, O you gates! And be lifted up, you everlasting doors! And the King of glory shall come in. Who is this King of glory? The Lord strong and mighty. The Lord mighty in battle. Lift up your heads, O you gates! Lift up, you everlasting doors! And the King of glory shall come in. (Psalm 24:7-9)

O you afflicted one, tossed with tempest, and not comforted. Behold I will lay your stones with colorful gems, and lay your foundations with sapphires. I will make your pinnacles of rubies, your gates of crystal, and all your children shall be taught by the Lord, and great shall be the peace of your children. (Isaiah 54:11-13)

"Pass through the camp and command the people saying, 'Prepare provisions for yourselves, for in three days you will cross over this Jordan, to go in to possess the land which the Lord your God is giving you to possess.' " (Joshua 1:11)

Thus says the Lord, who makes a way in the sea and a path through the mighty waters. Do not remember the former things, nor consider the things of old. Behold, I will do a new thing. Now it shall spring forth; shall you not know it? I will even make a road in the wilderness and rivers in the desert. The beast of the field will honor Me. The jackals and the ostriches. Because I give waters in the wilderness and rivers in the desert, to give drink to My people, My Chosen. This people I have formed for Myself, they shall declare My praise. (Isaiah 43:16, 18-21)

Because You have been my help, therefore in the shadow of Your wings I will rejoice. My soul follows close behind You. Your right hand upholds me. (Psalm 63:7-8)

Would you consider finding a song to sing to your son or daughter as I did? Would you consider seeking out and standing before your door of destiny, holding on to Ruby Red and the Great King's promise to walk through the door with you? Would you consider reaching for the Great King's hand and together guiding Ruby Red into the keyhole of your door? Would you?

Chapter 18

Eve of the Dawn

"**B**eloved, what do you see?"

"Oh! Great King! I cannot see a thing! It is as dark as a moonless, starless night in the middle of the desert! Truly I cannot even see my hand in front of my face!"

"Did I not tell you we would enter the Visions of Life when the seas heard My voice and the day turned into night?"

"Oh! Great King! We have passed through the wooden door? Oh! Tell me it is so!"

"Yes, My child, indeed we have. Here, take My hand and come with Me."

"Great King. What is this beneath my feet? It is not the golden street that I have become accustomed to...it...feels... like sand? Where is this Vision of Life?"

"It is in your heart, My child, in your heart."

"Oh! Great King! You have brought me to my favorite place on the planet! I just know You have! I hear the waves crashing on the shore! I smell the ocean breeze and feel it brushing against my cheek. Oh! Great King! The stars are coming out and the moon is rising! Your loving-kindness is beyond measure that this would be on the other side of destiny's door! May I walk along the shore barefoot in the sand? May I sing again to Chloe Renee?"

I dug my fingers and toes into the sand, imagining what the Great King might have in store for me. He said the Visions of Life are in my heart! Does that mean what I think it does? Where is Chloe Renee? I know for certain she is in the Visions of Life, for she is in my heart. She must not be far away! My heart longs to lay eyes upon her! My arms long to hold her tight! My ears long to hear her voice and her laughter. My legs want to run to her and scoop her up into the air just as the Great King did the day He twirled me around like a parasol! Oh! How every part of my being wants to embrace my daughter, the daughter that I rejected so long ago!"

"Patience, My child, patience!"

"Whatever do You mean, Great King?"

"I know the Visions of Life that you hold in your heart and your desire to see them with your eyes and experience them with your being. Although the visions are good and they are true, they are incomplete. Do not settle for less than your door of destiny has to offer. Impatience will cause you to run ahead of the plan and steer you off course. You have endured much to gain entrance. Sit with Me until the night turns into day and you will understand with great wisdom what I am saying. As dusk turns into dawn, the day of the unveiling of the Daughters of Destiny and the celebration of the occupants of the land will rise with the sun over the horizon. The mystery of the Daughters of Destiny is hidden in the horizon in the darkness of night."

"Great King! What good could possibly come from the night?"

I will give you the treasures of darkness and hidden riches of secret places that you may know that I, the Lord who call you by your name am the God of Israel. (Isaiah 45:3)

"It is in the treasures of darkness and the hidden riches of secret places that great miracles shall emerge."

"What is that snapping noise, Great King?"

"We must have a fire for warmth and light as we wait upon the horizon. The night air is cool and I know your heart's desire to sit on the shore beside a campfire is strong."

"Oh! But, tomorrow cannot arrive soon enough! I know…I just know I will see Chloe Renee after the rising of the sun! Tell me it is so, Great King!"

"Rest, My child. For you shall need strength for the unveiling of the treasures of darkness and the riches of secret places at the morning's light."

"Yes, Great King, I shall rest, for You know all things and show me all things in due time. I rest in knowing that Chloe Renee is in my heart and will be presented to me at the KAIROS time when I am ready. You have given me a campfire on the shore…surely You will not withhold Chloe Renee from me!"

"Surely not, My child. Surely not."

"Great King?"

"Yes? My child?"

"I am no longer the Beloved, but Your child?"

"You are always and forever My Beloved. It is for the mystery of the horizon and the Visions of Life in the morning light that you are My child. You shall see when the daystar rises and the mystery unfolds that it is the little child who leads you. Rest in this understanding and wisdom of the mystery. You are both My Beloved and My child. It is in the child's heart that miracles and visions of life live. It is in the child's heart that the door of destiny is always open."

"Tell me, Great King. It is from my child's heart that You have pulled out the ocean, the beach, the campfire, and the sunrise to be the place on the other side of the door of destiny? Is it not?"

"It is, My child. Indeed, it is. The desires of your heart pull you toward your destiny and are always in the center of child-like trust. Ruby Red has brought you here, and here is the foundation and stage for of all that will transpire tomorrow in the Visions of Life."

"My soul soars as the eagle with wings of thanksgiving and gratefulness. I shall sing a song for the Great King now or I shall burst. I hope it pleases You."

"I am certain it will warm My heart as does this fire from your destiny's door." Crackling sounds from burning wood competed with the crashing of the waves as He stirred the fire. I faced the rising moon and stars and began to sing…

*My soul magnifies the Lord, and my spirit
has rejoiced in God my Savior.
For He has regarded the lowly state of His maidservant;
For behold, henceforth all generations will call me blessed.
For He who is mighty has done great things for me,
and holy is His name.
And His mercy is on those who fear Him
from generation to generation.
(Luke 1:46-50)*

Light from the moon and stars danced upon the waves as I sang. The Great King grabbed my hand and said, "My beautiful child, you have warmed My heart with your song of adoration. On this, the eve of the day of the unveiling of the Daughters of Destiny, may you sleep peacefully until the horizon's light wakens and the ceremonies begin." He took His cloak and wrapped it around my shoulders. "I will keep watch over you until the morning's light."

I will lift up my eyes to the hills — from whence come my help? My help comes from the Lord, Who made heaven and earth. He will not allow your foot to be moved. He who keeps you will not slumber. Behold, He who keeps Israel shall neither slumber nor sleep. (Psalm 121:1-4)

The Lord is your keeper; The Lord is your shade at your right hand. The sun shall not strike you by day, nor the moon by night. The Lord shall preserve you from all evil. He shall preserve your soul. The Lord shall preserve your going out and your coming in from this time forth, and even forevermore. (Psalm 121:5-8)

Waves of peace washed over me the minute the Great King's cloak touched my skin. I was immersed in love and mercy way beyond anything I could have ever imagined as the sounds and smells of this time and place beaconed me to follow them into the land of peaceful dreams.

I reached for my bag woven in fine linen and brought forth the beautiful lapis lazuli stone the Great King gave me at the beginning of my journey. "Is this not the answer to the mystery of the waves of peace that wash over me now? The beauty of deep calling to deep and Your promise to release my destiny with Your Spirit and Your vision?"

"Yes! My child, yes! You have remembered well the mystery of the deep, deep blue lapis lazuli. Peaceful sleep, My child, peaceful sleep. For tomorrow the Visions of Life will reveal the promises contained in the beautiful stone."

Deep calls unto deep at the noise of Your waterfalls. All Your waves and billows have gone over me. The Lord will command His lovingkindness in the daytime, and in the night His song shall be with me. (Psalm 42:7-8)

His Night Song

Walk with me, O Lover of my soul.
Through the sands of time past, present, and future.
Create in me a longing for Your presence above all.
Above the cry of those in need.
Above the noise of the world.
Let me rest on the beach of Your love,
With the warm breeze of Your Word brushing my cheek,
The roar of Your demand causing my enemies to flee,
The rising of Your beauty as the sun peeks over the horizon,
Take my hand and walk with me, sit with me,
Let us make a sandcastle together.

By Lynn Potter, March 9, 2017

Journal Entry Part A March 7, 2017

Your ways, oh Lord, are beyond my human understanding—yet You invite me to follow You and listen to You as I journey along life's path. I have no understanding how this all works except to trust like a child that before You formed me in my mother's womb You KNEW me…

Before I formed you in the womb, I knew you. (Jeremiah 1:5)

It is this oneness I ponder. Just what is it? I cannot fathom this intimate being part of You in this oneness. No wonder my spirit/soul longs for something/Someone greater than this place of existence has to offer. No wonder abortion tears apart the deep, deep place of a woman's existence. If You knew me in this oneness before You formed me in my mother's womb, yes and amen, You knew Chloe Renee before You formed her in my womb! Chloe Renee, before the Lord formed you in my womb, He knew you. You came from Him and went back to Him…You are safe…you are whole…I rest in this…

My thoughts faded into the relaxing sounds of the crackling fire and faithful waves of the midnight tide. The moon had risen to its height of the night, casting beautiful rays on which my peaceful dreams would ride. It was in this moment of serenity that the oneness with my Creator and my daughter was restored, and the Great King whispered…

"Sleep well, My child, for the desires of your heart have been granted and it shall be that…"

A cord of three strands is not quickly broken. (Ecclesiastes 4:12, NIV)

REST-REFLECT-REFRESH

If you were to be asked where your *favorite place on the planet* is, what would your answer be, and why? Take a minute to think about this and journal your thoughts. It could very well be the place where the Lord would like to create your own *EVE OF THE DAWN* in order to prepare you for the unveiling of your Visions of Life!

We have come a long way, you and I. I trust by now we have become friends who have bonded through sharing the transparency of *Chloe's Cry*. We have entered the spiritual battle that surrounds anyone wishing to seek healing and wholeness from abortion, and have come out victorious by embracing everything the Great King has offered. We have unlocked the doors to our destinies through childlike trust, and have entered an atmosphere that only the Great King could have created. We now stand together on this, my *EVE OF THE DAWN*, anticipating what the Visions of Life will unveil as the sun peeks over the horizon announcing the start of a new day...

Do not remember the former things, nor consider the things of old. Behold, I will do a new thing. Now it shall spring forth. Shall you not know it? I will even make a road in the wilderness and rivers in the desert. (Isaiah 43:18-19)

As I contemplate what will come with the rising of the sun, the Great King instructs me with the wisdom of the treasures of darkness and the hidden riches of secret places. He has opened my eyes to the reality of what happened to the three-strand cord the day Chloe Renee died at the hands of an abortionist through my darkness-driven choice.

I would like to share with you what I wrote in my journal on March 7, 2017 and invite you to meditate on the words that are written. They are raw and uninviting, but powerfully freeing as the Great King promises us restoration of our ripped apart three-strand cords...

Repent, therefore and be converted, that your sins may be blotted out, so that times of refreshing may come from the presence of the Lord, and that He may send Jesus Christ, who was preached to you before, whom heaven must receive until the times of restoration of all things. (Acts 3:19-21a)

Journal Entry March 7, 2017 Part B

The interruption of this generational oneness is what I believe causes the deep emotional distress in every post-abortive woman. Not only was the oneness, the nurturing makeup of a mother's soul torn apart, but the oneness with God Himself, as He gave part of Himself to fill her womb—rejection of her own Creator results. Thus, the necessity for disassociation, pro-choice activism, and denial. Somehow, through these three self-preservation actions, we are duped into believing that this oneness with our Creator had never existed...

1 - Denial...It never happened.
2 – Disassociation...It happened, but I can separate myself from the event, living as though it has happened to someone else.
3 - Pro-choice activism...Complete separation from oneness with our Creator as a personal choice, inflicting generational curses of denial and disassociation on millions of men and women. We not only become rejecters of the life growing inside of our womb, but we become rejecters of the Giver of life Himself.

This is the deep two-sided dark wound that only Jesus' sacrifice can heal...

The Tender Shepherd's heart inside the Great King responds to the darkness of my soul on the day I penned those words...

"Come now, and let us reason together," says the Lord. "Though your sins are like scarlet, they shall be as white as snow; though they are red like crimson, they shall be as wool. If you are willing and obedient, you shall eat the good of the land." (Isaiah 1:18-19)

The Spirit of the Lord God is upon Me, because the Lord has anointed Me to preach good tidings to the poor; He has sent me to heal the brokenhearted, to proclaim liberty to the captives, and the opening of the prison to those who are bound; to proclaim the acceptable year of the Lord, and the day of vengeance of our God; to comfort all who mourn, to console those who mourn in Zion, to give them beauty for ashes, the oil of joy for mourning, the garment of praise for the spirit of heaviness; that they may be called trees of righteousness, the planting of the Lord, that He may be glorified. (Isaiah 61:1-3)

Journal Entry March 9, 2017

In response to the revelation of the two-sided rejection wound, He brought me out by a mighty hand and by an outstretched arm. Out of the land of denial, disassociation, and demonic oppression. My Redeemer lives, He lives to take away my shame... A little child shall lead them. His mighty hand, His outstretched arm...

When I find my completeness in Him, I can help other people without using them to meet my own needs. From Jesus Calling March 9, 2017.[2] Remember that you were a slave in the land of Egypt and the Lord your God brought you out from there by a mighty hand and by and outstretched arm. (Deuteronomy 5:15)

Behold, the Lord's hand is not shortened that it cannot save. Nor His ear too heavy that it cannot hear. (Isaiah 59:1)

Are you in your safe place? Have you responded to the invitation to enter your own *EVE OF THE DAWN*? Are you willing to risk the unknown as the daystar rises over your own horizon in order to receive the healing your ripped apart three-strand cord seeks?

The Great King desires more than anything that you would receive your son or daughter from Him so that you can lay them to rest and begin your grieving process. Take as much time as you need at this station of our journey.

---

[2] Sarah Young, *Jesus Calling* (Brentwood, TN: Integrity Publishers, 2004), 72.

You may want to get creative in your approach to this, your *EVE OF THE DAWN*. I call it preparing the atmosphere. My husband and I just came back from several days at Myrtle Beach, SC, and during the time we were there, I spent many quiet hours sitting on the beach contemplating this portion of *Chloe's Cry*.

I received several piecemeal pictures of what I would be writing during the "Eve of the Dawn" and "The Visions of Life," and jotted down some notes. Other than that, whatever comes alive from this point on, is a mystery to me. I am excited and anticipating great things for us ahead!

Would you stand in agreement with me that we will receive more than we could ever ask or think during the remaining portions of our journey through *Chloe's Cry*?

Now to Him who is able to do exceedingly abundantly above all that we ask or think, according to the power that works in us, to Him be glory in the church by Christ Jesus to all generations, forever and ever. Amen. (Ephesians 3:20-21)

Chapter 19

New Day Rising

Somewhere between a deep, deep sleep and a drowsy awakening, a moist, warm tongue swept across my cheek, over my eyes, and across my forehead. I turned toward this uninvited interruption of my blissful slumber, intending to halt any further invasion, only to receive a full-fledged canine welcome. With paws pulling at the Great King's cloak that covered me, wagging tail and all, this beautiful creature was starving for attention, and apparently, I was the one chosen to respond. Face-to-face with the friendliest female canine on the planet, there was only one course of action to take. Sit up and take notice or be slobbered on indefinitely and possibly miss the most important sunrise of my life!

A muffled chuckle came from the other side of the campfire that continued to burn under the brilliantly moonlit sky. The Great King threw another log on the fire and walked over toward us. "Enjoy your newfound friend, My child. For at the rising of the daystar she shall be hidden until the time of the memorial where she will seal its completion."

"Whatever are You talking about, Great King? Your mysteries continue to baffle me!"

"It will be in the laying to rest where the canine will seal its completion. It shall be several days from now when your receiving and releasing is complete. Until the daystar rises, let us enjoy her, for she has been sent from the Owner of the skies with joy and healing to share."

He reached for a piece of kindling wood and threw it over her head. She flew past me and lunged for it as it landed on the beach several yards away. Spinning like a top out of control, with sand flying all around, she stopped abruptly and pounced on top of it. We laughed and laughed and she lifted her head as if to say, *"What's so funny, y'all?"* Seemingly unimpressed with our response to her show of canine aerobics, she lowered her head and promptly began chomping on the stick, which made us laugh all the more!

What a delight to squish my feet in the cool sand and enjoy laughter as one set free from the tyranny of the king of darkness! What a treat to share the simple joy of watching one of God's creatures having fun on the shores of hope. What a perfect place to prepare for the rising of a new day! Surely freedom calls out from the carefree canine to this one, who just days ago, held Ruby Red tight and dared to face fear head-on and follow the Great King over the great divide.

"Great King! Look at her! She has more energy than the sea itself! She is simply delightful!"

Barking at the edge of the sea and spinning around with glee, my newfound friend demanded an audience that would engage in some more canine play. The Great King launched another stick high into the sky, which she skillfully caught between her teeth. I jumped for joy, clapping my hands in acknowledgement of her outstanding accomplishment. She ran to me in grateful response to my admiration and challenged me to follow her down the beach. I grabbed her beautiful face and said, "Most precious little friend, where are you taking me?"

Without missing a beat, she turned and proudly ran toward the north with her catch firmly secure in her mouth. The challenge was too much for me to ignore as I was growing very fond of this fun-filled fuzzy little friend, and my inner child screamed with joy at the chance to play with her. She ran and ran, never losing her prized possession, then stopped abruptly and began sniffing around. I laughed at the sight. She spun around several times, pounced on top of the stick, and began to dig. I turned to see the Great King siting by the fire with another stick in His hand, smiling ear to ear and laughing with joy.

"What fun! What fun! Oh! Great King! She is the life of our tailgate party on the beach under the brilliantly moonlit sky! Wherever did she come from?"

"She is in the heart of the Daughters of Destiny and guides those with broken hearts to the Keeper of the stars. She is laughter in the darkness, hope to the hopeless, and strength to the weary. She is a gift from the Father of the Great King to the Daughters of Destiny. Drink of her unconditional love and loyalty, for she was born in the heart of the Father and carries His DNA. As He has sent Me, so He has sent her. He shall hand you the gift of the Vision of Life at the ceremony of the Daughters of Destiny after the rising of the sun. This precious canine of laughter and joy has been given for the expansion of your heart."

"I am certain I cannot understand his, Great King, unless You reveal its meaning!"

"Your heart must expand, My child, to contain all that will fill it during the ceremony of the Daughters of Destiny. Come… it is soon time for the daystar to appear. We must be ready."

With the sound of my furry friend digging in the sand behind me, I slowly walked back toward the fire, leaving her behind. My heart was heavy at the possibility of yet another loss. I reached into my bag woven in fine linen and retrieved Ruby Red. As I held her close to my heart, the familiar feel of a warm, moist tongue made my heart skip. My precious little friend had left her prized possession and had come to escort me back to the place where I would watch the daystar rise.

Her unconditional love and loyalty flooded my soul. At that moment I realized she was a very special gift sent to me to learn from. She looked at me, then toward the campfire. I knelt at her side and nuzzled my face into hers, and we shook our heads together. "I will forever remember this smell," I said. "It is the smell of love, loyalty, and hope. I will forever remember what it felt like to have your warm, moist tongue against my skin when

I thought I had lost you forever. You just have no idea, my little friend!" I stood with head held high and tears flowing down my cheeks as we trotted back to the campfire where the Great King kept watch.

"Surely my little friend, because of you, I have received the expanded heart required to finish my journey over this great divide. Thank you for showing me what it is to receive, carry, bury, and walk away in order to journey with another. Thank you for the unconditional love and loyalty that would cause you to leave your most precious prize in order to escort me back to my place of receiving. Thank you, my precious little friend, for showing me that there is purpose and destiny in the receiving and releasing…"

To everything there is a season, a time for every purpose under heaven. A time to be born. A time to die. A time to plant, and a time to pluck what is planted. A time to kill, and a time to heal. (Ecclesiastes 3:1-3a)

"It is time to heal, My child."
My heart melted at the thought.
"We must prepare for the rising of the sun and the celebration of the Daughters of Destiny. Your heart has been expanded by the gift of unconditional love, loyalty, and understanding that there is purpose and destiny in receiving and releasing. Now we must seal the miraculous work with the body and blood of the cross of torture. Sit, My child. Let us partake together."

I sat on the blanket He had prepared by the warmth of the fire. "My child," He said, "we shall share the elements of the cross of torture as the daystar rises over the horizon. Prepare your heart to embrace the miraculous healing power that will enable you to receive and release Chloe Renee…

And He took bread, gave thanks and broke it, and gave it to them, saying, "This is My body which is given for you; do this in remembrance of Me." (Luke 22:19)

I heard whips, screams, and the cries from Mary, His mother. I heard shouting, cursing, and accusing from the frenzied crowd. I felt the anguish, loneliness, the agony of soul as I reached out my hand to receive the bread.

"This, My child, is what I endured so that you no longer need to suffer. Take, eat with Me. Receive all that My body has bought for you…"

I began to shake as the bread touched my lips and I gazed upon the King, the Lord of hosts…

So, I said, "Woe is me, for I am undone! Because I am a man of unclean lips and I dwell in the midst of a people of unclean lips. For my eyes have seen the King, the Lord of hosts. (Isaiah 6:5)

He wrapped His arms around me and touched my lips. "You are cleansed by My blood…"

Then He took the cup, and gave thanks, and gave it to them, saying, "Drink from it, all of you. For this is My blood of the new covenant, which is shed for many for the remission of sins." (Matthew 26:27-28)

He knelt in front of me and handed me the crystal goblet filled with the fruit of the vine which came from the royal table and said, "My child, My child. Take, drink. For the heavens will open shortly and our Father will present the daughter of your tears to you."

As I opened my mouth to receive the representation of His life-giving blood, the night sky began to surrender to the dawning of a new day…

REST-REFLECT-REFRESH

The King of the universe, The Great I AM, Jesus of Nazareth, through His Holy Spirit took me to a place where He knew He could get my attention and created an atmosphere where I would be open to receiving an expanded revelation of what He was about to do.

All my life I have been drawn to the beach and feel closer to my Creator there than anywhere else I have ever been. My husband and I have had several dogs, and in times of great distress, they have been an invaluable source of comfort to me. It should come as no surprise then, that much of the content of *Chloe's Cry* has had reference to the ocean, and most recently, the introduction of a fun-filled fuzzy little friend.

Because we are fearfully and wonderfully made, uniquely by the power of the most creative Being in existence, our stories should have their own unique details, birthed out of our individual personalities, preferences, and desires. As we move into the final steps of our journey over the great divide, I invite you to allow the King of the universe to surround you with His perfect healing atmosphere, uniquely created for you.

Since the day I held sleeping Candyce Skye in the presence of her grieving family, the Great King has been preparing me for these last final steps. During that most holy moment in time, He told me the key to the mystery of the great divide is in the receiving and releasing. He continued reinforcing that principle throughout my entire journey.

In preparation for the receiving and releasing, the Great King offered me the most intimate of relationships this side of heaven I could ever experience, and that is partaking of the body and blood of His cross of torture with Him. This act of sharing is mostly known as Communion or the Eucharist. I believe Communion is much deeper than the sacrament or service we traditionally engage in with fellow brothers and sisters in the context of a public gathering. Communion is a word formed by the union of two words: common and union.

As I sat on the beach with the Great King and He offered to partake of the elements of His cross of torture with me, I was being invited into a common union with Him. A personal and intimate union where we shared the experience of Chloe Renee's death and everything that event represented. We were partaking of the great exchange together. He took my sin, I received His righteousness. He took my sorrow, and offered me His joy. Everything in the parchment of my Rite of Passage was solidified the moment we partook together. There is no greater intimacy in the course of human life than to be asked by our Creator to become one with Him in the common union.

It was in the context of this common union that I was able to fully embrace Ruby Red. I *felt* our hearts beat as one with every wave that crashed upon the shore. I *saw* our combined tears produce the mist of the sea as the waves resided. I *heard* His heart for me as the dance of the dolphins echoed over the sea with His heavenly love songs. I *smelled* His unconditional love and loyalty as my fun-filled furry friend stood faithfully by my side.

I was able to trust Him fully because our hearts had become one, and my human senses were awakened to the oneness I shared with Him. Yes! Touching, seeing, hearing, and smelling had been brought to their heavenly completeness as we partook of His body and blood together. My heart soared high above every bird of the sea as my fifth sense awakened and I cried out…

Taste and see that the Lord is good! Blessed is the woman who trusts in Him! (Psalm 34:8a)

Let's review my first statement in this Rest-Reflect-Refresh section…

The King of the universe, The Great I AM, Jesus of Nazareth, through His Holy Spirit took me to a place where He knew He could get my attention and created an atmosphere where I would be open to receiving an expanded revelation of what He was about to do…

That place was on the beach for me. Where would it be for you? I invite you to search your heart and seek such a place. Seek it with all your heart. There is nothing like becoming one with the One who knows our pain and sorrow and being able to trust Him fully. He offers a *New Day Rising* to all who have suffered at the dark hand of abortion and will stand by any who come.

As you begin to seek Him, meditate on the following Scriptures and journal your thoughts…

But he who is joined to the Lord is one spirit with Him. (1 Corinthians 6:17)

For I know the thoughts that I think toward you, says the Lord, thoughts of peace and not of evil, to give you a future and a hope. Then you will call upon Me and go and pray to Me, and I will listen to you. And you will seek Me and find Me, when you search for Me with all your heart. I will be found by you, says the Lord. (Jeremiah 29:11-14a)

All that the Father gives Me will come to Me, and the one who comes to Me I will by no means cast out. (John 6:37)

Behold, I will do a new thing, now it shall spring forth; shall you not know it? (Isaiah 43:19a)

But to you who fear My name, the Sun of Righteousness shall arise with healing in His wings. (Malachi 4:2a)

Chapter 20

Daughter of My Tears

"Great King! Look! The last embers of the fire are going out and we have no more wood!"

"Fear not! Beloved, the embers burn only until they hear the voice of the One who owns the skies, as He will be rising with the daystar and commands nothing to share His light. We shall no longer need the fire when He appears. He brings light for the day and warmth in His heart."

"But what of the elements and my newfound friend? They have gone from my sight."

"The elements are in the hands of the occupants of the land in preparation for the celebration, and your beloved friend is waiting in the shadows until she is summoned. Fear not! You shall see them both in due time at their designated positions of service."

"Great King! I shall think my heart will race away from me waiting for the daystar to rise! How much longer, my King? How much longer must I wait?"

"Sweet mother of Chloe Renee, the Keeper of the stars and the Owner of the skies knows your heart well. He has called the night to give up its reign. Look! The crystal river that hovers over the sea shall be as a golden street for you to walk on toward the Visions of Life."

"Who are these that answer the cry of my heart? The Owner of the skies and the Keeper of the stars? You have not mentioned them before!"

"Beloved, He and they are one in the same, called by many names. Just as you are daughter, beloved, and child, to name a few. You shall understand this mystery when the song of the unborn rises from the inhabitants of the land. Focus on the horizon and wait. All the questions of your heart shall be answered in the Visions of Life."

"Would You stand with me at the edge of the sea, Great King? For I know I shall need support at the unveiling! Oh, my! What is happening under my feet? The sand is raising me up! I must sing to the Keeper of the stars and the Owner of the skies! Surely these words belong to Him!"

I waited patiently for the Lord, and He inclined to me, and heard my cry. He also brought me up out of a horrible pit, out of the miry clay, and set my feet upon a rock, and established my steps. He has put a new song in my mouth. Praise to our God. Many will see it and fear, and will trust in the Lord! (Psalm 40:1-3)

"Ah! Yes! My Beloved! The words belong to the Keeper of the stars! He has heard them and prepares to rise in response to song of your heart! He brings with Him the precious strand that was ripped from your cord so long ago. She is in the company of Keeper of the stars and carries in her soul the song of the unborn. Here, Beloved. You must wear these in order to shield your eyes from the perfection of the Visions of Life." He handed me the most beautiful pair of emerald-green contact lenses I had ever seen.

"You shall see the Visions of Life through the eyes of emerald green...the precious stone of the Great Exchange. You shall see things differently, with more clarity. These lenses will expand your vision past your lifetime, allowing you to view your story as a vital part of My redemptive plan for all who suffer from the dark hand of abortion. You shall step into the receiving and releasing ballroom of the Daughters of Destiny with hope, peace, and joy. You shall see that I have turned your tragedy into victory. This is the song of the glistening green emerald lens, Beloved. Sing, oh daughter of the Great King! Sing! Oh! Mother of Chloe Renee!"

As I placed the lenses upon my eyes, I fell to my knees and raised my hands toward the horizon in anticipation of the unveiling of this glorious victory. Already I was seeing things differently, more clearly. I sang with all that is within me the song of the glistening green emerald lens…

But as for you, you meant evil against me; but God meant it for good, in order to bring it about as it is this day, to save many people alive. (Genesis 50:20)

"Oh! Great King! There are teardrops falling from the crystal river that hovers over the sea! And from where the teardrop falls, that place in the river turns into gold! What a magnificent sight! Oh! How wonderful are Your works, oh Great King, that You would swallow up my river of tears in the depth of the sea and turn them into streets of gold!"

"You say rightly, My Beloved. Yes, the crystal river that has held the tears of your incarceration for decades is being transformed before your very eyes! The glistening green emerald of sight has brought forth the interpretation of the golden street. Today, you shall rejoice that death is swallowed up in victory, and walk on streets of gold to receive the daughter of your tears…"

"I know this to be true, Great King! For I have read it in the Great Book of Promises!"

He will swallow up death forever, and the Lord God will wipe away tears from all faces. (Isaiah 25:8a)

"A song in my heart, a melody in my soul rejoices at this most precious gift of sight! It is the wisdom, the understanding of the unfolding of the Visions of Life that You have given me!

How great is Your compassion on this one who seeks healing and wholeness from the pain and suffering of abortion! How tender is Your heart toward this one who will receive the daughter of her tears in the Visions of Life! How utterly liberating are Your promises of this new day rising! I shall sing and shout for all the heavens to hear…"

And God will wipe away every tear from their eyes; there shall be no more death, nor sorrow, nor crying. There shall be no more pain, for the former things have passed away. Then He who sat on the throne said, "Behold, I make all things new." And He said to me, "Write, for these words are true and faithful." (Revelation 21:4-5)

"Yes, Great King! I receive the wisdom, understanding, and promises of clarity of sight through Your gift of the emerald lens! I answer Your call to write the Visions of Life for all to read, that those who would embrace Ruby Red may walk the golden streets formed out of their tears of incarceration into their land of victory. I choose this day not to remove the emerald lenses no matter what they reveal. In this, I shall follow the footsteps of my fun-filled furry friend in order to escort another to their place of receiving…."

"You ravish My heart, My Beloved, with your words of courage and strength. The Father has allowed Me to see the fruit of My sacrifice and I drink in the living water of His kindness…"

He shall see the labor of His soul and be satisfied. (Isaiah 53:11a)

"And together we sing with the golden tears of Samaria and shout to the Keeper of the stars the words of the sons of Korah…"

There is a river whose streams shall make glad the city of God. The holy place of the tabernacle of the Most High. God is in the midst of her, she shall not be moved. God shall help her, just at the break of dawn. (Psalm 46:4-5)

The great cloud of witnesses and the armies of light joined us in the song of the sons of Korah, causing the ocean to erupt in a deafening roar and thunder and lightning to rule the skies.

"What is this rumble I feel beneath my feet, oh Great King?"

"It is the earth making way for the golden street that shall connect you to the Owner of the skies and the Keeper of the Stars. Beloved, prepare you heart. Prepare ye the way..."

The great cloud of witnesses and the armies of light shouted to the heavens and the earth...

The voice of one crying in the wilderness; "Prepare the way of the Lord. Make straight in the desert a highway for our God. Every valley shall be exalted and every mountain and hill brought low. The crooked places shall be made straight. And the rough places smooth. The glory of the Lord shall be revealed. And all flesh shall see it together. For the mouth of the Lord has spoken." (Isaiah 40:3-5)

"Oh! Great and Mighty King!" I fell to my knees.

Out of the sea rose what appeared to be a massive auditorium with the capacity to hold millions upon millions. Its span and height no man could measure. It had no walls, nor ceiling. It hung suspended in the heavens above the sea much like the golden door I passed through earlier.

"Oh! Great King! Whatever is this place?"

"Beloved! Let us rejoice with the great cloud of witnesses and the armies of light! The Owner of the skies and the Keeper of the stars has called forth the rising of the auditorium for the celebration of the Daughters of Destiny. Your time has come!"

I looked, and behold, a rainbow covering the horizon grew as the daystar rose until it covered the entire auditorium and all the sea.

"Oh! Great King! The beauty of the rainbow! It knows no end!"

"Yes, My Beloved. But there is more! There is no end to its promises." He removed His cloak and wrapped it around my shoulders. The brilliance of its glory called the colors of the rainbow to itself and the robe became as a rainbow around me.

"Beloved, receive the robe of celebration of the Daughters of Destiny. You shall be covered with the promises of the Rite of Passage every step of the way. Go forth with Ruby Red as the daystar rises and the mystery of the celebration unfolds."

"Oh! Great King! The beauty of the robe! I feel like royalty!"

The royal daughter is all glorious within the palace. Her clothing is woven with gold. She shall be brought to the King in robes of many colors. (Psalm 45:13-14a)

"Come, let us proceed to the King's table which holds the Ballroom's Book of Life. There we will release the occupants of the land and usher in the start of the celebration."

"Great King! However will we get there?"

"The golden highway has been constructed through the oneness of our tears and sorrow during the common union. It is in your heart, My Beloved, the way to the King's table is in your heart."

"Oh! Yes, Great King. Yes, it must be! This morning my heart swells with gratefulness for the common union and what it has done for me! Oh! Great King! The way is in my heart! We are one and You know the way! I trust You to take me to the King's table and the Ballroom's Book of Life! Surely, that is where I shall see the joy of my heart, the daughter of my tears…"

Let the morning bring me word of Your unfailing love, for I have put my trust in You. Show me the way I should go, for to You I entrust my life. (Psalm 143:8, NIV)

The sand beneath my feet gave way to a golden highway that lifted toward the heavens like an airplane taking off into the sky. If I wasn't wearing the emerald contacts the Great King had given me, I'm sure that I would have been blinded by its beauty. I held tight to Ruby Red and watched as it reached the auditorium suspended above the seas.

"We are ready now, Beloved. You have activated the King's highway by the childlike trust of Ruby Red. Shall we go?"

"Oh! Yes, Great King! Let's hurry! I see the table in the distance, and the Ballroom's Book of Life. Oh! Great King! My heart is about to burst...for real!"

The moment I stepped onto the golden street, the great cloud of witnesses and the armies of light took the same positions they had when they guarded the edges of the bridge over the great divide. But instead of offering protection from a deadly fall, they were lining up as though they were waiting for a holiday parade!

I walked the King's highway with head held high, heartbeat racing, and a skip in my step. Instead of serious looks on their faces, my faithful heavenly companions were waving banners and throwing the most brilliant colors of confetti I had ever seen! I looked at my robe of many colors and wondered if the confetti got its brilliance from the same rainbow...

Shouts of joy and celebration faded into the distance as we approached the King's table. Reverential awe struck the very core of my being as the atmosphere turned from jovial to surreal. I took a deep breath. Was this the same banqueting table that the Great King invited me to the day He gave me my Rite of Passage?

Instead of the aroma of fresh bread baking leading me to the table, the Bread of Life Himself led. There were no crystal goblets with wine or plates or parchments wrapped in golden twine. There was no basket woven with strips of fresh-cut cedar. The only element on the table was the Ballroom's Book of Life, which I could not bear to look at.

"Beloved, you must open the book upon the King's table. Herein lies the mystery of the purpose of receiving and releasing, the strength and courage to leave the celebration, and follow destiny's door into the future."

"Oh! Great King! However shall I do it? I am not worthy to open such a book!"

"No one is worthy in and of themselves, Beloved, to open such a book. But you are found in Me and I in you in the oneness of the Great Exchange and in the common union. The Rite of Passage that permitted you passage this far has been written on your heart and shall move your hands to open the book. Receive the words of the Great Book of Promise…"

I will put My law in their minds, and write it on their hearts, and I will be their God, and they shall be My people. No more shall every man teach his neighbor, and every man his brother saying, 'Know the Lord,' for they all shall know Me, from the least of them to the greatest of them, says the Lord, For I will forgive their iniquity, and their sin I will remember no more. (Jeremiah 31:33-34)

"Yes, Great King. I receive. I will open without fear, for You have forgiven all my iniquity, and my sin You remember no more. I shall open the Ballroom's Book of Life with joy!"

"Great King?

"Yes, Beloved."

"Am I mistaken or are these rainbows of color different than the ones hovering over the seas?"

"Yes, Beloved. Your emerald lenses serve you well. These are the healing colors of your journey over the great divide as they have followed you for such a time as this. You shall be surrounded from the north to the south, and from the east to the west, as you open the Ballroom's Book of Life. Healing promises have been created with both rainbows to aid you as the daystar continues to unfold the celebration. Breathe in their essence and receive what they have to offer. Behold My everlasting words and promises to you are yes, and amen…"

Be of good courage, and He shall strengthen your heart, all you who hope in the Lord. (Psalm 31:24)

HOPE and PEACE, my two archangels, stationed themselves on either side of the table with trumpets near their lips. An angelic choir began to sing softly in the distance as I silently walked toward the book. The Great King stood behind me, reaching around my back in order to assist me in opening the cover. When His hand touched mine, HOPE and PEACE sounded their trumpets and the leader of the angelic choir announced…

THE SONG OF HOPE OF THE UNBORN…
THE DAUGHTER OF DESTINY
IS WORTHY TO OPEN THE BOOK
FOR THE GREAT KING
HAS PLACED HIS HAND UPON HERS!

We opened the book together and millions upon millions of the unborn rose from inside a cavern so deep that again, no man could measure. Of all colors, all ages, all cultures, and races, they kept rising and rising. With names, beautiful, glorious, individual names written on their foreheads, one after another they took their places in the stands in the great auditorium.

A watershed full of tears spilled into the cavern from which the unborn sang as they rose…

O death where is your sting?
O Hades, where is your victory?
(1 Corinthians 15:55)

Let not your heart be troubled, you believe in God,
believe also in Me.
In My Father's house are many mansions;
if it were not so, I would have told you.
I go to prepare a place for you.
And if I go and prepare a place for you,
I will come again and receive you to Myself,
that where I am, there you may be also.
(John 14:1-3)

And God will wipe away every tear from their eyes;
there shall be no more death, nor sorrow,
nor crying. There shall be no more pain,
for the former things have passed away.
Then He who sat on the throne said,
"Behold, I make all things new..."
(Revelation 21:4-5a)

"Oh! Great King...Chloe Renee is missing from this book, is she not?"

"Yes, Beloved, yes she is."

"I cannot bear it, I cannot." I fell to the floor in front of the King's table where the unborn continued to rise, singing their songs of hope. "I cannot bear it," I repeated, holding my head.

A rumble slowly started and escalated to a full-fledged roar. The golden street below me began to shake. The same voice that announced the song of the unborn shouted with authority...

THE DAYSTAR HAS RISEN!

THE OWNER OF THE SKIES AND
THE KEEPER OF THE STARS
HAS IN HIS ARMS, THE DAUGHTER OF THE ONE
WHO HAS FACED EVERY FOE AND WALKED
THROUGH THE GOLDEN DOOR

ALL RISE FOR THE PRESENTATION
OF THE DAUGHTER OF HER TEARS

OCTOBER 16, 2017

I reached for the edge of the King's table and slowly pulled myself up. My body was like water. My face swollen with tears. Millions and millions of the unborn pounded their feet in response to the announcement, then stood with me in solidarity. I watched in utter amazement as wave upon wave of red roses were held into the air in honor of every life affected by abortion in this massive place. Oceans and oceans of red roses lifted to the Owner of the skies, and the Keeper of the stars flooded the atmosphere with a sweet-smelling aroma.

The Great King walked me to the center of the auditorium where the cloud of witnesses and the armies of light had been stationed on either side of the King's highway. They were now dressed in US military uniforms, which I easily recognized as Army, Navy, Air Force, and Marine. These were the faithful soldiers of the Great King who had fought on my behalf in the heavenly war against the king of darkness. They would now stand with the King of Light, and witness the victory they had been commissioned to secure.

The holy hush I started to recognize as evidence that something spectacular was about to happen washed over the sea of millions, and no one moved. It was way beyond my ability to stand at this point, and very apparent by the posture of the millions, that sitting would not be acceptable. I leaned into the chest of the Great King who stood behind me, every nerve in my body standing on edge.

We all faced the rainbow, which hovered over the eastern sky waiting for the Owner of the skies and the Keeper of the stars to enter the King's highway. Its golden hue developed a door-like frame where the archangels HOPE and PEACE were now stationed with their trumpets at their sides. They stood with the rest of us under the weight of the holy hush.

For a few minutes we waited. The golden hue expanded and contracted as if it had a heartbeat of its own and I felt drawn toward it. I leaned forward as it pulled me to itself and felt strength come to my weakened legs. I was standing on my own! The Owner of the skies and the Keeper of the stars had sent me a message! He was about to come through with Chloe Renee just like the leader of the angelic choir had said!

The golden hue expanded and contracted one last time and I felt as though my heart would split in two. There she was! A tiny figure emerged, carrying something over her right shoulder and a rose in her left hand.

"Oh! Great King! Oh! Great King! Is it so? Is it so? I cannot bear it! I cannot bear it! It is too glorious! Too awesome! Too wonderful for words! Oh! Great King! Oh! Great King! Look at her! Look at her! Look at her! Oh! How long, Great King? How long till I hold my precious daughter? Whatever is that over her mouth?"

"It is for the ceremony of the Presentation of the Daughters of Destiny that we wait."

The Owner of the skies and Keeper of the stars followed the tiny figure through the golden hue and lifted the holy hush. "Papa! Papa! Papa!" Shouts of joy rose from the masses. "Oh! Papa, Papa, Papa! Today another daughter joins in the celebration of receiving and her mother will write her name in the Ballroom's Book of Life! Oh! Papa! She will be held by her mother, be recognized, loved, and honored! Oh! Papa! Her mother has made it through the golden door and the door of destiny! Our sister will no longer wear the red tape of anonymity, but will join us in the song of the unborn! You are such a good, good Papa!"

As Chloe Renee stood beside Him, His hand resting on her shoulder, the Keeper of the stars said, "Great company of the unborn whose voices have been released! Receive unto the masses your sister Chloe Renee whose mother has made it over the great divide and entered through the doorway of the Great King. May her voice be known and her song be sung throughout the land! Today we celebrate with her and the King's Beloved the removing of the silence of the red tape! Prepare the King's table and the Great King's beloved for the ceremony of receiving!"

Attendants dressed in robes of many colors proceeded to the King's table, carrying elements for the ceremony in their hands. One brought a crystal goblet filled with water and a crystal plate and placed them in the center of the table. Another brought a parchment similar to my Rite of Passage and carefully laid it on the crystal plate. The last attendant placed five books beside the Ballroom's Book of Life.

The leader of the attendants said, "If the Great King's Beloved should desire all of the gifts of the door of destiny, please present yourself to the King's table, and bring with you the canister of hope you carry in your bag."

As I brought forth the canister of hope and gave it to the attendant, Chloe Renee squealed from her place beside the Keeper of the stars. This caused the masses to shout with joy, "The union of the Daughters of Destiny has transpired and the celebration shall begin! Chloe Renee, we call you to the celebration of the union of the Daughters of Destiny! Papa, we ask that You present our sister to the Great King for the Beloved's receiving!"

"And so, it shall be!" said the Keeper of the stars. "Son, come forward!"

The Great King bowed. The masses cheered. "Praise be to the Great King who has brought His Beloved to the highway of the Keeper of the stars! Praise to the Great King who gave His life so that we all may live! Praise to the Great King who redeems, restores, and reunites Chloe Renee with her mother today! Praise to the Great King for this sight that we are about to see!"

The masses waved their roses and began to sing...

You are worthy, O Lord, to receive glory and honor and power for You created all things, and by Your will they exist and were created! (Revelation 4:11)

Worthy is the Lamb who was slain to receive power and riches and wisdom, and strength and honor and glory and blessing! (Revelation 5:12)

And they sang a new song, saying, "You are worthy to take the scroll, and to open its seals. For You were slain, and have redeemed us to God by Your blood out of every tribe and tongue and people and nation, and have made us kings and priests to our God, and we shall reign on the earth." (Revelation 5:9-10)

The Keeper of the stars bent down, kissed Chloe Renee on the forehead, and said, "Go to your mother by way of the Great King on the King's highway until I call for you. Enjoy her. Tell her everything that is in your heart. Do not forget to show her the way of the receiving and releasing!"

"I will Papa, I will! I promise I will!"

The masses cheered and cheered as the Great King lifted Chloe Renee high up into the air and spun her around like a parasol! She squealed with delight, much like I had days ago. My heart soared with her in unison at the remembrance, and I cried with joy at the sight. Oh! The love of this Great King and His Father, the Keeper of the stars! How glorious are the Visions of Life! Look at my precious Chloe Renee! She is healed! She is whole! She is happy! She is loved! Thank You, Keeper of the stars, and Your Son, the Great King, for this day of celebration! Thank You! Thank You! Thank You!

The Great King turned to me, golden tears freely flowing down His face. "My Beloved, I have waited many, many years for the Daughters of Destiny to be united in the dance of the parasol. Today the broken strands of the cord have been restored and the hearts of the broken mended. It is in the power of the dance that you shall soar with wings as eagles until the day the Owner of the sky calls you to Himself. The success of the dance has been acknowledged by the Keeper of the stars and its power to receive has been granted to you."

The auditorium erupted with more shouts of joy, "We celebrate the reunion of the Daughters of Destiny over the head of the Great King in the dance of the parasol! Great are Your ways, Owner of the skies and Keeper of the stars! You have granted us joy beyond measure!"

As the Great King lowered Chloe Renee to the ground, the Keeper of the stars turned to walk back through the golden hue.

"Papa! Papa! When shall we see You again?" A chant erupted from the auditorium, as millions of the unborn waved their roses in celebration of the success of the dance of the parasol and in honor of the Keeper of the stars.

"When another mother or father passes through the door of destiny by the way of The Rite of Passage of My Son. Until then, be diligent! Be strong! Raise your voices! Sing the song of the unborn until another mother or father hears your cry! Today is a day of celebration! Another abandoned star will be embraced by her mother, the red tape will be removed, and she will sing her song of the unborn…and her song shall be called *Chloe's Cry!*

Chloe's Cry! Chloe's Cry! Chloe's Cry! The chanting, foot-stomping, rumbling of the stands in the auditorium escalated as millions of the unborn shouted *Chloe's Cry! Chloe's Cry! Chloe's Cry!* As my body responded to this magnificent tribute to my precious daughter, I fell to my knees in honor of the Owner of the skies, who truly is the Keeper of the stars.

"Mother of Chloe Renee!" The leader of the singers of the songs of the unborn shouted. "The Son of the Owner of the skies presents the daughter of your tears to you…"

I looked, and behold, this beautiful tiny figure who came from the golden hue walked toward me hand in hand with the Great King, a big smile on her face, and a rose in her hand…

REST-REFLECT-REFRESH

My fellow sojourner, it is time to take a break! This was some chapter to write! It is fresh off the press so to speak as I am typing it right now with no journal entries or notes to aid me. It is fresh manna from the Visions of Life! Wow! Parts of it had me weeping, weeping real tears of healing, even this far in my journey. And, I am so okay with that! I welcome the opportunity to shed tears. The outcome is always healing for me.

As I wrote about the Great King touching my hand to aid me in opening the book, I could barely see the keys on the keyboard to type. Most of this chapter was extremely emotionally charged for me. And, I mean that in a good way! I have received additional healing as the events unfolded, and for that I am very grateful. I also received more understanding into the nature of the *Keeper of the stars* and what that really means in the context of abortion.

Our Father God is the Father of the unborn. He receives them the day they die. He keeps watch over them, cares for them, and loves them. They are safe and whole in His presence, with identity, dignity, and purpose. Knowing that Chloe Renee has been safe in His care since the day of her death brings me great peace. Knowing that she has identity, dignity, and purpose in His presence brings me great joy. Knowing that one day we will be reunited in a place where death and destruction, tears and regret, cannot exist, brings me great hope. I suspect this might be what the canister of hope contains.

This has been an eye-opening experience as it unfolded while I wrote. I am grateful for the Visions of Life the Lord has given me to share with you. I realize now that there are not only millions of unborn children who have songs to sing, but there are millions of mothers and fathers who would love to have the opportunity to sing with them.

The Keeper of the stars told the masses of the unborn in the heavenly auditorium that my daughter's song would be *Chloe's Cry*. Your unborn child has a song! Take some time to meditate on this concept. Do you hear a song in your spirit? Journal your thoughts.

There was reference to removing red tape from Chloe Renee's mouth so she would be able sing her song. Many right-to-life organizations place red tape on their mouths with the word LIFE written on it to identify with the silence of the pre-born who have no voice to defend themselves. For more information you may visit: bound4life.com.

For thirty-eight years, Chloe Renee did not have a voice. And, for most of that thirty-eight years, only a handful of people even knew she existed. Today, she has a voice! Today, I stood in the midst of an auditorium in the Visions of Life with millions upon millions of the unborn celebrating her life and her song!

Whatever way the Lord may lead you, I encourage you to honor your child by removing the tape from his or her mouth and allow them to sing their song of the unborn! I promise you there will be much healing!

The cries of the unborn are before the Lord day and night!

Hear my prayer, O Lord! Listen to my cry for help! Do no ignore my sobbing! For I am dependent on You, like one residing outside his native land. I am at Your mercy, just as all my ancestors were. (Psalm 39:12, NET)

The book you hold in your hands is the answer to Chloe Renee's song and her cry for a voice!

"Not everyone is called to write a book, but every post-abortive parent is called to give dignity, honor, and a voice to their unborn star," says the Keeper of the stars!

May this be your prayer as we move on...

Today, Lord, I commit to giving my unborn child a voice. In any way You desire."

Chapter 21

Celebration of the Receiving

I stood at the edge of the golden street, tears streaming down my face. "Oh! Great King!" I sobbed. "She is the child of the photo…the child of the photo…over and over I said, "She is the child of the photo…"

"Look at her! She's beautiful!" I raised my eyes to the masses, pleading for their recognition of her beauty. I fell to my knees under the weight of the holy hush that had returned. In silence they lifted unlit candles high above their heads in her honor. There was no need of fire, for the glory of the Great King's countenance lit the candles as He walked hand in hand with the daughter of my tears.

"Let the procession of lights and the cry of the unborn begin!" He proclaimed.

The faithful soldiers stationed on either side of the golden highway stood at attention as the Great King escorted Chloe Renee during the procession. One by one, the holders of the candles left their seats in the great auditorium and formed a circle around the golden highway as far as I could see. Their faces glowed from the countenance of the Great King much like the moon does from the sun, and I drank in their light. One by one they began to sing the cry of their hearts until I was surrounded by the unified song of the unborn, drinking in its sound.

The echo of their songs reverberated through every fiber of my being, causing even the strongest bone to weep at what it heard. The cries of those who have been unknown and forgotten had now become part of my DNA through the procession of lights and the cry of the unborn. Oh! How I wept! My precious daughter had not yet been given the honor and dignity of recognition in this great company! How I longed for her cry to be heard in this powerful voice!

The leader of the choir announced to the holders of the candles, "The songs of the unborn have prepared the way for the Beloved's receiving of the cry of the daughter of her tears. Let their hearts beat as one in preparation for the ceremony."

The Great King shouted, "Let the ceremony of the receiving begin!"

There was a rumble like nothing I had ever heard as all the occupants of the great auditorium responded to this most anticipated announcement.

I looked, and behold, every candle in the hands of the occupants of the great auditorium became as a trumpet, which they held to their lips waiting for the command to sound. PEACE and HOPE took their places on either side of the Great King and Chloe Renee, preparing to lead the millions of the unborn in the call to the celebration of the receiving...

The leader of the singers of song of the unborn stood in the midst of the auditorium and shouted...

COMFORT, YES COMFORT MY DAUGHTER,
SAYS THE KEEPER OF THE STARS.
SPEAK COMFORT TO THE KING'S BELOVED
AND CRY OUT TO HER!
THAT HER WARFARE HAS ENDED
THAT HER INIQUITY IS PARDONED!
(From Isaiah 40:1-2)

"Yes! Yes! We comfort the Great King's Beloved! We comfort her and cry out to her! Your warfare has ended! Your iniquity is pardoned! You shall, this day, receive your Certificate of Occupation and join our parents in the City of the Forgiven! You are forgiven! You are forgiven! You are forgiven! We say collectively, YOU ARE FORGIVEN! Let us raise our trumpets born out of the candles of the songs of the unborn and usher in the ceremony of the receiving! Blessed be the name of the Great King who escorts the daughter of her tears to His Beloved!"

The noise was deafening, exhilarating, energy producing! I was beside myself as the Great King released Chloe Renee's hand and she came running toward me! Trumpets sounded, shaking the very heavens themselves; rifles shot and cheers erupted. The masses left their seats in the stands and ran to the floor waving banners, throwing confetti, laughing, dancing, and shouting…

I thought I would explode! Here she comes! Here she comes! Yes! She is the child of the photo! Here she comes running in her bare feet! Oh! I laughed and laughed! My own mother, her grandmother, always, and even to this day, yells at me for running around in my bare feet! And, I'm sixty years old! What a hoot! What joy! What happiness!

Here she comes! Her curly, blonde hair flying in the breeze! The Great King runs after her! She's got the bucket! Oh! Dear Owner of the skies and Keeper of the stars! She's got the bucket from the picture! Is this for real? Oh! Great King! Look! She's got the sand bucket! She's got fair skin like me and loves the ocean! Oh! My Great King…

This daughter of my tears, this unborn beauty, ran toward me screaming and laughing without a care in the world, carrying the bucket of my dreams. She *wanted* to run into my arms, I could *feel* it. All I could do was get on my knees and open my arms…the arms that have been empty for thirty-eight years. The mystery of the great divide is in the receiving and releasing, the Great King said. I could not bear to think of the releasing. I would stay in the moment of the receiving and trust the Great King with the rest. I clutched Ruby Red with all I had as she threw the bucket and the rose down and ran into my arms screaming, "Mommy! Mommy! Mommy!"

"Chloe Renee! Chloe Renee! Chloe Renee!" I screamed with joy. We fell back onto the golden highway and rolled around together while the masses continued to celebrate.

"Chloe Renee, is it really you?"

"Yes! Mommy it is! Yes! Mommy it is me, Chloe Renee! Oh! How I have waited for you to come through the door! Look at the tears running down your face! Here Mommy, I brought this for you." The daughter of my tears reached into the little pocket on the side of her dress and pulled out a tissue. "Here Mommy. Let me wipe your tears away."

"Oh! Chloe, Oh! Chloe Renee! That will make me cry all the more!" I picked her up and held her for the longest time. I sobbed into her neck, holding her tight. "Mommy, please don't cry. We don't have a lot of time. Please don't cry it all away!" she said as tears fell from her little eyes.

I breathed in her scent. Soft as the dew of a fresh spring morning; peaceful and cool as an afternoon rain; relaxing and serene as the dusk of the evening. This is the scent of my Chloe Renee. Soft, peaceful, relaxing, and serene. "How I will forever remember your scent! When my day brings strife, anxiety, or stress, I shall remember burying my nose in your neck and breathing in the soft, peaceful, relaxing, and serene essence of the daughter of my tears. When I am sad and the fields of regret call me to lie in their pastures full of thorns and bristles, I will remember this time with you. I will remember your laugh, your smile, and your scent! I will always remember, Chloe Renee, always!

"PEACE!" the Great King said. "Present the parchment of the King's table."

Chloe sat with me on the golden highway as PEACE retrieved the parchment and walked toward us. "Chloe Renee, daughter of the beloved, have you forgiven your mother for her crimes against you?"

"Oh Yes! Servant of the Great King, for sure I have! She's my mommy! Of course, I have!"

"Chloe Renee, today in the presence of all the unborn in this great auditorium, I present to you the parchment from the King's table. At the sound of the trumpet, you may present it to your mother and say anything you wish." The leader of the singers of the songs of the unborn sounded his trumpet and Chloe Renee accepted the parchment.

"Mommy, in front of all my brothers and sisters in the land of the forgiven, I want to give you this piece of paper. They call it a Certificate of Occupancy. This means, Mommy, that I forgive you unconditionally! Always remember that you live in the City of the Forgiven. I seal it with a kiss, Mommy. Here, take it and eat. They tell me when you are sad or feeling bad because of me it will help you."

"Chloe Renee...it is sweet to the taste, and healing to my soul. I shall remember your words always."

Chloe Renee picked up her sand bucket and grabbed my hand. "Come, Mommy, the Great King is calling us to His table! I have so much to show you and tell you there!" She stopped and said, "Oops! I left my rose on the King's highway. Don't move! Stay here till I go and get it!" She looked at me with a look that only my own mother could appreciate! "You promise?" She ran back before I could answer. I smiled as I realized my daughter was just as impulsive me!

Again, I responded to the Great King's invitation, but this time it was in the presence of my precious daughter. It was at this very table He had given me the parchment of the Great Exchange for safe passage over the great divide. I was certain that Chloe Renee's Certificate of Occupation was just as important to my survival, if not more so.

The leader of the singers of the songs of the unborn announced, "Let the celebration of the restoration of the broken cord begin!" Shouts of joy filled the great auditorium.

The Great King opened the Book of Promises from which the foundation of my journey had been built. When He found the place He was looking for, He said, "Beloved and Chloe Renee, Daughters of Destiny, for thirty-eight years the three-strand cord has been separated by the dark hand of abortion.

Today we celebrate at this table in the presence of the company of the unborn, the great cloud of witnesses, and the armies of light, the restoration of this cord. Chloe Renee, please present the bucket and your reason for bringing it to the King's table…"

"Oh! Great King! You know all things! I love the beach! You love the beach! And, Mommy loves the beach! Look! Great King! My bucket has three hearts painted on it. One for me. One for You. And, one for Mommy! I brought this bucket to the King's table to tell you both I love you and someday I want us all to build a sandcastle on the shores of hope! This is why I brought my bucket to the King's table, oh Great King!"

"You say well, daughter of My Beloved's tears. We are three hearts that belong together. This is a gift that pleases the Great King, and the request shall be granted by the Owner of the skies and Keeper of the stars when He sees fit. Let us partake of the elements of the power of the cross of torture from which this request can be filled. May our hearts be as one from this moment on as the Scriptures say…"

But she who is joined to the Lord is one spirit with Him. (From 1 Corinthians 6:17)

The leader of the singers of the song of the unborn shouted, "Let the ceremony of song of the remembrance begin! Stand, oh daughter of the Beloved's tears, and prepare for the presentation of the rose of remembrance."

Chloe Renee stood.

The Great King brought forth the crystal plate on which Chloe Renee had placed her red rose and held it high above His head. "Owner of the skies and Keeper of the stars, grant these, our Daughters of Destiny, restoration of the cord by the receiving of the rose of remembrance." He kissed the rose and handed the crystal plate to Chloe Renee. "Chloe Renee, I charge you this day as the daughter of the Beloved's tears to receive this rose of remembrance and release it to your mother in the celebration of the restoration of the broken cord."

"Yes! Great King! I shall! Oh! Mommy, will you receive my rose of remembrance?"

The auditorium became as dark as night, for the moon had passed over the sun. As the singers of the song of the unborn began to hum, the countenance of the Great King once again lit the candles of the masses. Beautiful soft, glowing light surrounded my precious daughter as she knelt at my feet with the rose of remembrance, her innocent eyes looking into mine.

"Beloved, the daughter of your tears kneels at your feet with forgiveness in her hand. Will you receive her forgiveness in the form of the rose of remembrance?"

"Indeed, I will, Great King. Indeed, I will," I said and received the rose.

"Chloe Renee, you may sing your song to your mother now..."

Mommy, Mommy, I heard you calling my name,
From the other side of the wooden door
Now nothing will be the same...

I have a name! I have a name!
I'm no longer hidden away!
You've given me honor, you've given me joy!
You've made my heart smile today!

I waited for you... I waited for you...
and you finally came to the door...
You gave me a name! You gave me a name!
I love you forevermore!

You came to the door! You came to the door!
I heard you calling my name...
Mommy, you came to the door! You came to the door!
Now nothing will be the same!

By Lynn Potter

She could not finish. We were all sobbing. The Great King gathered us together in a big bear hug and put Chloe Renee's prized bucked in the center of the table to catch all of our tears.

"Beloved and Chloe Renee, it is time for the ceremony of the entrance of the daughter of tears into the Ballroom's Book of Life. Come, let us sit at the King's table and receive the blessing of the Keeper of the stars for the releasing." My heart stopped at the Great King's talk of the releasing for I knew this is what I had journeyed over the great divide to accomplish.

"Do not be troubled, Beloved, for your precious Chloe Renee has watched many of these ceremonies from afar. She knows the way, and will strengthen you. Come, let us enjoy the blessing of the Keeper of the stars, for it will sustain you in the days to come."

"Why, Great King, would she have to watch from afar?"

"Beloved, until the mothers of the unborn journey over the great divide into the auditorium of celebration by way of the Great King, the daughters and sons of tears must wait with the Keeper of the stars. Because you have held tight to Ruby Red and passed through the valley of the shadow of death, the Keeper of the stars has commissioned Me to present Chloe Renee to you today for the receiving and releasing."

"Great King, I must hold tightly to Ruby Red, for this shall be the hardest thing ever asked of me." I reached into my bag woven in fine linen and clutched my precious stone.

"All rise for the ceremony of the entrance into the Ballroom's Book of Life!"

Chloe Renee rushed to my side and pulled on my pant leg. "Mommy!" she said. "Don't look so sad! This is what has to happen! I want you to get better and you can't if you don't! Please! Mommy! Come with me to the Ballroom's Book of Life! I will help you!"

I took her little hand in mine. It was soft and tender. My heart melted and my legs turned to water. "Be strong, Mommy! Look! Look at all the unborn in this place! All their mothers came to the King's table and put their kids' names in the book! Don't I deserve to be in there?"

"The Keeper of the stars promised me that when you came through the door of destiny I would be able to join all my brothers and sisters in singing the songs of the unborn. But Mommy, I can't until you write my name in the Ballroom's Book of Life. That's what the red tape is about! It's not about me talking to you; it's about you talking to everybody about me! I have no voice until you write my name in this book!"

"Oh, Chloe Renee! I had no idea. I had no idea. That is why they were chanting *Chloe's Cry, Chloe's Cry, Chloe's Cry!* I am torn in two, my precious one, torn in two! However shall I do this thing that will cause me to have to let you go?"

"Look, Mommy! Look! There are books stacked by the Ballroom's Book of Life! They will help you! They are stories of the unborn and their mothers who have completed the ceremony of the releasing. Their stories will give you strength to get better and tell the other mothers who are thinking about sending their babies to the land of the unborn what the deep, dark prison is like. We have a story to tell, Mommy! Our story gives me a voice; it takes the red tape off my mouth! As soon as you write my name in this book, I will be able to laugh, sing, and shout! We will sing together the song the Keeper of the stars gave me until the Owner of the skies tells you it is time to come build sandcastles with me by the shore…"

We walked hand in hand, tears streaming down my face, toward the Ballroom's Book of Life. Surely enough, the books that the attendants placed there earlier awaited our arrival. There was a golden pen and inkwell sitting beside the Ballroom's Book of Life.

"Go ahead, Mommy," Chloe Renee said.

I opened the book. Pages and pages filled with names and dates met my eyes. Millions of precious children whose identity, dignity, and destiny had been restored by the Great King's sacrifice and the courage of their mothers. *Oh! Yes! Chloe Renee! I must not deny you! I shall!*

As I reached for the golden pen in the golden inkwell, Chloe Renee began to weep. "Mommy," she said, "do you remember when you had to put Buddy to sleep? When the vet brought him into the room on the table? Do you remember? I saw it all! You loved him so!"

Warm, comforting tears freely flowing now. "Yes, sweetheart, I sure do."

"Well, do you remember what you thought when they wheeled him in and you saw his face?"

"Oh, Chloe Renee, yes I do. Indeed, I do."

"Well, Mommy. This is kind of the same thing."

"No! Chloe Renee! No! It is not! This cuts deeper than anything could ever! You are *my child*!"

"But, Mommy! Lean down here, please!" she said, and brought another tissue out from the pocket in her dress. "You did it for Buddy; you can do it for me! You must let me go!"

I lifted her up and nuzzled my face into her neck one last time. I took deep, long breaths and breathed in her scent. *I shall honor your life and death and lay you to rest with dignity…*

Crying uncontrollably, I said, "Yes, Chloe Renee. I will do this for you, for me, for us. I shall give you identity, dignity, and honor. I shall write your name in this Ballroom's Book of Life and then let you go. Oh, sweetheart, how shall I ever find the place where it should be written?"

The Great King walked up behind us, took my hand, and placed it in hers.

"Beloved, let this little child lead you, and you shall find the way…"

REST-REFLECT-REFRESH

As I wrote this chapter, "Celebration of Receiving," Chloe Renee became so real to me that it was as though her smell, touch, and voice had left their heavenly home and entered mine. The place where *Chloe's Cry* was being birthed in the Spirit became one in the same with my dining room where I sat for days on end being transferred from the natural into the spiritual realm. Again, I found myself on holy ground in the midst of the Holiest of Holies where the Great King resides, and Chloe Renee's life and death are not in vain.

In this Holiest of Holies, forgiveness surrounded me. Chloe Renee's, the Great King's, and the great company of singers who sang the songs of the unborn. It was so thick, so compelling, that I *had* to release any residue of self-loathing in order to embrace the child I could not embrace thirty-eight years ago. The Great King paid the ultimate price for me to walk free from this evil, destiny-destroying spirit. I had to fight to the death with self-loathing when I saw her precious face, by using the keys and stones I had been given for my journey.

Symbolically receiving our children from the Great King, writing their names in His Ballroom's Book of Life, and bonding with them for a period of time before we lay them to rest is the most life-changing experience I believe any post-abortive parent could have. I can testify that this is true in my life! As Chloe Renee's and my "Celebration of Receiving" unfolded, every part of the vision was as real to me as the keyboard I was typing it on.

Would you take time to meditate on what you have read in "Celebration of Receiving" and allow the Great King access to your deepest thoughts, desires, and emotions concerning your precious unborn child? Would you receive all the forgiveness the Great King's sacrifice on the cross of torture purchased for you, including your child's? Would you fight to the death against the spirit of self-loathing with Ruby Red's trust by receiving them in their fullness from the Great King?

The Great King tells us the mystery of the great divide is in the receiving and releasing. As we receive our unborn children from Him and release them back to Him, there is yet another step we must take that is vital to crossing the great divide...

RELEASING OF UNFORGIVENESS THROUGH FORGIVENESS

Unforgiveness is an invisible cancer that threatens our very lives until it is exposed and dealt with. Abortion has stolen so much from us. When reality hits, and we are faced with the cold, hard facts concerning the loss of our children, a door of bitterness, resentment, and unforgiveness swings wide open. In order to deal with this life-threatening condition, *we must extend forgiveness* to those who had a part in either forcing us into, or helping follow through our abortion decision. The Great King reminds us as we have received His forgiveness...

Freely you have received, freely give. (Matthew 10:8b)

This may seem impossible at first, but I can tell you from experience, it is a *necessary step* we must take in order to cross the great divide. Take some time to think about those with whom you are bound to through unforgiveness. Pray for the ability to extend forgiveness toward them. Many post-abortive parents have found that writing their feelings out in a letter and burning the letter has brought great relief and the ability to extend forgiveness. Their recommendation is...DO NOT MAIL THE LETTER! The letter is to free you by freeing them!

With man this is impossible, but with God all things are possible. (Matthew 19:26, NIV)

FORGIVENESS IS NOT A FEELING! IT IS AN ACTION THAT FREES US BY FREEING THEM!

Chapter 22

Silent No More

Chloe Renee had seen thousands of these ceremonies and knew exactly what to do. "Mommy," she said. "Come! I will help you find the page that belongs to us!" She flipped through the Ballroom's Book of Life with ease and understanding. "Here it is!" She pointed to a page that was blank except for the date August 8, 2017, which was written in gold letters at the top.

"Mommy, you must use the golden pen with the golden ink to write my name on the page that will receive the details of the Celebration of the Memorial. Don't cry, Mommy. I know this is hard, but you aren't alone. It was hard for all the other mothers too. You'll be okay, I promise."

My precious daughter wrapped her little arms around my leg, leaned against my side, and said, "Mommy, thank you. I love you." With a peace that passes all my understanding, I proudly, and without hesitation, wrote Chloe Renee's name under the date in the Ballroom's Book of Life.

The singers of the songs of the unborn shouted with joy, *"Chloe's Cry! Chloe's Cry, Chloe's Cry!* Chloe Renee joins us now as a singer of the songs of the unborn! We celebrate the mercy of the Great King, the courage of the mother of the daughter of her tears! Oh, Keeper of the stars! Another star has been given her voice! All rise for the celebration of the removal of the tape of silence! Servants of the Great King, erect the tent of removal in the presence of the singers of the songs of the unborn!"

HOPE and PEACE surrounded us, providing a wall of privacy while the great cloud of witnesses and the armies of light hovered over us. We were enclosed by heaven itself where no darkness could penetrate. A soft glow from the countenance of the Great King filled the tent of removal.

He said, "Father, My Beloved stands before You and this heavenly host, in the presence of the singers of the songs of the unborn. She has written Your star, Chloe Renee's name, in the Ballroom's Book of Life and desires to remove the tape from her mouth."

The heavens opened above us with thunder and lightning indicating the Keeper of the stars had granted His permission. "You may now remove the tape," the Great King said.

The holiest of hushes yet to be fell upon all in the great auditorium as I gently removed the red tape from her mouth. Our eyes met and tears of unity slowly filled our eyes, dripping onto our cheeks. The Great King took the tape from my hand and said, "Beloved, this day you have chosen to give voice to your unborn daughter in the presence of all who wish her song to be heard. Seal the celebration of the removal by the mother's kiss..."

The beautiful scent that I had come to love filled my soul with peace as I leaned forward to kiss this most precious gift from the Keeper of the stars. The moment the roughness of sixty years touched the smoothness of innocence, she began to sing with a tenderness that only heaven could produce...

"Mommy, Mommy, this is my song. This is your song. This is our song. O death, where is your sting? O Hades, where is your victory? O death, where is your sting? O Hades, where is your victory? O death, where is your sting?"

As I joined her in singing *Chloe's Cry*, the Great King lifted the tent of removal. In beautiful harmony, millions upon millions of the unborn joined the daughter of my tears and myself in our song of restoration and hope. Lifting their candles toward the Keeper of the stars, they flooded the floor of the great auditorium with tears of joy.

I stood with Chloe Renee by my side, wondering what August 8, 2017 would bring and what its page would hold once the memorial of the releasing had been completed. Warm, comforting tears had become my closest companions during the most difficult parts of my journey, and I gratefully welcomed them now. As these freshly flowing tears of release dripped upon our special page, comfort like I had never known washed over me.

"Let the ceremony of the rose and the canister begin!" the unborn shouted from the stands.

The Great King declared, "We shall now prepare the rose of remembrance and the canister of hope. Chloe Renee, place your rose upon the crystal plate. Beloved, remove the canister of hope and the precious stones from your bag. Place them beside your daughter's rose of remembrance on the crystal plate."

We did as we were told. The Great King lifted the crystal goblet that held the heavenly water and said, "Keeper of the stars, I ask You to grant these, Your Daughters of Destiny, Your blessing on this, their ceremony of preparation. May the water that spilled from My side on the cross of torture cleanse these, the elements of releasing."

He sprinkled the rose of remembrance, the canister of hope, and every precious stone that lay on the crystal plate with the heavenly water from the crystal goblet. He then took the books lying beside the Ballroom's Book of Life and said, "May the songs of the unborn which have been released throughout the pages of these books provide the mother of Chloe Renee strength, peace, and hope in the days following the completion of her ceremony of releasing. This, oh Mighty Keeper of the stars, completes the sprinkling of the elements. "

But one of the soldiers pierced His side with a spear, and immediately blood and water came out. (John 19:34)

Let us draw near with a true heart in full assurance of faith, having our hearts sprinkled from an evil conscience and our bodies washed with pure water. (Hebrews 10:22)

"It is for the exchange of the elements of the releasing we have prepared them with the water of the cross of torture. Beloved, present to the daughter of your tears, the rose sprinkled with the water of life."

Chloe Renee reached her soft little hand out toward me and I gently laid it in her palm. She took the rose and placed it on top of the Ballroom's Book of Life. "Chloe Renee," the Great King said, "the rose upon the book is the sealing of your name upon its pages and the date of the ceremony of the releasing. You shall join the singers of the songs of the unborn when the ceremony of the exchange of the elements is complete."

"Yes, Great King, this I know." She ruffled her little dress and brushed a curl from her eyes.

"Chloe Renee, daughter of the Keeper of the stars, present your mother the Books of Strength that have been sprinkled with the water of life. They total five in number. Remove them from the Great King's table and hand them to your mother one by one." He touched her lips and said, "Seal the strength of the books of the library of the unborn with the victory of your song. Mother of Chloe Renee, open your bag woven in fine linen to receive these gifts from the daughter of your tears."

Chloe Renee stood in front of me, with the comfort of her innocence. "Mommy," she said, "receive these books with my kiss of love and forgiveness. Receive their strength and hope for your journey through life until the day we build sandcastles by the sea." One by one she lifted the books to her lips and kissed them, leaving a bright red imprint on the cover.

The books were warm to the touch. Warm, with the tenderness of heaven's healing and wholeness. I received more than I could ever ask or think. I received strength, love, and forgiveness from the child whose father and I thought we could not possibly afford. I received the ability to move on toward the memorial of the releasing without fear, guilt, shame, or regret standing in my way. I received the unconditional love of the Great King and the Keeper of the stars through an abandoned child who wanted her mommy to be healed and whole.

I knelt before her, my empty arms reaching toward her tiny little hands. "Chloe Renee," I said, "I receive these gifts from you with hope, joy, and peace, my precious little one. I shall cherish these gifts you have given me all the days of my life. I shall often touch the place where your innocent lips have left their mark." Through clouded eyes filled with tears, I read the titles out loud as she placed them in my bag one by one…

Will I Cry Tomorrow? By Susan M. Stanford
Unplanned By Abby Johnson
Empty Arms By Wendy Williams and Ann Caldwell
The Scarlet Lady By Carol Everett
Shattered into Beautiful By Jeannie Scott Smith

"Mommy, these books have helped so many mothers of the unborn. Remember I love you and forgive you when you read them. The Keeper of the stars told me before He brought me through the door of the golden hue that you would write a book for the library of the unborn. He said other mothers would receive it in their ceremony of the exchange of the elements. He said the book will be our story, Mommy, and it will be called, *Chloe's Cry.*"

"And so, shall it be," said the Great King.

I bent to kiss her forehead. The place where my lips touched her innocent skin left a red imprint identical to the ones she left on the Books of Strength. I held her tight, so tight she gasped for air. I buried my face in her curly blonde hair. I stroked her cheeks. She pulled away and brushed her little hands across my face, wiping my tears away. She said, "Mommy, it is time for the completion of the exchange of the elements at the King's table. Don't be sad, Mommy! You made it! You made it! You crossed the great divide and passed through the door of destiny! You gave me my voice! You gave me my song!

"Oh! Chloe Renee! I am so sorry…I am so very sorry…"

"Mommy, there is no time to be sorry! There are millions and millions of people that need to read our story and hear our song! Mommies and daddies everywhere are living in the same dark dungeon, crying out for freedom like you were! Millions of my unborn brothers and sisters are still waiting for their mothers to cross the great divide and come through the door of destiny! They are waiting for their roses of remembrance to be placed on the Ballroom's Book of Life! They are waiting for the tape to be removed, for their voices, and for their songs!

"Oh! Mommy! You can't be sad! There is no time! Mommy! *Chloe's Cry* has to be sung to the masses and used to help the Great King rescue many more from their deep, dark dungeons! There's no time to be sad! We *will* build sandcastles in the sky someday. But, now we have work to do! I must take my place in the Keeper of the star's choir of the unborn and you must take your place in the Great King's rescue of the incarcerated! Come! Mommy! Come! We must present ourselves to the Great King at the King's table! It is time for us to celebrate the ceremony of the exchange of the stones in preparation of the releasing."

The leader of the singers of the unborn shouted, "All rise for the song of the exchange of the stones! Sound the trumpets! Lift up your voices! Celebrate and honor the Great King for what He has done! Let us join our sister, Chloe Renee, as she sings for the first time, our song in honor of the Great King in the presence of her mother! We shall rejoice and be glad."

You are worthy, O Lord, to receive glory and honor and power. For You created all things and by Your will they exist and were created. (Revelation 4:11)

"Chloe Renee," said the leader, "what song have you chosen to begin the ceremony?"

"It is the song of chapter 139 of the Psalms in the Great Book of Promises, Noble One…"

O Lord, You have searched me and known me. You know my sitting down and my rising up. You understand my thoughts afar off. You comprehend my path and my lying down. And are acquainted with all my ways. For there is not a word on my tongue, but behold, O Lord, You know it altogether. You have hedged me behind and before, and laid Your hand upon me. Such knowledge is too wonderful for me. It is high, I cannot attain it.

Where can I go from Your Spirit? Or where can I flee from Your presence? If I ascend into heaven, You are there. If I make my bed in hell, behold You are there. If I take the wings of the morning, and dwell in the uttermost parts of the sea, even there Your hand shall lead me. And Your right hand shall hold me.

If I say, "Surely the darkness shall fall on me, even the night shall be light about me. Indeed, the darkness shall not hide from You. But the night shines as the day. The darkness and the light are both alike to You.

For You formed my inward parts. You covered me in my mother's womb. I will praise You, for I am fearfully and wonderfully made. Marvelous are Your works, and that My soul knows very well.

My frame was not hidden from You when I was made in secret, and skillfully wrought in the lowest parts of the earth. Your eyes saw my substance, being yet unformed. And in Your book, they all were written, the days fashioned for me, when as yet there were none of them.

How precious also are Your thoughts to me, O God! How great is the sum of them! If I should count them, they would be more in number than the sand, when I awake, I am still with You... (Psalm 139:1-18)

"Oh! Great King! The song of an angel, my angel! My precious Chloe Renee! What a glorious thing to hear her voice among the singers of the songs of the unborn! Oh! The wisdom and understanding of my precious daughter! My heart bursts with joy at the sound of her voice!"

"Beloved, it is for your comfort and peace that Chloe Renee, the daughter of your tears, has chosen to sing this song. The words are Spirit and they are truth. They will comfort you when the ache of her loss pulls at your heart. They will dry your tears when regret threatens to consume you. They will remind you that she is alive and well in the care of the Keeper of the stars, singing the songs of the unborn. Receive her chosen song, protect it, draw strength from it, and walk into your destiny with her declaration in your heart. This is the mystery of the canister of hope and the exchange of the jewels of the journey."

"This song is life to me, peace to me, hope for me! I receive! I receive! I receive! Oh! Chloe Renee! I receive your song of hope! You truly are fearfully and wonderfully made! I shall forever hold these words and the sound of your voice close to my heart! For that is where you shall forever live!"

"Oh! Mommy! Yes! Mommy! I will forever be in your heart! It is because you made it over the great divide I no longer stand on the other side of the door of the golden hue without a voice! I can sing! I can sing! I can sing! I can sing the song of the unborn! We must now complete the exchange of the jewels of the journey in the ceremony of the stones."

The Great King took my hand. He lifted His face toward heaven and said, "Oh Keeper of the stars, watch over us as we seal the ceremony of the stones and prepare My Beloved for the releasing. Grant us Your mercy, peace, and comfort for the body and blood of the cross of torture's sake. Sit, My Beloved, beside your precious daughter. Drink in her scent. Gaze into the depths of her soul. Prepare your heart for the releasing."

He lifted the canister of hope and said, "Beloved, this canister shall receive the jewels of destiny in the precious stones you have carried. It was in the receiving of these stones that you activated the hope that lies within. We shall begin the Divine Exchange now."

"Beloved, place your hand upon your heart, and receive the hope of lapis lazuli, the deep blue stone of transparency, where deep calls unto deep. As destiny takes you places that you do not know, you shall search for Me and find Me. Nothing shall harm you as you reach into the place in your heart where transparent hope resides. This is the exchange of the lapis lazuli stone into the jewel of transparency. You shall be transparent with yourself, others, and Me, and this transparency shall cause others to desire the healing and wholeness found in this journey over the great divide."

"Yes. Great King. Let it be so," I said. "I receive this jewel for destiny's sake."

"Chloe Renee, place your hand upon your mother's hand." The warmth of her tiny little hand prepared my heart to receive. The Great King placed His left hand upon hers and His right hand upon His heart.

"Today, the body and blood of the cross of torture has restored the broken cord. Three hearts shall beat as one in the hope of the lapis lazuli. Deep has called to deep. Deep has answered deep. Beloved, I seal the exchange of the stone of hope into a jewel for your journey by My hand upon My heart, which releases the healing of heaven to flow." A surge of warm oil flowed from the King's heart, through Chloe Renee's hand, and into my heart. "The exchange of the lapis lazuli is complete. "Beloved, walk in newness of life. Chloe Renee, place the lapis lazuli back into the canister and sing to your mother the canister's song of hope…"

This hope we have as an anchor of the soul, both sure and steadfast, and which enters the Presence behind the veil…we are children of God, and it has not yet been revealed what we shall be, but we know that when He is revealed, we shall be like Him, for we shall see Him as He is. (Hebrews 6:19, 1 John 3:2)

"Chloe Renee! Your voice is as the voice of an angel! Your song of hope is peace to my soul!"

The Great King took the crimson sapphire from the crystal plate, lifted it up toward heaven and said, "Great cloud of witnesses, armies of light, and singers of songs of the unborn! Rejoice! And again, I say rejoice! For today the body and blood of the cross of torture has reunited My Beloved, her unborn daughter, and Myself for the restoration of broken cords all across the land! Rejoice at the sound of your sister's song! *Chloe's Cry* shall sing My song of redemption, restoration, and redirection! Mothers and fathers of the unborn shall be redeemed! Broken cords shall be restored! Paths of parents of the unborn shall be redirected! I have spoken!"

The Great King placed His hand upon my heart and said, "Beloved, receive destiny's jewel of the Great Exchange from the crimson sapphire. In the presence of the great cloud of witnesses, the armies of light, and the singers of the songs of the unborn, I seal this exchange and the voice of the Beloved." He touched my lips and said, "Mother of Chloe Renee, the Great Exchange of the crimson sapphire into destiny's jewel is complete. I charge you, this day! Go, be a voice of hope to the parents of the unborn! Shout the testimony of the power of the cross of torture, and My willingness to guide them over the great divide!"

"Mommy! Mommy! Mommy! Look! The black tape of the deep, dark dungeon has completely dissolved at the Great King's touch! You can sing! You can shout! You can tell our story without fear, guilt, shame, or regret! We shall sing and shout our song together, only it will be in different places. Oh! Mommy! Mommy! Destiny's jewel says I shall surely join the choir of the unborn, and you shall sing to the parents of the dungeon! Oh! Mommy! Mommy! The time of the releasing of our destinies is near!"

"Chloe Renee," the Great King said, "place the crimson sapphire back into the canister of hope and sing the song of the Great Exchange..."

Now then, we are ambassadors for Christ, as though God were pleading through us, we implore you on Christ's behalf, be reconciled to God. For He made Him who knew no sin to be sin for us, that we might become the righteousness of God in Him. (2 Corinthians 5:20-21)

"Oh! Chloe Renee! It is because of the Great King's love for us that we are reunited this day in order to prepare my heart for the release into the memorial of celebration of your life. Yes, the time of our releasing is near. I shall carry your scent and your song with me all the days of my life. They shall be part of me until the Owner of the skies brings me to you."

The Great King placed His hand upon my eyes and said, "Receive destiny's jewel of sight from the glistening green emerald. From this day forward, you shall see the pain of the parents of the unborn with the eyes of a heart that has been healed by crossing the great divide. You shall have heaven's clarity of vision to guide them in their own journey. I charge you, this day, to follow Me with eyes sharpened by the jewel of the glistening green emerald. Together, we shall guide the wounded parents of the unborn safely over the great divide."

"Chloe Renee," He said, "place the glistening green emerald back into the canister of hope and sing to your mother the song of sight and commissioning..."

The people who walked in darkness have seen a great light. Those who dwell in the land of the shadow of death, upon them a light has shined. I, the Lord, have called You in righteousness, and will hold Your hand. I will keep You and give You as a covenant to the people, as a light to the Gentiles. To open blind eyes, to bring prisoners from the prison, those who sit in darkness from the prison house. Peace to you! As the Father has sent Me, I also send you. (Isaiah 9:2, Isaiah 42:6-7, John 20:21)

"Great King! Great King! I shall heed the words of Chloe Renee's song of sight and commissioning! I shall honor you! I shall honor her! I shall honor the three-strand cord that has been restored! Yes! Great King! I shall go to the incarcerated parents of the unborn!"

"The exchange of the emerald stone and destiny's jewel of sight is complete."

I grabbed Chloe Renee as the Great King held Ruby Red high into the air. We held each other tight. We knew this was the last stone to be exchanged before the ceremony of releasing.

"Keeper of the stars," He said, "we rejoice with My Beloved and the star of Your heart, Chloe Renee, for what has been accomplished through the successful journey over the great divide. We have cried, cheered, laughed, and sat in holy silence. Now, as we prepare for the releasing, grant Our Beloved, the mother of Chloe Renee, peace that passes all understanding as our eyes turn toward the ceremony of the releasing. Grant her power, strength, and childlike trust beyond anything she could ever ask or think as she walks through destiny's new door."

"Oh! Chloe Renee!" I stared in awe at the depth and beauty of the Ruby Red. "Oh! Look! The majesty of Ruby Red! I shall forever remember her strength and determination, her power over darkness, and her willingness to lead me over the great divide! She, by far, is the most treasured of all the stones! Without her, I would still be crying in the dungeon of the parents of the unborn, and you, Chloe Renee, would never have received your voice! Without her, I would never have touched your face, held your hand, or breathed in your scent! Oh! Great King! The stone of Your sacrifice on the cross of torture sings its own song! Chloe Renee, listen…"

Surely, He has born our griefs and carried our sorrows. Yet we esteemed Him stricken, smitten by God and afflicted. But He was wounded for our transgressions, He was bruised for our iniquities. The chastisement for our peace was upon Him, and by His stripes we are healed. (Isaiah 53:4-5)

"Beloved, My Beloved! Beloved of the Owner of the skies and the Keeper of the Stars, receive destiny's jewel of childlike trust in Ruby Red where all the promises of the Great Book are stored. May her tenacity to trample on serpents and scorpions serve you as you walk through destiny's new door. May she forever reign in your thoughts, hopes, and dreams. May she take you from this place of celebration out to the dungeons of the parents of the unborn where you will sing *Chloe's Cry* and offer the incarcerated freedom from their chains."

Sobbing uncontrollably, I said, "Oh! Great King! Ruby Red has done more for me than I could have ever thought or imagined! She has been mined from the depths of the cross of torture where crimson blood poured out of Your heart. Victorious by the way of the cross, she rules over darkness, fear, and death. Her song is sung in the choir of the unborn day and night…

"Come now, and let us reason together," says the Lord. "Though your sins are like scarlet, they shall be white as snow. Though they are red like crimson, they shall be as wool…O Death, where is your sting? O Hades, where is your victory? (Isaiah 1:18, 1 Corinthians 15:55)

"Great King! My friend, my confidant, my guide, and my Lord! How can I ever thank You enough for the gift of Ruby Red and what You have done through her? I receive destiny's call with her childlike trust and all the promises of the Great Book! I shall cherish her always. I shall look to her for strength as we approach the releasing, for surely, I could not survive it without her. I receive everything You have for me in this jewel of childlike trust from the stone of Ruby Red…"

"Beloved, the exchange of the Ruby Red stone and the jewel of childlike trust in the promises of the Great Book is complete. Chloe Renee, place Ruby Red back into the canister of hope and seal it with the song of Ruby Red…"

Trust in the Lord with all your heart, and lean not on your own understanding. In all your ways acknowledge Him, and He shall direct your paths. (Proverbs 3:5-6)

"Mommy! Mommy! Mommy! Look! The ceremony has begun! The King's highway is being prepared for the releasing! Destiny in the stones and jewels is calling us!"

HOPE and PEACE stood on the east and west side of the King's highway directly in front of me, their wings spread over the highway, creating a canopy under which the rainbow colors of healing danced. The great cloud of witnesses and the armies of light stood on either side of the highway, positioned exactly as when Chloe Renee emerged from the golden hue.

"All rise for the preparation of the Daughters of Destiny through the ceremony of the robes!"

The Great King, Chloe Renee, and I stood at the edge of the King's highway that leads to the door of the golden hue from where the Keeper of the stars would come. Attendants chosen by the Owner of the skies walked toward us with the robes of transformation and presented them to the Great King. "All hail the Great King! He has received the robes for the ceremony of the release! Let us rejoice as the ceremony begins!"

Let us be glad and rejoice and give Him glory...And to her it was granted to be arrayed in fine linen, clean and bright, for the fine linen is the righteous acts of the saints. (Revelation 19:7a, 8)

"Chloe Renee, daughter of the Beloved. You have received your voice today. You have received your song. Destiny's new door has been unlocked for you by your mother's successful crossing over the great divide. She shall release you back to the Keeper of the stars and you shall join the company of the singers of the songs of the unborn. Your story and your song, *Chloe's Cry*, shall be heard across the land. It shall be sung until the Owner of the skies ushers in the new day. Receive your robe of transformation in preparation for the ceremony of the release."

Chloe Renee reached out her tiny little soft hands that had brought me so much comfort and peace to receive her robe. "Great King," she said, "I will forever remember this day as the day I wiped my mommy's tears away and our broken three-strand cord was mended. I shall forever sing in the company of the unborn my song, *Chloe's Cry,* until the Owner of the skies calls my mommy home and we build sandcastles along the shores of heaven with You."

"Chloe Renee, I seal your words of destiny with My love and My heart."

"Beloved, mother of Chloe Renee and successful sojourner in the journey toward healing and wholeness from abortion, you have received your voice today. You have received your song. Destiny's new door has been unlocked for you by clutching Ruby Red and following Me over the great divide. You shall release Chloe Renee to the Keeper of the stars by way of the King's highway through the door of the golden hue. *Chloe's Cry* shall be sung in the great auditorium throughout the land until the Owner of the skies ushers in the new day. Receive your robe of transformation in preparation for the ceremony of the release."

With trembling hands and tears in my eyes, I reached for the robe. My heart soared as on wings of eagles with joy unspeakable. Its touch was warm, soft, and comforting, just as my precious Chloe Renee's tiny little hands were. Every thread, strategically woven with Ruby Red and a promise from the Great King's Book, gave me the strength I needed to face releasing Chloe Renee back to the Keeper of the stars.

"Great King," I said, "I will forever remember this day as the day my precious daughter, Chloe Renee, wiped my tears away and our broken three-strand cord was mended. I shall go from this place and sing *Chloe's Cry,* the song of the daughter of my tears, throughout the land. I shall go to the dungeons of the parents of the unborn and offer them Your freedom from their chains. I shall sing the song of the daughter of my tears until the Owner of the skies calls me home and we build sandcastles along the shores of heaven with You."

"Beloved, mother of Chloe Renee, I seal your words of destiny with My Love and My Heart," He said. "Come near, we must present ourselves to the Keeper of the stars."

I stood at His right, Chloe Renee in front of us, leaning against our legs. The Great King put His left hand on her left shoulder. I put my right hand on her right shoulder. We faced the King's highway, one heart, one mind, one spirit, waiting for the Great King to address the Keeper of the stars.

He lifted His face toward heaven and said, "Great Keeper of the stars, the ceremony of transformation is complete. My Beloved and the daughter of her tears, Chloe Renee, have received their robes of transformation. Their words of destiny have been sealed with My love and My heart. We are prepared for the ceremony of the releasing. Come, Keeper of the stars, to our place of release! We invite You to receive Your precious Chloe Renee from the hand of her mother in the ceremony of the releasing. Grant us Your favor! Grant us Your peace and comfort!"

"I present My body and My blood that endured the cross of torture on their behalf to You this day. Oh! Great Keeper of the stars, receive My sacrifice that My joy may overflow, that I may see the labor of My soul and be satisfied. That Chloe Renee may return to the company of the unborn, singing her song of freedom from her mother's silent secret. That her mother may return to the dungeons of the parents of the unborn to offer them freedom from their incarceration. This is the desire of My heart, oh Keeper of the stars."

The holders of the candles steadied themselves as thunder rumbled through the heavens. The great cloud of witnesses and the armies of light bowed as the golden highway reached into the clouds in preparation for the entrance of the Keeper of the stars. The Great King held us tight. I could feel His chin resting on my head. Oh! What comfort! Oh! What peace! Chloe's face was buried in my chest, her little arms barely fitting around my waist. The Great King softly sang…

O death where is your sting? O Hades, where is your victory? Let not your hearts be troubled, you believe in God, believe also in Me. In My Father's house are many mansions. I go to prepare a place for you, and God shall wipe away every tear from your eyes. There shall be no more death, nor sorrow, nor crying. There shall be no more pain, for the former things have passed away…

I lifted my tear-stained face toward the heavens. Chloe Renee said, brushing my tears, "Mommy, the time of the release is here! Look! Heaven is preparing to receive me! The sun is going down and the moon shall soon rise. Look how the skies kiss the rainbow's healing colors under the archangel's canopy! Oh! Mommy, I've watched this thousands of times, wondering if it will ever be my turn! Mommy! You made it! We made it! Thank you, Mommy, for facing your fears! Thank you for holding onto Ruby Red and making it across the great divide! Thank you, for giving me identity, honor, and purpose! Thank you! Thank you! Thank you! Thank you for everything! Mommy! Look! The golden hue is rising from the healing colors! He is almost here! The Keeper of the stars is almost here to receive me. Oh! Mommy! Look!"

The healing colors followed the King's highway into the most glorious sunset I have ever seen, where they formed a golden frame. I held her close. "Oh! Great King!" I said.

"Beloved, the time has come. Let us stand at the King's table for the dedication of the gifts of release. Chloe Renee, you shall dedicate the canister of hope and the door of destiny it represents and present it to your mother. Beloved, you shall dedicate Chloe Renee's rose of remembrance and the door of destiny it represents and present it to your daughter."

Chloe Renee picked up the canister of hope and stood in front of me. "Mommy, I dedicate this canister of hope and the door of destiny you will walk through once you release me to the Keeper of the stars. I am so proud of you, Mommy! I love you so much! You will always be in my heart!" I took the canister and placed it in my bag.

As I picked up Chloe Renee's rose of remembrance, a thorn on its stem pricked my hand and I smiled. It is because of a crown of thorns and spilled blood that I made it over the great divide. It is because of a crown of thorns and spilled blood that I stood in front of my daughter free of fear, guilt, shame, and regret. It is because of a crown of thorns and spilled blood that my daughter and I have a voice and a destiny to share.

Chloe's Cry will be heard because of a crown of thorns and spilled blood.

"Chloe Renee, I dedicate this rose of remembrance and the door of destiny that awaits you on the other side of the golden hue. I am so proud of you! I thank God for you! You have filled my heart with hope and joy! You shall always be in my heart, daughter of my tears!"

Chloe Renee took the rose from my hand and said, "Mommy, this has been the best day of my life! Don't cry, Mommy! Remember, we have work to do!" She pulled away from me and stood at the edge of the King's highway.

"Beloved," the King said with compassion and care, "it is time to present the daughter of release to the Keeper of the stars. Take your place beside Chloe Renee at the edge of the King's highway. Stand on her right, holding her right hand. This is the position of the release. I shall stand behind you both in the position of the completion of the three-strand cord. It is in unity of the Spirit that we release Chloe Renee into the golden hue and you through destiny's new door."

"Keeper of the stars," the Great King said, "the dedication of the gifts for the release is complete. May all the earth rejoice! Freedom for the beloved and the daughter of her tears has come! It is in the receiving and releasing that true healing flows. Beloved, you have received your daughter by the crossing of the great divide. Now release her to the Keeper of the stars who has come through the golden hue…"

I kneeled and pulled Chloe Renee close to me. "I love you! I love you!" I said.

"I love you too, Mommy! I love you too! I have to go now, Mommy. I have to go."

"I know, beautiful, I know."

Her smell and her touch lingered on long after I released her warm, soft, little hand.

The Great King stood behind me in silence with His hands on my shoulders as we watched her walk up the King's highway toward the Keeper of the stars.

"Look, Great King. Her curly blonde hair bounces as she walks."

"Yes, it does, Beloved. Indeed, it does."

"Great King! She is in her bare feet!"

"Indeed, she is, Beloved. Indeed, she is!"

When she reached the Keeper of the stars, she stopped, turned, and said, "Mommy, the Great Book of Promises says…"

"But, Beloved, do not forget this one thing, that with the Lord one day is as a thousand years, and a thousand years as one day." (2 Peter 3:8)

"We shall be building sandcastles together before the rising and setting of the sun! I love you always and forever!"

With her rose of remembrance held close to her heart, she blew me a kiss, turned toward the Keeper of the stars, and walked hand in hand with Him through the golden hue…

REST-REFLECT-REFRESH

Silent no more. This is *Chloe's Cry*. Silent no more. This is my cry. I trust it has become your cry. I want to encourage you to meditate on these three powerful, life-changing words…

SILENT NO MORE

SILENT NO MORE – SILENT NO MORE – SILENT NO MORE – SILENT NO MORE – SILENT NO MORE

Silent no more! Chloe Renee has received her voice! The red tape of my silent secret has been removed! I have received my voice! The black tape of my incarceration has been removed! *Chloe's Cry* shouts throughout the land that passage over the great divide is possible when one *intentionally* follows the Great King and receives everything His cross of torture offers.

Silent no more. Has your son or daughter received his or her voice? Have you received yours?

CHLOE RENEE AND I ARE SILENT NO MORE.
HOW ABOUT YOUR CHILD AND YOU?

Would you join me in honoring the short life and death of my precious daughter, Chloe Renee...

Chapter 23

Ceremony of the Release

Journal Entry August 8, 2017

*I*t is the eighth day of the eighth month, August, 2017. The *date is not lost to me—day and month of new beginnings. I must face reality. I must walk through the wilderness of the field of regret and gather manna daily. I do not walk alone— this I am promised and in this I take great comfort.*

Yesterday, 8/7/17, is also not lost to me. With Divine Providence speaking tenderly through little Stacey, I am able to enter this field full of briars and bristles. I am willing to lay Chloe Renee to rest even as I stood by Stacey with Candyce Skye. I held Candyce Skye without understanding or wisdom to know the Divine purpose. As I held Candycy Skye's still body, she was already with Jesus. Her perfect little eyes would not open, her perfect little feel and hands would not move, her chest would never rise and fall, but in that moment—heaven met earth in that tiny body as I held her and walked around the room with her. I must do as Stacey had to do. I must lay Chloe Renee to rest. I must honor her short life and move on, knowing and being fully aware that I was, I am, and I always will be her Mommy.

Stacey stood before me and said when she walked into church, the anger, the questions, and the pain disappeared. Jesus, the Comforter and Healer, had met her. Through her words, He gently told me it is time for this part of my abortion recovery. That it is okay and necessary. That it is the KAIROS time, that I will not be alone. They will walk with me, Chloe Renee and Jesus.

I invite you to read the "Bulletin" That I wrote for Chloe Renee's memorial...

MEMORIAL SERVICE
FOR
CHLOE RENEE
AUGUST 8, 2017

O Death, where is your sting?
O Hades, where is your victory?
(1 Corinthians 15:55)

Let not your heart be troubled.
You believe in God, believe also in Me.
In My Father's house are many mansions.
If it were not so, I would have told you.
I go to prepare a place for you.
And, if I go and prepare a place for you,
I will come again and receive you to Myself,
that where I am, there you may be also.
(John 14:1-3)

And God will wipe away every tear from their eyes.
There shall be no more death, nor sorrow, nor crying.
There shall be no more pain, for the former things have
passed away. Then He who sat on the throne said,
"Behold, I make all things new..."
(Revelation 21:4-5a)

ORDER OF SERIVCE

Sing, "I'm No Longer a Slave to Fear, I Am a Child of God,"[3] about twenty times in preparation.

Go to shed to look for a flowerpot.

Separate and dig up a shoot from a tiger lily plant.

Prepare deck—gather plants, move water fountain to the corner—set up memorial atmosphere.

Arrange plants and candles on tables. Light candles. Turn water fountain on.

Place plaque that reads, "A Triple-Braided Cord Is Not Easily Broken" in corner above table.

Turn phone on and speak to Chloe Renee for seven minutes.

Print the cover of this book, *A Little Child Shall Lead Them*, put it in Buddy's frame, and set it on the table beside the lit candle.

Plant green tiger lily shoot in green pot. Place on memorial table.

Bring stuffed bear and ceramic bears and place by table.

Speak to Chloe Renee by video.

Prepare communion elements.

Place communion elements on floor beside the stuffed bear; Place "A Little Child Shall Lead Them" picture, root beer candle, tiger lily shoot; and ceramic bears around metal church with lit candle.

Prepare for candlelight service.

Get pink prayer shawl and put over my head.

Read Scriptures that are sewn into prayer shawl...

For He who knew no sin became sin for us that we might become the righteousness of God in Him (2 Corinthians 5:21), (was sewn on right side of prayer shawl).

---

[3] Jonathan Helser, Joel Case, Brian Johnson, "No Longer Slaves" (Redding, CA: Bethel Music Publishing, 2014).

But to you who fear My name, the Sun of righteousness shall arise with healing in His wings (Malachi 4:2), (was sewn on left side of prayer shawl).

Receive bread and wine, communion. The sun came out after communion!

Blow out candles. Place all memorial plants, candles, and items back to original places.

Prepare to lay Chloe Renee to rest...

Proceed to the burial...

REST-REFLECT-REFRESH

August 8, 2017 was the day I truly begin to grieve the loss of my daughter as any mother would at the death of her child. My spirit was quickened by the touch of the Great King. *Today is the day. Today is the day. Today is the day. You shall have the memorial today.*

I wasn't prepared for this! It was too final! It was almost eight months since the Christmas party and I had just gotten to know my daughter! *Oh! Great King! Why today?*

Nothing. No response. Just an urge in my spirit that I *must* honor Chloe Renee *today!*

Okay, I thought. I had no idea how to go about it, what I should do, or what I should say. I remembered reading in several abortion recovery books that having a memorial service for the child helps bring closure to post-abortive parents who could not experience it otherwise.

I knew true closure for me would not happen by reading someone else's story or attending abortion recovery classes. At the beginning of *Chloe's Cry*, we discussed at length being *intentional* about seeking healing and wholeness from our abortion experience. Chloe Renee's memorial service had to be an *intentional* act on my part to follow the lead of the Holy Spirit in how it was to be orchestrated.

At first, I was just going have a short memorial, thrown together quickly, without much thought, not even showering or changing out of my night clothes! As I walked through the house, I was convicted by the Holy Spirit. "Had she been born *sleeping* as Candyce Skye, would you not have had the best for your daughter? Would you not shower and prepare yourself? Would you not use the creativity I have given you to prepare an atmosphere for My Spirit to honor your daughter, My daughter? She deserves the best and so do I."

Immediately, I went upstairs to take a shower. Heavenly ideas flowed through my mind as warm water cleansed my body. I started having visions of what items in our home were to be used, how they were to be placed, and what to do!

Chloe Renee's memorial could very well be one of the longest memorials ever recorded! It was a healing journey beyond anything I could possibly put words to as we began at 9:30 a.m. and ended at 4:00 p.m.! Almost eight hours! One hour for every month following the Christmas party! Doesn't the Great King just make you smile? He does me!

I encourage you to ask the Great King to reveal to you how to go about preparing a memorial service for your son or daughter. Chloe Renee's memorial was private here at the house, with the Holy Spirit guiding me and with no one else in attendance. Perhaps you have a prayer partner that could join you in petitioning heaven for the details of your child's memorial.

Chloe Renee conceived October, 1978 – Passed in October 1978
– Laid to rest August 8, 2017…

Chapter 24

Chloe's Resting Place

Journal Entry October 23, 2017

A gentle rain fell all day as Chloe Renee's memorial was taking place. Its light sound, along with the peaceful flow of the water fountain on the deck soothed my aching soul. I walked around outside gathering the elements without an umbrella, welcoming the cleansing I felt from heaven's tears. *Surely, this is the day that the Lord has made for laying Chloe Renee to rest.*

The memorial was beautiful. I took my time with each step, moving forward only when the Holy Spirit led. After approximately eight hours, I felt a release from the Holy Spirit to go back into the woods to where Buddy is buried and symbolically lay Chloe Renee to rest. The same gentle rain that fell upon me while preparing for the memorial returned. I smiled. *Surely, the Lord knows I need to feel the cleansing of heaven's tears right now…*

Buddy was the first dog we had ever owned, a gentle black Labrador retriever. He came to live with us at six weeks of age and passed away thirteen years later. He did not die naturally; we had to put him to sleep. When they opened the door to roll him in on the gurney, his eyes met mine and I thought my heart would burst. *This is the greatest act of love you are showing right now.* I held his cheek and buried my face in his head while the veterinarian gave him the shot. I remember whispering, "It's okay, Buddy-boy, it's okay. You can go to sleep now." We came home and buried him the in woods behind the house. I wept for days. I would not be comforted. Only now do I realize the deep-rooted cause of the intensity of the trauma.

You shall symbolically bury Chloe Renee in the back woods beside Buddy...

I printed out the picture of "A Little Child Shall Lead Them" and carried it along with my garden spade down the path through the woods toward Buddy's grave. I knelt to dig a hole, and the Spirit said, *"No, this is not the one...go back up and print out the one of you holding the fetus..."*

Oh. Yes, Lord. Yes. That's the one. I was reminded of a picture I had in my phone of me holding an eight-week-old fetus in my hand, the age Chloe Renee was when she died. I had taken the picture one day while I was touring a satellite facility of Palmetto Pregnancy Center. It was another *holy hush, Holy of Holies* experience. I was being ushered into an ultrasound room, and before I knew it, I was face-to-face with a model that could have been Chloe Renee.

I wept as I asked if I could hold it. *Oh! Holy hush! Oh! Holy moment! Oh! Chloe Renee!* The tenderness and compassion of my guide moved her to share my tears. Oh. Yes. This is the picture I will bury beside Buddy. *Thank you, Holy Spirit; You are always right. Always.* Unspeakable peace, comfort, and hope fell upon me as I journeyed back up to the house with tears of heaven still washing over me.

*The Holiest of Holies...*A sixty-year-old wrinkled hand cradling an eight-week-old fetus. *Oh! Holy hush...Oh Holy of Holies.* Representation of Chloe Renee's form safe in the palm of my hand and close to my heart, I picked up the garden spade, and slowly walked toward her resting place. As tears from heaven mixed with mine, my soul sang over and over again, *I am no longer a slave to fear, I am a child of God.*

I knelt beside Buddy's grave, remembering clearly the day we placed him there. *Buddy-boy, you aren't alone out here anymore.* I took the garden spade and began to dig. *I am no longer a slave to fear, I am a child of God! I am no longer a slave to fear, I am a child of God!* I dug and dug and dug. The sound of the garden spade scooping up dirt was almost too much to bear. *I am no longer a slave to fear, I am a child of God!* On my knees I sang it over and over.

The rain kept falling, I kept crying, the spade kept digging. When the hole was deep enough to bury the picture, I started covering it up. More tears. More healing. More tears. More healing. *Oh Chloe! Oh! Chloe Renee! Oh Chloe! I am no longer a slave to fear, guilt, shame, and regret…I am a child of God…*

I searched for a stone to mark her grave and laid it on the ground in line with Buddy's. I did not want to leave. I stood. *I am no longer a slave to fear, I am a child of God.* So many emotions, so many thoughts, so many unanswered questions. *I am a child of God. I am a child of God…*

> **I come to the garden alone,**
> **While the dew is still on the roses.**
> **And the voice I hear falling on my ear**
> **The Son of God discloses.**
>
> **And He walks with me and He talks with me.**
> **And He tells me I am His own.**
> **And the joy we share as we tarry there,**
> **None other has ever known.**[4]

"This is my spot to remember you, Chloe Renee. You are with the Keeper of the stars. The Great King has taken me out of the dungeon, and brought me this far. I will walk through destiny's new door. I will sing your song and tell our story. Your voice and the songs of the unborn shall be heard. I shall forever sing, *Chloe's Cry…*"

There is a rustling in the woods. I look up. In the distance watching over me and Chloe Renee is my fun-filled fuzzy little

---

[4] C. Austin Miles, "In the Garden," 1912 song, public domain.

friend with a stick in her mouth. Surely, heaven's shores and the daughter of my tears are not far away…

My heart skips a beat and my spirit soars…Mommy! Mommy! Mommy! I am barefoot in the sand! Jesus is with me! We are building a great big sandcastle where all three of our pink hearts can live together forever…

REST-REFLECT-REFRESH

As I stood beside Chloe Renee's resting place, tears of thankfulness flowed freely, mixing with the gentle rain that continued to wash over me. In wonder and awe of the kindness, gentleness, and compassion of my Savior, I felt Chloe Renee and He were truly with me. Three hearts beating as one sang the song of the unborn…

O Death, where is your sting?
O Hades, where is your victory?
(1 Corinthians 15:55)

Let not your heart be troubled,
you believe in God, believe also in Me.
In My Father's house are many mansions.
If it were not so, I would have told you.
I go to prepare a place for you.
And if I go and prepare a place for you,
I will come again and receive you to Myself,
that where I am, there you may be also.
(John 14:1-3)

And God will wipe away every tear from their eyes,
there shall be no ore death, nor sorrow, nor crying.
There shall be no more pain, for the former things have passed
away. The He who sat on the throne said,
"Behold I make all things new…"
(Revelation 21:4-5a)

We have come a long way, my beloved friend. It has been an honor beyond anything I have ever done in my life to share my story of healing and wholeness from the tragic death of my precious daughter, Chloe Renee.

You have been part of my journey, because you were on the heart of the Great King the entire time I was writing. It is because of His love for you that *Chloe's Cry* has made it to print.

We have unearthed our secrets, and been *intentional* about seeking healing and wholeness. We have faced our fears, guilt, shame, and regret. We have invited God into our recovery journey. We have faced the cold, hard facts of what abortion is and received forgiveness from God and our children. We have received, named, bonded with, and released our precious children. We have been commissioned to share our stories with others so they too may find healing and wholeness. It has been a struggle. It has been a battle. But, the victory is ours!

Our unborn children now have identity, honor, and purpose. Our lives can never be the same!

Our silent secrets are no more silent! We have a voice! Our unborn children have a voice!

As the Great King commissioned me, I also commission you…

Peace to you! As the Father has sent me, I also send you. (John 20:21)

Will you go wherever the Great King leads to show the traumatized parents of the unborn the way over the great divide?

A Special Note from Chaplain Potter...

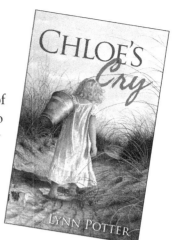

It is my desire to provide copies of *Chloe's Cry* to men and women who are in jail or prison if they feel they would benefit from its contents. To request a gift book, or for information on how to sponsor a book for someone in need, please fill out the form below and mail it to:

Chaplain Lynn Potter
Potter's Heart Ministry
PO Box 11
York, SC 29745
www.pottersheartministry.org
lynnpotter222@yahoo.com

Requests for gift books will be filled as sponsors become available.

Name _____

Address _____

_____ I would like to request a gift copy of *Chloe's Cry*.

_____ I would like more information on how to sponsor a gift book for someone in need.

Please tell me a little about yourself and your interest in *Chloe's Cry*.

_____

_____

_____

_____

Made in the USA
Columbia, SC
12 March 2019